The Little World of
Don Camillo

Giovannino Guareschi, known as Giovanni to his millions of readers, was born at Fontanelle in the Valley of the Po on the 1st of May, 1908. His father wanted him to become a naval engineer. He, for the very enjoyment of going the opposite way, determined to become a lawyer, but found his vocation when he sent some cartoons he had drawn to the satirical magazine, *Bartoldo*. Later he founded his own magazine, *Candido*, and between 1946 and 1966 he wrote 346 stories featuring Don Camillo, a character who has done for Italy what Cervantes' Don Quixote did for Spain.

Beloved all over the world by readers from 10 to 100, *The Little World of Don Camillo* has been feted not only in books but in films, in series on TV, on radio and most recently on YouTube. Now, in this new authorised edition, stories never before translated into English are published alongside the classic tales for the very first time.

Adam Elgar, the translator of this the first new English translation of *Don Camillo* since 1952, is a young poet and award-winning translator with a profound empathy with the spirit of Italy, past and present. Since 2008 he has been translating the Italian novelist Alessandra Lavagnino, whose particular talent is for capturing spirit of place. Adam's other main translating interest is Italian sonnets. His own poetry is published widely in Europe, America and on the Internet, where he has been translation moderator at Eratosphere online literary forum since 2009.

Some Reviews

'These haunting stories about this haunting place... Somehow Guareschi made people laugh at their own predicament at a time when humour was sorely needed.' *BBC Radio 4*

'Written with such warmth and simplicity, so concerned with the trivialities of everyday life and giving us so shrewd a glimpse into the minds of the people ...' *London Evening News*

THE LITTLE WORLD OF DON CAMILLO

GIOVANNI GUARESCHI

PILOT PRODUCTIONS

Published by Pilot Productions
Grove Farm Sawdon, North Yorkshire Y013 9DY

2 4 6 8 10 9 7 5 3 1

A catalogue record for this book is available

from the British Library

ISBN 978-1-900064-07-1

Jacket design by Berni Stevens

Typeset in Galliard by Mark Heslington Ltd,
Scarborough, North Yorkshire YO11 3PU

Printed in Great Britain by
Clays Ltd, Elcograf S.p.A.

Contents

Editor's Preface

Reading *The Little World of Don Camillo* is to travel to the Valley of the River Po, Italy's widest and most fertile plain, with its unique atmosphere, culture and natural history. And to do so in the incomparable company of a cast of characters who testify to the exquisite humour and humanity of their creator.

Giovanni Guareschi, himself a native of the Lower Plain, first drew breath in Fontanelle di Roccabianca on May Day, 1908, returning to buy a house there in Roncole Verdi in 1952, after a decade of getting himself arrested, variously by Mussolini's Fascists, Hitler's Nazis, and Italy's President, Luigi Einaudi.

The Einaudi arrest occurred after Giovanni's satirical magazine, *Candido*, which had helped engineer the defeat of the 'Fronte Popolare' (the Communists) in '48, depicted Einaudi at the Quirinal Palace, surrounded by a presidential guard of giant bottles of Nebbiolo wine, suggesting perhaps that his love for the wine he produced on his farm near Dogliani might have eclipsed his commitment to the people.

The cartoon was judged a *lese-majesty* (an offence against the dignity of a reigning sovereign or State). Giovanni received a suspended prison sentence, later imposed after a further bust-up with the authorities, when Prime Minister Alcide De Gasperi sued him for libel. (See the *Biographical Afterword* at the end of this book for further details.)

Conflict marked Giovanni's life. The combination of a humorously provocative nature and the creative talents of a cartoonist and writer was always bound to get him noticed, and quite possibly into trouble. That he survived his detractors and became not only bed-time reading for Pope Benedict XVI but also a household name across the world, was down to something else.

The Don Camillo stories reflect Giovanni's life of conflict, but also his search for enlightenment. In episode after episode, the hot-headed Catholic priest, Don Camillo, and the equally pugnacious Communist mayor, Peppone, confront one another, sometimes in a serious and violent manner. But the clever bit is the way Giovanni not only engineers a resolution to this, but transforms the situation to the great benefit of the local community, so that the two men put their political convictions aside and, however begrudgingly, develop respect for each other.

To enable this, Giovanni created a third main character, his finest creation and the most surprising. *Il Cristo* presides over proceedings from a crucifix above the altar of the town church and counsels Don Camillo, exposing and undermining the stubborn priest's personal politics and prejudices and, with fascinating insights and gentle humour, suggests paths of action which, with the benefit of hindsight, we come to see make things right.

Giovanni claimed that the voice from the crucifix was merely the voice of his own conscience, but in the stories it is a living reality which enables solutions so simple that they are beyond the reach of political minds clouded with ideology and the need to win.

Victory, as such, is never sought; the wry wisdom of *il Cristo* seeks not supremacy but equanimity within the Little World, which is achieved through an understanding and acceptance of what being human means. Giovanni's message is that what works at the micro level of the Little World can be made to work universally, the world over.

Another aspect of the appeal is that the Little World is inspired by the spirit of a real place and its people. The Lower Plain is a region where often 'the passion for politics is so intense that it becomes worrying,' as Giovanni once said. But its people 'are pleasant and hospitable and generous, and have a high sense of humour.' Creating his fictional world was second nature to him, because he himself was imbued with the spirit of it.

In 1942, four years before conceiving Don Camillo, Peppone, Brusco, Smilzo and the rest, Giovanni wrote three stories about this region, prefacing the original Italian edition with them to give the reader a preliminary sense of the ethos of the Lower Plain and the character of its people, and to explain why unusual things can happen there.

These three stories, along with sixteen about Don Camillo, appear together in English for the very first time. The present volume, translated by Adam Elgar, is the first complete edition of *The Little World of Don Camillo* ever to be published in the English language.

Piers Dudgeon, September 2013

Introduction

(Here, by means of A Quotation and Three Stories, the world of The Little World of Don Camillo *is explained)*

WHEN I was young I was a reporter for a newspaper and I went around on my bicycle all day long looking for stories worth reporting.

Then I got to know a girl, and I began to spend my days in a state of wonder, thinking about what she would do if I became Emperor of Mexico, or if I should die. And in the evenings I began to fill my pages with made-up pieces of news, and people liked these a lot because they were more plausible than the real news.

Back then I must have had a vocabulary of more or less 200 words, and I used the same ones to report an old man being knocked over by a cyclist and a housewife losing a fingertip as she peeled potatoes.

So there was none of that literary malarkey, and in this book I am that same reporter, and I still confine myself to reporting items of news, made-up stuff but so realistic that on loads of occasions I've written a story and then seen it happen in real life a couple of months later. There's nothing extraordinary about this. It stands to reason: you consider the time of day, the time of year, the current fashion and the psychological moment, and conclude that, things being as they are, in Situation X this or that event could actually take place.

So the stories in this book come out of a particular climate and a particular environment: the Italian political climate of the period from December 1946 to December 1947; the story, in other words, of a political year. They are set in a part of the Po Plain: and here I need to state that for me, the River Po properly begins at Piacenza. The fact that upstream from Piacenza it's the same river is neither here nor there: the road from Piacenza north-west to Milan is the same road as the one which goes from Piacenza south-east to Rimini, but only the latter is properly the Via Emilia, built as it was in 187 BC.

You may object that you cannot make a comparison between a river and a road because roads belong to history, while rivers belong to geography.

But men don't make history any more than they do geography. They *undergo* history, as they undergo geography. And in the end, history is no more than geography in action.

Men make holes through mountains and divert rivers, deluding themselves that in this way they are changing the course of history, but ultimately they are changing nothing at all, because one fine day everything is going to collapse, and the waters will swallow up the bridges and burst the dykes, and fill up the mines; they'll pull down the houses and the palaces and the hovels, and grass will grow on the rubble, and everything will turn back to earth. And the survivors will have to fight off wild animals with stones, and the story will begin all over again.

The same old story.

Then, after three thousand years, they'll discover a household tap and a lathe from the Breda foundry in Milan buried under more than 100 feet of mud, and they'll say, 'Look at this incredible stuff!'

And they'll set to work, organising the same nonsense as their distant ancestors. Because men are unfortunate creatures condemned to 'progress', progress which leads inevitably to replacing the old Eternal Father with the latest chemical formulae. And so, in the end, the old Eternal Father gets annoyed, moves the last digit of the little finger on his left hand a fraction of an inch, and the whole world goes up in smoke.

So, the Po begins at Piacenza! And it has every right to do so; for it is the only respectable river in Italy; and as any self-respecting river knows, the plain is where a river comes into its own, for water is stuff that is supposed to stay horizontal, and only when it is perfectly horizontal does it preserve all of its natural dignity. The Niagara Falls is a fairground attraction, like men who walk on their hands.

The Po begins at Piacenza, and so does the world of my stories, a little world situated on that slice of the Plain that stands between the river and the Apennines, and was described by the notary Francesco Luigi Campari in his history of Roccabianca and the Province of Parma, *Un Castello del Parmigiano Attraverso i secoli* (1910):

'. . . The sky is often a beautiful azure-blue, as everywhere in Italy, except in the less good season, when dense mists develop . . . The soil is for the most part soft, sandy and cool, somewhat firmer upstream and occasionally clayey. Lush vegetation envelops the area and not one single palm is less than luxuriantly green, as the species seeks to extend its dominion over the broad sandbanks of the Po.

'Fields of waving corn, all bordered by rows of vines, punctuated at intervals with small field-maples and crowned with banks of mature mulberry trees, attest to the fecundity of the earth here . . . Wheat, maize, a profusion of grapes, silk from the cocoon of the silkworm, hemp and clover are the principal products, but every kind of plant can be propagated. There was a time when oaks and all sorts of fruit tree thrived.

'Thick clumps of willow bristle on the river banks, along which, in the past more than now, broad rich stands of poplar put forth their green leaves, interspersed here and there with alders and osiers or prettily adorned with perfumed honeysuckles, which embrace them and form arbours and steeples, sprinkled with tiny coloured bells.

'Oxen and pigs abound, as do poultry and their enemies, the marten and weasel. The hunter flushes out no small quantity of hare, the prey of foxes also. And from time to time the air is cloven by quails, turtle doves, partridges with grizzled plumage, woodcocks that peck the earth into a sieve, and other birds of step. Overhead, great flocks of fleet starlings, and in winter schools of duck, pattern the sky across the Po, and the alert white gull, gleaming watchful on the wing, swoops and grabs for fish.

'Riverside, the reeds conceal the many-coloured kingfisher, reed warbler, water-loving moorhen and crafty coot. You can hear the curlew's distinctive cry and spot herons, plovers, lapwings and other waterfowl, rapacious falcons and circling buzzards (terror of brooding hens), possibly at night even the barn owl and silent nightjar. In former times, larger winged creatures, carried up along the Po or down from the Alps by winds from strange lands, were the sport of admiring hunters.

'In the valley mosquitoes may sting you ("from muddy/ Swamps the frogs sing their ancient lays"),[1] but in the brilliant nights of summer the enchanting nightingale echoes the

---

[1] From Virgil, *Georgics I.*

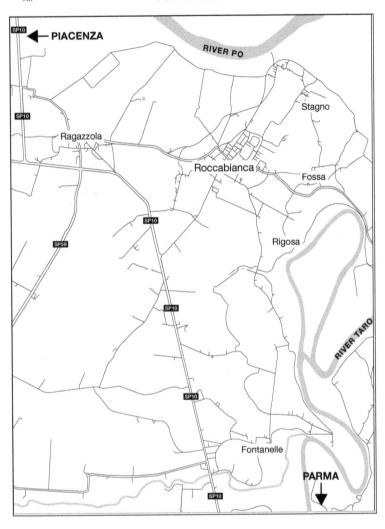

divine harmony of the universe with his sweet song, lamenting perhaps that it does not also soften the hearts of men.

'In the river, heavy with fish, dart barbels, tench, voracious red-finned pike, silver carp, exquisite perch, and slippery eels; and at one time great sturgeon, sometimes weighing more than 300 pounds, made their way upriver here, goaded by little lampreys.

'. . . On the beach are remnants of the town of Stagno, formerly extensive, now almost completely submerged beneath the encroaching water. On the side where the territory of Roccabianca touches the stream of the Stirone near the River Taro, the town of Fontanelle rises, broad and open to the sun. And where the main road crosses the dyke beside the Po, stands the hamlet of Ragazzola. While to the east, where the ground drops ever lower, lies the little village of Fossa and small, lonely Rigosa, humbly tucked away among white and grey poplars and other plants, not far from where the Rigosa brook flows into the Taro. In amongst all these is the town of Roccabianca.'

When I re-read this page written by Francesco Luigi Campari, I seem to become a character in a story he is telling, because I was born in Fontanelle, 'broad and open to the sun'.

Yet the little world of *The Little World* isn't exactly here: it is not in any specific place. The village of *The Little World* is a black dot which moves, along with its Peppones and its Smilzos, up and down the river through that chunk of land that stands between the Po and the Apennines. But its climate is the same, the landscape is the same; and in a village like this one, it is enough to stop on the road and look at a farmhouse, inundated by maize and hemp, and right away a story is born.

First Story –
Plain Madness

I lived on the farm known as Boscaccio in the Po basin with my father, my mother and my eleven brothers. I, the eldest, was coming up for twelve and Chico, the youngest, was nearly two. Every morning my mother supplied me with a basket of bread and a little bag of apples or sweet chestnuts, and my father would line us up on the threshing floor to recite the Lord's Prayer: and then we'd go with God and come back at sunset.

Our fields were never-ending. We could run all day without once moving off our property and my father barely had half a word to say if we walked through three whole acres of wheat in bud, or pulled up a row of vines. But still we'd trespass on other people's land and find plenty of mischief to get up to. Even the cherubic Chico, barely two years old, with his little red mouth, big eyes, long eyelashes and curls on his forehead, never let a gosling escape once it came within range. Old women used to flock to the farmhouse with baskets full of massacred goslings, hens and chicks. It became a regular event, and my mother would dutifully replace every dead bird with a live one. We had a thousand hens scratching about in our fields, but whenever we needed a few chickens for the pot, they had to be bought.

My mother shook her head and carried on exchanging live goslings for dead ones. My father would scowl, twirl his long moustache, and brusquely interrogate the little old women to see if they could remember which of the twelve of us was responsible for the killing.

When one of them said it had been Chico, the tiniest among us, my father made her tell the story three or four times over: how Chico would throw the stone, if it was a big one, and if he killed with the first shot.

I found these things out a long time afterwards: back then they never crossed my mind. I remember once being behind a bush with the other ten while Chico went after a gosling that was strolling stupidly around a bare patch of lawn, when I saw my father twenty yards away, smoking his pipe in the shade of a huge oak tree.

When Chico had despatched the gosling, my father sauntered off with his hands in his pockets, and my brothers and I gave thanks to God. I said to them in a low voice, 'He didn't see a thing!' I didn't realise that our father had been on our trail all morning, lurking like a thief, just so he could see for himself how Chico slaughtered goslings.

But I'm losing my thread: that's the trouble with having so many memories.

I have to tell you that Boscaccio was a place where no-one ever died, because of the extraordinary air we breathed there.

So it seemed impossible that a two-year-old child could fall ill at Boscaccio.

And yet Chico became very ill indeed. As we were going home one evening, he lay down suddenly on the ground and started to cry. Then he stopped crying and fell asleep. He wouldn't wake up, so I took him in my arms. He was red-hot, as if he was on fire inside: and we were gripped by fear. The sun was setting, the sky was black and red, and the shadows were long. We left Chico in the grass and fled, yelling and crying as if some unknown terror was after us.

'Chico's asleep and he's burning up!' I sobbed as soon as I was in front of my father.

My father – I remember this clearly – took down his shotgun from the wall, loaded it, put it under his arm, and followed us without a word. We walked in a tight cluster around him, no longer afraid because our father could hit a rabbit at eighty yards.

Chico was lying on the dark grass where we had left him, and in his long white smock and with his curls over his forehead, he seemed like one of the good Lord's angels who'd damaged a wing and tumbled down into the clover.

When it became known that Chico was ill, everyone was thrown into dismay. People talked in whispers even in their own homes. It was as if a dangerous stranger was haunting the village. Nobody risked opening a window at night for fear of seeing him on the threshing floor in the moonlight, wrapped in his old black gown with a scythe in his hand.

My father sent the gig to fetch three or four famous doctors. And they all touched Chico and put their ears to his back, then looked at my father without speaking.

Chico went on sleeping and burning, and his face became whiter than his sheet. My mother was weeping with us all around her; my father wouldn't sit down, and just kept on pulling at his moustache without saying a word.

On the fourth day, the last three doctors, who had arrived together, spread their arms and said to my father, 'No one but the good Lord Himself can save your child.'

I remember it was morning: my father nodded, and we followed him onto the threshing floor. Then with a whistle he called the farm workers and their families; fifty people altogether, men, women and children.

My father was tall, thin and powerful, with a long moustache, a big hat, a short close-fitting jacket, trousers that clung to his thighs, and high boots. (As a young man, he had been in America, and he dressed in the American style.) He'd strike fear into anybody when he planted himself in front of you with his legs apart. My father planted himself in front of the families and said: 'Only the good Lord can save Chico. On your knees: we need to pray to the good Lord, to save Chico.'

Everyone knelt and started praying aloud. The women took turns to say things, and we and the men answered, 'Amen.'

My father stayed with his arms folded, still as a statue in front of us until seven that evening, and everybody prayed because they were afraid of my father, and because they loved Chico.

At seven in the evening, as the sun was setting, a woman came to call my father. I followed him.

The three doctors were sitting palely around Chico's bed: 'He's getting worse,' said the oldest one. 'He won't last till morning.'

My father said nothing, but I felt his hand tightly squeezing mine.

We went out: my father took his shotgun, loaded it, slung it over his shoulder, picked up a big pack and handed it to me.

'Let's go,' he said.

We walked through the fields: the sun was now hidden behind the last of the undergrowth. We climbed over a low garden wall and knocked on a door.

The priest was alone in his house, eating by the light of an oil lamp. My father went in without taking off his hat.

'Reverend,' said my father, 'Chico is ill, and only the good Lord can save him. Today, sixty people have prayed to the good Lord, but Chico is getting worse and won't make it to tomorrow morning.'

The priest was looking at my father wide-eyed.

'Reverend,' my father went on, 'only you can talk to the good Lord and make Him understand the way things are. Get Him to realise that if Chico doesn't get better I shall blow everything up. There are eleven pounds of dynamite in that pack. The church won't have a single brick left standing. Come on!'

The priest didn't say a word: he went out, followed by my father, entered the church, knelt in front of the altar, and clasped his hands.

My father stood in the middle of the church with his gun

under his arm, his legs apart, immovable as a boulder. A single candle was burning on the altar, and all the rest was dark.

Towards midnight my father called me: 'Go and see how Chico is, and come straight back.'

I flew through the fields and reached the house with my heart in my mouth. Then I ran back even faster.

My father was still there, motionless, legs apart, his gun under his arm, while the priest was mumbling his prayers on the altar steps.

'Papa!' I shouted with my last breath, 'Chico's getting better! The doctor says he's out of danger. It's a miracle! Everyone's laughing and happy.'

The priest stood up: he was sweating and his face was crumpled.

'Good,' said my father gruffly.

Then, while the priest watched open-mouthed, he took a thousand lira note from his wallet and slipped it into the collection box.

'I always pay for my pleasures,' said my father. 'Good evening.'

My father never boasted about what he'd done, but there are still a few from outside the community of Boscaccio who say that on this occasion God was scared.

This is the Lower Plain, a land where there are people who don't baptise their children, and where blasphemy is not to deny God, but to spite God. It is only twenty-five miles or less from the city, but out on the plain, criss-crossed by dykes, where you can't see over a hedge or beyond the next bend, every mile counts for ten, and the city is something from another world.

I remember:

Second Story –
The Miracle of the Lower Plain

Sometimes we'd see city types at Boscaccio: mechanics, brick-layers. They'd go to the river to tighten the bolts on the iron bridge, or to the canal on the reclaimed land to re-point the walls of the locks.

They wore straw hats or cloth caps pulled down on one side; they sat outside Nita's bar and ordered beer and steaks with spinach. Boscaccio was a place where people ate at home and only went to the bar to swear, play bowls and drink wine with their friends.

'Wine, soup with bacon fat, and eggs with onion,' answered Nita appearing at the door. And then those men pushed back their straw hats and caps and started shouting that Nita had a very nice this and a very nice that, and slamming their great fists on the table and racketing like geese.

Those townies didn't understand anything: they went roaming through the countryside creating uproar and outrage like sows in a field of maize. In their own houses, they ate horse-meat rissoles, and came to Boscaccio wanting beer when the most you could expect there was wine in a soup dish; and they tried to bully men like my father who had 350 head of livestock, twelve sons and 1,500 acres of land.

It's different now because even in the country there are people who wear their caps pulled down to one side, eat horse-meat rissoles, and shout at the barmaids that they have a very nice this and a very nice that: telegraph wires and railways have a lot to answer for in that respect. But it was different then, and when those blokes from the city turned up in Boscaccio, there were people who couldn't decide whether to load their shotguns with buckshot or with bullets.

Boscaccio was a blessed place in that way. We were sitting in front of the threshing block once, watching our father carve a grain shovel from a piece of poplar wood, when Chico came running up.

'Ooh! Ooh!' said Chico, who, being only two, couldn't manage long speeches. I'm still amazed at how my father always understood what he was babbling about.

'It's either a stranger or some animal,' said my father and, picking up his shotgun, he set off, pulled by Chico towards the meadow in front of the first ash tree.

We found six no-goods from the city: they had trestle tables and poles marked in red and white, and they were measuring I don't know what as they trampled the clover.

'What are you doing?' my father asked the nearest one, who was holding up one of the red and white poles.

'I'm doing my job,' replied the idiot without turning around, 'and if you were doing yours we'd all save our breath.'

'Get away from there!' shouted the others, who were standing around their tripods in the middle of the meadow.

'Go!' said my father pointing his gun at these six idiots from the city. When they saw him standing there, tall as a tree, in the middle of the cart track, they picked up their equipment and ran off like hares.

That evening, as we sat around the threshing block watching my father give the last blows of his mattock to the shovel blade, the six men from the city came back, accompanied by two officers who they'd gone all the way to Gazzola to dig up.

'That's him there,' said one of the wretches, pointing at my father.

My father went on chiselling without even lifting his head, and the senior officer said he couldn't understand how all this had come about.

'It came about because I saw strangers ruining my clover, and I sent them off my land,' explained my father.

The senior officer said that the engineer and his assistants had come to take measurements for the tracks of the steam train.

'They should have told me. People have to ask permission before they come into my house,' declared my father, admiring his work with satisfaction. 'And no train is coming through my fields.'

'The track is going to come through,' laughed the engineer angrily, '. . . if you'll be so kind.' My father had noticed that the shovel had a lump on one side, and was now very busy smoothing it.

The senior officer stated that my father had to let the engineer and his staff onto his land. 'It's government level stuff,' he added.

'When I have an official piece of paper from the Government, I'll let these people through,' muttered my father. 'I know my rights.'

The senior officer agreed that my father was within his rights, and that the engineer would bring him an official piece of paper.

The engineer and the other five men from the city came back the next day: they came onto the threshing floor with their straw hats tipped back and their caps over one ear.

'Here's the authorisation,' said the engineer, handing my father a piece of paper.

My father took the paper and went back to the house: we all followed him.

'Read it slowly,' my father ordered me when we were in the kitchen. So I read it, and read it again.

In the end my father said darkly, 'Go and tell him he can come.'

Back in the house, I followed my father and the others up into the attic, and we arranged ourselves in front of the round window which gave onto the fields.

The six idiots were walking along the cart track towards the ash tree, singing to themselves: all at once we saw them gesticulating angrily. One of them made as if to run towards our house, but the others held him back.

City types still act like that, even today: they make as if to run towards somebody, but the others hold them back.

They stood there arguing on the cart track for a while. Then they took off their shoes and socks, and rolled up their trousers. Finally they went hopping into the clover meadow.

It had been a horrible slog from midnight until five in the morning: four heavy ploughs pulled by eighty oxen had churned up the entire clover meadow. Then some drainage ditches had been blocked and others opened in order to flood the ploughed area. Last of all, ten tanks of slurry had been carried over, and emptied into the waterlogged field.

My father stayed with us at the attic window until midday to watch the men from the city tottering about.

Chico chirped like a little bird every time he saw one of the six lose his balance, which pleased my mother, who had come up to tell us that lunch was ready.

'Look at him: he's got his colour back this morning. He just needed something to cheer him up, poor little chick. May the good Lord be thanked for putting that idea into your head last night,' said my mother.

Towards evening, the six men from the city came back again

accompanied by the officers and a gentleman dressed in black that they'd dug up from who knows where.

'These gentlemen allege that you have flooded a field in order to obstruct their work,' asserted the man dressed in black, irritated that my father had stayed sitting down, and wasn't even looking at him.

My father whistled and all the workers and their families came onto the threshing floor, men, women and children, fifty people in all.

'They say I flooded the meadow by the ash tree last night,' explained my father.

'That field's been flooded for twenty-five days,' said an old man.

'Twenty-five days,' they all said, men, women, and children.

'They must have mixed it up with the clover meadow near the second ash tree,' added the dairyman. 'It's easy to go wrong when you're not used to the place.'

They went off, gnashing their teeth with rage.

Next morning, my father had the horse hitched up to the wagon and went to the city, where he stayed for three days. He came back with a face like thunder.

'The track has to pass through here,' he explained to my mother. 'There's nothing we can do.'

More men came from the city and started planting stakes in the now dry soil: the track was supposed to cross the entire clover field before rejoining the road and running alongside it as far as Gazzola station.

The train would travel from the city all the way to Gazzola station, and it was a fine amenity: but it would pass right through my father's estate. And it was coming through by force; that was the worst of it. If only they'd asked nicely, my father would have let them have the land without even asking for money: my father had no objection to progress.

Who was the first to buy a modern double-barrelled shotgun with internal hammers? It was him, at Boscaccio. Well, good God, who else would it have been!

The main road was lined with gangs of men from the city laying stones and sleepers, and screwing in rails: and every time the track lengthened, the locomotive pulling trucks of materials took another step forward; at night the men slept in covered wagons at the end of the convoy.

Now the line was approaching the field of clover, and one morning the men started to cut down part of a hedge. My father and I were sitting under the first ash tree, and with us was Gringo, the mongrel that my father loved as if he had been one of us. As soon as the spades started digging up the hedge, Gringo hurled himself towards the road, and when the men had opened up a gap in the acacia bushes they found him right in front of them, threatening them with bared teeth.

One of the idiots took a step forwards and Gringo flung himself at the man's neck.

There were thirty of them with picks and spades: they didn't see us because we were behind the ash tree.

The engineer came forward with a stick and shouted, 'Get away, you filthy beast!' but Gringo bit him on the calf and made him fall down, yelling.

The others attacked *en masse*, dealing blows with their spades. Gringo didn't yield an inch. He was bleeding, but he carried on biting, tearing calves, crunching hands.

My father was chewing his moustache; he was pale as a corpse, and sweating. If he'd whistled, Gringo would have come back straight away and his life would have been saved. My father didn't whistle: he went on watching, pale as a corpse, with his forehead bathed in sweat, squeezing my hand while I sobbed.

The shotgun was leaning against the trunk of the ash tree, and that's where it stayed.

Now Gringo had no strength left, and was only fighting with the ferocity of his spirit: one of the men split his head open with the edge of a shovel.

Another pinned him down with his spade. Gringo moaned a little and then lay stone dead.

Now my father stood up, put his shotgun under his arm, and slowly moved towards the men from the city.

As if he'd suddenly appeared out of the blue, tall as a tree, with his pointed moustaches, his big hat, his short jacket and his thigh-length boots, the men all took a step backwards and watched him in silence, holding tightly onto their tools.

My father walked up to Gringo, bent down, grabbed him by the collar, and dragged him away like an old rag.

We buried him at the foot of the dyke, and when I'd stamped down the earth and everything was back the way it had been, my father took off his hat.

And I took off my hat, too.

The track never made it to Gazzola: it was autumn and the river had swollen and was flowing yellow with mud. One night the dyke burst, and the water ran through the fields and flooded all the lower part of the estate; the clover field and the road became a lake.

So they suspended the work, and to avoid any future danger they stopped the line at Boscaccio, five miles from our house.

And when the river had calmed down and we were going with our men to repair the landslide, my father squeezed my hand hard.

The dyke had burst exactly where we had buried Gringo.

Look what the spirit of a dog can do!

I call this the miracle of the Lower Plain.

Francesco Luigi Campari was a generous-hearted man, and one who loved the Plain, but he was a notary, a man of the law, and he wouldn't have allowed a single turtle dove into his description of it, if turtle doves hadn't actually formed part of the local fauna. Into a scrupulously realistic scenario like the one he painted, a journalist interpolates his own invented story. Which has more truth, the notary's factually true description or the journalist's imaginative story?

This is the world of *The Little World*: long straight roads, little houses painted red, yellow and ultramarine vanishing amidst the rows of vines. On August evenings when an enormous red moon rises slowly behind the dyke, it looks like something from another age. Someone is sitting on a heap of gravel beside the ditch, with his bicycle leaning against a telegraph pole. He rolls himself a cigarette. You pass, he asks you for a light. You talk. You tell him you're going to the 'festival' to dance, and he shakes his head. You tell him there'll be beautiful girls there, and he shakes his head.

Third story –
The Third Telegraph Pole on the Fabbricone Road

Girls? No, no girls. If you're after a bit of a knees-up in a bar, a bit of a sing-song, I'm your man. But that's it: I've already got a girl of my own waiting for me every evening by the third telegraph pole along the Fabbricone road.

When I was fourteen years old I used to come home on my bike along the Fabbricone road. There was a plum tree with a branch stretching out from a wall, and I stopped there once.

A girl came from the fields with a basket in her hand, and I called her. She must have been about nineteen because she was much taller than me and very shapely.

'Give me a leg-up,' I said.

The girl put down her basket, and I hoisted myself up onto her shoulders.

The branch was heavily laden and I filled my shirt with yellow plums.

'Hold out your apron and we'll go halves,' I said to the girl.

The girl said there was no need.

'Don't you like plums?' I asked.

'Yes, but I can pick them whenever I want,' she explained. 'It is my tree. I live here.'

I was fourteen, and still in short trousers, but I was a builder's labourer, and not scared of anyone. She was much taller than me, and shaped like a woman.

'I know the kind of stuff you get up to,' says I, giving her a nasty look, 'but I could smash your ugly face, beanpole!!'

She didn't say a word.

I saw her two evenings later, on the same little road.

'Hello, giraffe!' I shouted. Then I made a rude noise at her, one I wouldn't be capable of now, but back then I did it better than the foreman, who'd learned it in Naples.

I met her on other evenings, but I never said anything, until finally I lost patience, jumped off my bike, and blocked her way.

'What's up with you, looking at me like that . . . if you don't mind me asking?' I said, shoving the peak of my cap to one side.

The girl opened her two eyes, blue as water, two eyes like no others I'd ever seen.

'I'm not looking at you,' she answered shyly.

I got back on my bike.

'Just watch out, lanky!' I said. 'I mean it.'

A week later I saw her a long way ahead of me, walking beside a young man, and I flew into a great rage. I stood up on the pedals and hurtled down like a bat out of hell: six feet from the boy I did a sudden turn, and whacked him with my shoulder as I passed, laying him out like a fig skin.

I heard the son of a bitch shouting at me, so I got off my bike and leaned it against a telegraph pole near a heap of gravel. I saw him running towards me like a man possessed: he was about twenty years old, and could have flattened me with one punch. But I was a builder's labourer, and not scared of anyone. I picked my moment and chucked a stone right in his face.

My father was an amazing mechanic, and with a spanner in his hand he could see off a whole village: but even my father, once he knew I'd managed to pick up a stone, always did an about-face and waited till I was asleep to give me a beating. And that was my father, never mind this clodhopper! I covered his face in blood, then easy as you like, jumped onto my bike and rode away.

I roamed around for a couple of evenings, and then on the third I went back along the Fabbricone road, and as soon as I saw the girl I went up to her and did an American dismount, jumping backwards off the saddle.

Boys on bikes these days make me laugh with their mudguards, bells, brakes, lights and gears, and all the rest of it. I had a rust-covered Frera, but I didn't even dismount to go down the sixteen steps of the piazza: I just gripped the handlebars like the Red Devil, Gerbi, and flew down like a thunderbolt.

I dismounted, and there I was in front of the girl. I had a bag hanging from the handlebars, and I reached into it and pulled out a mason's hammer.

'If I catch you with someone else, I'll smash your head in, and his too,' I said.

The girl looked at me with those damned bright eyes, blue as water.

'Why do you say things like that?' she asked quietly.

I didn't know, but what did that matter.

'Just because,' I replied. 'You either go out on your own, or you go out with me.'

'I'm nineteen and you're fourteen at the very most,' said the girl. 'If you were at least eighteen it would be different. But I'm a woman now, and you're a boy.'

'So you wait till I'm eighteen,' I shouted. 'And you'd better not let me see you with anyone, or you're done for.'

I was a builder's labourer and I wasn't scared of anything: whenever I heard people talking about women, I cleared off right away. I couldn't give a dried fig for a woman: but I wasn't going to let this one act the fool with other men.

I kept seeing the girl for about four years, every evening except Sunday. She was always there, leaning against the third telegraph pole on the Fabbricone road. When it rained she put up her trusty umbrella.

I never stopped, not once.

'Hello,' I'd say as I passed.

'Hello,' she'd answer.

The day I turned eighteen, I got off my bike.

'I'm eighteen,' I said. 'Now you can go out with me. If you play the fool, I'll smash your head in.'

She was twenty-three now, and a complete woman: but she had the same bright eyes, blue as water, and she still spoke in the same low voice as always.

'You're eighteen,' she answered, 'but I'm twenty-three. The boys would throw stones at me, if they saw me with someone as young as you.'

I let my bike fall, scraped a flat stone off the ground, and said, 'You see that insulator there, the first one on the third pole?'

She nodded.

I hit it bang in the middle, and all that was left was the iron hook, bare as a worm.

'If the boys want to throw stones at us,' I shouted, 'they'll have to match that.'

'It was just an expression,' the girl explained. 'It's not right for a woman to go around with a child. If you'd at least been a soldier . . .'

I turned the peak of my cap all the way to the left: 'Listen my girl, do you think you can make a fool out of me? When I've finished soldiering I'll be twenty-one and you'll be twenty-six, and it'll be the same old story.'

'No,' replied the girl, 'eighteen to twenty-three is one thing, but twenty-two to twenty-six is something else. Differences in age don't matter so much as you get older. A man aged twenty-one is the same as a man aged twenty-six.'

That seemed reasonable: but I wasn't the type to let myself be led by the nose.

'All right. We'll talk again when I've finished being a soldier,' I said jumping onto my bike. 'But remember, if I don't find you here when I get back, I'm coming to smash your head in, even if you're hiding under your father's bed.'

Every evening I saw her standing still by the third telegraph pole, and I never stopped. I'd say good evening and she'd answer good evening. When I was called up, I shouted to her, 'I'm off to the army tomorrow.'

'See you when you get back,' replied the girl.

This isn't the place to tell you all about my military career: I got through eighteen months of national service, and I was no different in the regiment from how I was at home. I must have had three straight months without privileges, when I was either confined to barracks or in the clink.

As soon as eighteen months had gone by, they sent me home.

I got back in the late afternoon, and without even changing into civvies, I jumped onto my bike and headed for the Fabbricone road.

If she came up with more excuses, I'd smash her over the head with my bike.

It was slowly getting dark and I was going like the clappers, wondering where the hell I'd have to dig her up from, but I didn't have to bother, because there she was, on the dot, waiting under the third telegraph pole.

She was exactly as I'd left her, and her eyes were just the same, identical.

I dismounted in front of her.

'Finished,' I told her, showing my discharge papers. 'There's a picture of Italy sitting down, and that means unconditional discharge. When it's Italy standing up it means provisional discharge.'

'That's wonderful,' replied the girl.

I'd cycled like the wrath of God and my throat was dry.

'Could I have a couple of those yellow plums from before?' I asked.

The girl sighed, 'I'm very sorry, but the tree was burned down.'

I was amazed. 'Burned? Since when do they burn plum trees?'

'It happened six months ago,' answered the girl. 'One night the straw in the barn caught fire and the house and all the plants in the garden went up like matches. Everything got burned. After two hours there were just the walls left. Can you see them?'

I looked where she was pointing, and saw a piece of black wall with a window opening onto a red sky.

'What about you?' I asked.

'Me too,' she answered with a sigh, 'me too, like all the rest. A little pile of ashes, and it's all over.'

I looked at the girl leaning against the telegraph pole: I looked hard, and through her face and her body I could see the grain of the wood and the grass in the ditch.

I put a finger to her forehead and touched the telegraph pole.

'Did that hurt?' I asked.

'Not at all.'

We stayed there a while in silence as the sun turned an ever darker shade of red.

'What now?' I said finally.

'I waited for you,' the girl sighed, 'to show you it's not my fault. Can I go now?'

I was twenty-one now and big enough to present arms with a field cannon. When the girls saw me go by, they thrust out their chests as if they were in a march past, and watched me till their eyes became slits.

'May I go now?' repeated the girl in a low voice.

'No,' I replied. 'You must wait for me till I finish this other service. Don't try to make a fool of me, my lovely.'

'All right,' said the girl. And she seemed to be smiling.

But I didn't have much time for this sort of nonsense and I got straight back onto my bike.

Now we've been seeing each other every evening for twelve years. I pass by and never get off my bike.

'Hello.'

'Hello.'

Do you understand? If you want a sing-song in a pub, a bit of a knees-up, I'm your man. But that's it: I've got a girlfriend already, waiting for me every evening by the third telegraph pole on the Fabbricone road.

Now someone says: brother, why are you telling me these stories?

Because I am, I answer. Because you need to realise that in this bit of land between the river and the mountains, things can happen which don't happen anywhere else: things which are always in tune with the landscape. And the air you breathe there is special, inspiring both the living and the dead; and even the dogs have souls. Now you'll be able to understand Don Camillo and Peppone and all the other goings-on. And you won't be surprised that Jesus speaks, or that one man can split the head of another like a pumpkin, but do it honestly: by which I mean, without hatred. And two enemies can find that, in the end, they agree on everything that matters.

Because it's the rich, everlasting breath of the river that cleanses the air. The calm majestic river where, towards evening, Death passes quickly along the dyke on his bicycle. Or you pass by at night along the dyke, and you stop, and you decide to sit and look over at a little cemetery which is right there at the foot of the dyke. And if the shadow of a dead person comes and sits beside you, you won't get frightened and you'll talk tranquilly together.

That's the kind of air you'll breathe in this out of the way bit of land: and you'll find it easy to understand the way the business of politics can turn out down there.

Now these stories often talk about the crucified Christ. They do so because the main characters are three: the priest Don Camillo, the communist Peppone, and *il Cristo Crocifisso*.

Well, at this point I'd better make myself clear: if priests are offended by Don Camillo, they're welcome to break a candlestick over my head; if communists are offended by Peppone, they're welcome to break a crowbar on my back. But if anyone is offended by what my Christ has to say, there's nothing to be done about that; because it's not *the* Christ who speaks in my stories, but *my* Christ – in other words, the voice of my conscience.

My personal stuff; my affair.

And so: every man for himself, and God for all.

Giovanni Guareschi, 1948

The Little World of Don Camillo,
Il Cristo, Peppone and the rest

'This is how they told it to me.'

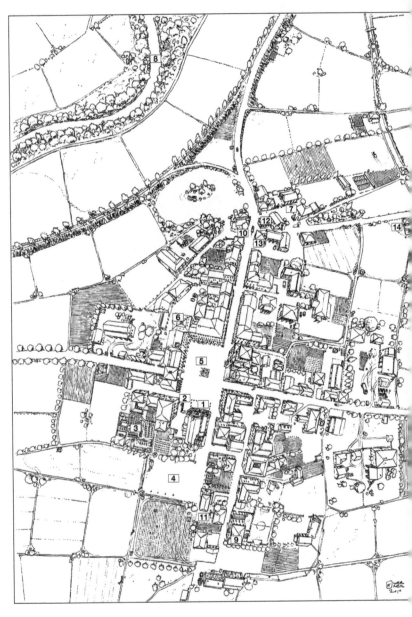

1 Church
2 Presbytery
3 Cemetery
4 Public piazza
5 Principal piazza
6 Theatre
7 Peppone's house

8 River
9 People's Palace
10 Police station
11 School
12 Post Office
13 Barchini's print shop
14 Smilzo's house

A Sin Confessed

DON CAMILLO was one of those straight-talkers who are incapable of knowing when to hold back. On one occasion during Mass, after some unseemly goings-on in the village involving young girls and landowners far too old for them, he threw caution to the wind. Having started an agreeable homily on matters in general, he happened to catch sight of one of the guilty parties sitting right there in the front row. Breaking off from what he'd been saying, he draped a cloth over the Crucifix above the high altar, and planting his fists on his hips he finished his sermon in his own unique style. So blunt was the language of this great brute of a man and so thunderous the delivery that the very roof of the little church had appeared to shake.

Naturally, at election time, Don Camillo expressed his opinions about leftwing activists in a similarly explicit manner, with the consequence that, just about sunset, as he was coming back to the presbytery, a great hulk of a man wrapped in a cloak darted out from a hedge behind him and, making use of the fact that the priest was encumbered by his bicycle and a bundle of seventy eggs hanging from the handlebars, gave him a whack with a stick before vanishing as if the earth had swallowed him up.

Don Camillo said nothing about this to anyone, but once he was back in the presbytery and the eggs were in a safe place, he went into the church to ask Jesus for advice, as he always did in moments of doubt.

'What should I do?' asked Don Camillo.

'Rub a bit of oil and water on your back and say nothing,' answered Jesus from above the altar. 'You must forgive those who offend you. That is the rule.'

'Yes, but in this case we're talking about beatings, not offences,' objected Don Camillo.

'And what does that mean?' whispered Jesus. 'That offences to the body are more painful than those done to the spirit?'

'All right, Signore. But you should bear in mind that by beating me, your minister, they have committed an offence against you . . . I'm more concerned for you than for me.'

'And am I not even more God's minister than you are? And did I not forgive those who nailed me to the cross?'

'It's pointless arguing with you, you're always right. Thy will be done. We'll forgive. But remember, if my silence makes that lot think they can get away with anything, and then they smash my head in, it'll be your responsibility. I could quote you passages from the Old Testament . . .'

'Don Camillo, you come here telling *me* about the Old Testament! I take full responsibility for whatever happens. But, just between ourselves, it serves you right. That little misfortune will teach you to play politics in my house.'

So Don Camillo forgave. But one thing stuck in his craw like a fishbone: the burning desire to know who had given him that tap on the back.

Time passed, and late one evening, while he was in the confessional, Don Camillo saw on the other side of the grille, the face of Peppone, the local boss of the far left.

Peppone coming to confession! – a jaw-dropping event. Don Camillo was delighted.

'God be with you, brother: with you who, more than any other, have need of His sacred blessing. Is it a long time since you have made a confession?'

'Not since 1918,' replied Peppone.

'Just imagine the sins you've committed in those twenty-eight years, with all those ideas filling your head.'

'Yes, well, quite a few,' sighed Peppone.

'For example?'

'For example, two months ago I hit you with a stick.'

'That is serious,' replied Don Camillo. 'By offending a minister of God you have offended God.'

'I regretted it afterwards,' Peppone exclaimed. 'I didn't beat you as a minister of God though, but as a political opponent. It was a moment of weakness.'

'Apart from this – and belonging to that diabolical Party of yours – do you have other serious sins to confess?'

Peppone spilled the beans.

All told, it wasn't much, and Don Camillo absolved him with ten Our Fathers and ten Hail Marys. Then while Peppone was kneeling at the altar rail to say his penance, Don Camillo went to kneel beneath the Crucifix.

'Jesus,' he said, 'forgive me, but I am going to beat him to a pulp.'

'Do not even dream of it,' answered Jesus. 'I have forgiven him, and so must you. Deep down he is a good man.'

'Don't trust the Reds, Jesus. They lure you in just so they can take advantage of you. Take a good look at him. Can't you see what a villainous mug he's got?'

'It is a face like any other. Don Camillo, you have let your heart be poisoned.'

'Jesus, if I have ever served you, grant me one thing: let me at least break that big candle over his back. Dear Jesus, what is one candle?'

'No,' replied Jesus. 'Your hands are made to bless, not to strike.'

Don Camillo sighed. He bowed and went through the little gate, turned towards the altar to make the sign of the cross again, and so found himself right behind Peppone who was kneeling there, deep in his prayers.

'Perfect,' groaned Don Camillo putting his hands together and looking at Jesus. 'My hands are made for blessing, but my feet aren't!'

'That is also true,' said Jesus from the high altar. 'But I am warning you, Don Camillo, just one!'

The kick flew like lightning and Peppone took it without batting an eye.

Then he stood up and sighed with relief: 'I've been waiting ten minutes for that,' he said. 'I feel better now.'

'Me too,' exclaimed Don Camillo, whose heart felt light and pure as the clear blue sky.

Jesus said nothing, but you could tell he was happy too.

The Baptism

OUT OF THE BLUE one day a man and two women came into the church. One of the women was the wife of Peppone, leader of the Reds.

Don Camillo, who was up a ladder polishing St Joseph's halo with Brasso, looked down and asked them what they wanted.

'This here needs baptising,' replied the man. And one of the women showed him a bundle with a baby inside.

'Whose is it?' asked Don Camillo, coming down.

'Mine,' said Peppone's wife.

'With your husband?' enquired Don Camillo.

'I should think so!' retorted Peppone's wife angrily. 'Who else would I have it with?'

'There's no need to get angry,' observed Don Camillo as he headed for the sacristy. 'I know a thing or two, and they say free love's all the rage in your Party.'

Passing the altar, Don Camillo bowed and winked at the crucified Christ.

'Did you hear that?' he chuckled. 'I slipped one to the Party of the Godless!'

'That is rubbish, Don Camillo,' replied Jesus in annoyance.

'If they were godless, they would not come here to have their children baptised. If Peppone's wife had slapped your face it would have been no more than you deserved.'

'If Peppone's wife had hit me I'd have grabbed all three of them by the neck and . . .'

'And?' asked Jesus sternly.

'Nothing, just a figure of speech,' said Don Camillo hurriedly as he stood up.

'Take care, Don Camillo,' Jesus warned.

Don Camillo put on his vestments and went up to the font.

'What do you want to call him?' asked Don Camillo.

'Lenin Libero Antonio,' replied Peppone's wife.

'Then go and have him baptised in Russia,' said Don Camillo, calmly replacing the cover on the font.

Don Camillo had hands as big as shovels, and the man and the two women left without a word. The priest then tried to sneak off to the sacristy, but a voice stopped him short.

'Don Camillo, you have done a terrible thing! Go and call those people back and baptise the child!'

'Jesus,' replied Don Camillo, 'baptism is no laughing matter. It is a sacrament. Baptism . . .'

'Don Camillo!' Jesus interrupted him. 'Are you seriously trying to teach me about baptism? I am the one who invented it! Now listen. You are behaving like an arrogant bully. Just suppose that baby were to die this moment, you'd be to blame if it was denied admission to Paradise!'

'Let's not over-dramatise the situation,' retorted Don Camillo. 'Why should the baby die? He's got ruddy cheeks like roses!'

'That has nothing to do with it,' Jesus countered. 'A roof tile could fall on his head; he could have an apoplectic fit. You *must* baptise him.'

Don Camillo flung wide his arms.

'Dear Lord, think about it for a moment. None of this would matter if we knew the child was definitely destined for Hell. But even though his parents are a bad lot, he could, if baptised, end up in Heaven. Now tell me this: how can I allow people called Lenin to join you in Heaven? I'm doing this for the good name of Heaven.'

'Leave the good name of Heaven to me,' cried Jesus in irritation. 'All I care about is that the child becomes an honest man. It does not matter to me if he is called Lenin or Coco the Clown. All you are entitled to do is point out to the parents that giving eccentric names to children can often cause them trouble, sometimes big trouble.'

'All right,' replied Don Camillo. 'It's always me who is wrong. We'll try and sort it out.'

Just then someone was heard entering the church. It was Peppone, alone but for the baby in his arms. He bolted the door behind him.

'I'm not leaving here,' he said, 'until my son is baptised with the name I want.'

'Well?' whispered Don Camillo to Jesus with a smile. 'You see now what these people are like? One can have nothing but the loftiest intentions, and look how they react.'

'Put yourself in his shoes,' replied Jesus. 'Peppone's way of life is not something for you to approve or disapprove, but to understand.'

Don Camillo shook his head.

'I said I'm not leaving until you baptise my son the way I want,' repeated Peppone, putting the bundle with the baby onto a pew. Then he took off his jacket, rolled up his sleeves, and came menacingly towards Don Camillo.

'Jesus,' implored Don Camillo, 'I appeal to you. If you think it right that one of your priests should assent to the threats of private individuals, then I will defer. But in that case, don't complain when they come back tomorrow with a calf they want baptised. You know as well as I do, precedents are dangerous . . .'

'Well,' said Jesus, 'in this case you must try to make him understand . . .'

'And if he attacks me?'

'Accept it, Don Camillo. Bear it. Suffer as I did.'

So Don Camillo turned around. 'All right, Peppone,' he said. 'The baby will leave here baptised, but not with that damnable name.'

'Don Camillo,' muttered Peppone, 'remember I've got a delicate stomach ever since I took that bullet in the mountains. No low blows, or I'll give you a good going over with a pew.'

'Don't worry, Peppone, I'll address myself only to your upper storey,' replied Don Camillo, landing a punch by Peppone's ear.

They were a pair of bruisers with arms of iron and their blows whistled through the air. After twenty minutes of furious, silent combat, Don Camillo heard a voice at his shoulder: 'Now, Don Camillo! Get him on the jaw!'

It came from above the altar. Don Camillo aimed a blow at the jaw, and Peppone fell to the ground.

He stayed sprawled out there for ten minutes, then he got up, massaged his chin, dusted himself off, put his jacket back on, retied his red kerchief, and picked up the baby.

Don Camillo, by then in his vestments, was waiting for him, solid as granite, beside the font.

'What shall we call him?' asked Don Camillo.

'Camillo Libero Antonio,' muttered Peppone.

Don Camillo shook his head.

'No, let's call him Libero Camillo Lenin,' he said. 'Yes, Lenin too. His sort cannot get up to mischief when he's got a Camillo as his neighbour.'

'Amen,' muttered Peppone, feeling his jaw.

When it was all done and Don Camillo was passing the altar, Jesus said smiling, 'Don Camillo, I have to admit it, you're better at politics than I am.'

'And at trading punches too,' answered Don Camillo loftily, putting a nonchalant finger to a big lump on his forehead.

The Proclamation

LATE ONE EVENING, old Barchini turned up at the presbytery. He was the village stationer, but being also the proud owner of two cases of type and a foot-operated press from 1870, he had added the word 'Printer' above his shop. There must have been something big to report because he stayed in Don Camillo's study for quite a while.

When Barchini had gone, Don Camillo ran to share the information with Jesus above the altar.

'Important news!' he exclaimed. 'The enemy is going to publish an announcement tomorrow. Barchini's printing it and he's brought me a proof copy.'

Don Camillo pulled a freshly printed sheet of paper from his pocket and read it aloud:

FIRST AND LAST WARNING

Again yesterday evening a cowardly anonimus hand wrote an ofensive insult on our news buletin bord. That hand had better keep a lookout, because if the good for nothing it belongs to, who takes advantage of the shadows to preform acts of provocation, doesn't stop he will regret it when its too late to make amends.

All patients has it's limits.

Branch Secretary
Giuseppe Bottazzi

Don Camillo gave a mocking laugh.

'What do you think of this? Quite a work of art isn't it? Just imagine the fun people will have tomorrow when these manifestoes go up. What's Peppone playing at, making such proclamations? It's enough to make you crack a rib laughing!'

Jesus made no reply, and Don Camillo stared in astonishment.

'Didn't you catch the style? Do you want me to read it again?'

'I heard you the first time,' said Jesus. 'People express themselves as best they can. It is hardly fair to expect someone who left school at the age of nine to cope with the subtleties of style.'

'Lord!' exclaimed Don Camillo, with his arms outspread. 'How can you speak of subtlety in the same breath as this verbal hotchpotch!'

'Don Camillo, the lowest tactic you can employ in a debate

is to latch onto your opponent's spelling mistakes and bad grammar. What counts in a debate is the argument. You would do better to question his threatening tone.'

Don Camillo put the sheet of paper back into his pocket.

'Of course,' he mumbled. 'The really reprehensible thing is the threatening tone of the statement. But what can you expect from people like that? Violence is all they understand.'

'And yet,' observed Jesus, 'for all his exuberance, Peppone doesn't have the air of someone who is just a troublemaker.'

Don Camillo shrugged. 'It's like pouring good wine into a rotten barrel. When somebody gets himself into a certain kind of company and adopts the sacrilegious thinking of the rabble, he ends up fit for nothing.'

But Jesus did not seem convinced.

'I would say that in Peppone's case, you should look beyond appearances if you want to find out where the truth really lies. Is Peppone being mischievous or has he been provoked into this? Which do you think it is?'

Once again Don Camillo spread his arms. Who could possibly tell?

'All we need to know is what caused the offence,' insisted Jesus. 'He talks about an insult that someone wrote on his news bulletin yesterday evening. So, yesterday evening, when you went to the tobacconist, you didn't by any chance go past the notice board? Try and remember.'

'Well, yes I did go past it,' Don Camillo freely admitted.

'Good. And did you happen to stop for just a moment to read the bulletins?'

'Not to read them, definitely not: more a quick squint. Was that wrong?'

'Not in the least, Don Camillo. You need to keep in touch with what your flock is saying and writing and, if possible, thinking. I was only trying to find out if you noticed anything strange written on the board while you were there.'

Don Camillo shook his head.

'I can assure you that when I stopped there, I didn't see anything strange written on the notice board.'

Jesus thought for a while.

'And when you *left*, Don Camillo, did you see anything out of the ordinary written there?'

Don Camillo concentrated.

'Ah, yes,' he said at last. 'Thinking back, I have a feeling that as I left I did see something scribbled in red crayon on one of the bulletins. Oh! Please excuse me, I think I hear somebody in the presbytery.'

Don Camillo bowed hastily and made to slip away, but the voice from above the altar stopped him.

'Don Camillo!'

Don Camillo came slowly back and stopped sulkily in front of the altar.

'Well?' asked Jesus sternly.

'Well, yes,' mumbled Don Camillo. 'It may be that . . . I did happen to write "Peppone is an ass" . . . But if you'd read that bulletin, I'm sure you'd have . . .'

'Don Camillo, you seem to know nothing about your own actions, and yet you claim to know what the *Son of God* would do?'

'Forgive me. I've been foolish, I realise that. But now Peppone's being foolish too, sending out posters with threats, and so we're quits.'

'You are nothing of the kind!' exclaimed Jesus. 'You called Peppone an ass yesterday evening, and tomorrow the whole village will be doing the same. Just think of the people who will pour in from all directions to laugh at the howlers committed by local boss Peppone, of whom everyone is scared to death! And it is all your fault. Does that look good to you?'

Don Camillo plucked up the courage to say, 'You're right, but from the wider political point of view . . .'

Jesus cut him off. 'I care not at all about the wider political point of view! From the point of view of Christian charity, giving people an excuse to laugh at a man for no better reason than that he left school at the age of nine is a complete disgrace. And you, Don Camillo, are the cause of it!'

'Tell me, Lord,' sighed Don Camillo. 'What can I do?'

'Well it was not I who wrote "Peppone's an ass"! It is the sinner who must do the penance. See to it, Don Camillo!'

Don Camillo retreated to his study and started to walk up and down the room, imagining that he could hear people stopping in front of Peppone's proclamation to laugh. 'Idiots!' he exclaimed in fury.

He turned to the small statue of the Virgin Mary.

'Mother of God,' he prayed, 'help me.'

'This is strictly my Son's concern,' whispered the little Madonna. 'I cannot become involved.'

'Put in a good word for me.'

'I will try.'

And all of a sudden, in came Peppone.

'Listen,' he said. 'This has got nothing to do with politics. This is about a Christian who finds himself in trouble and comes to ask a priest for his advice. I'm sure . . .'

'I know my duty,' said Don Camillo. 'Who have you killed?'

'I don't kill people, Don Camillo,' replied Peppone. 'But if someone treads on my corns, my fists are bound to blaze into action.'

'And how is little Libero Camillo Lenin?' inquired Don Camillo slyly. And Peppone, remembering the pounding he'd been given on the day of the baptism, shrugged his shoulders.

'You know how it is,' he grumbled. 'Fist fights go both ways. You win some, you lose some. But never mind that, this is a different matter. In short, the fact is that in the village there's a good-for-nothing lowdown coward, a Judas with poison fangs who, every time we pin up a bulletin on our board with my signature as Secretary, thinks it's amusing to write "Peppone's an ass" on it!'

'Is that all?' exclaimed Don Camillo. 'Not exactly a tragedy.'

'I'd like to know what *you'd* say if for twelve days on the trot you found someone writing "Don Camillo's an ass" on the order of service.'

Don Camillo said the comparison didn't stand up at all. A Church notice board was one thing, the news bulletin board of a political party quite another. It is one thing to call God's priest an ass, quite another so to discredit the leader of a bunch of rampaging lunatics.

Finally, he asked, 'Don't you have any idea who it might be?'

'It is better that I don't,' replied Peppone with some force. 'If I did, that Barabbas would be going around with both his eyes as black as his miserable soul. That vandal has been having his fun with me for twelve days – I'm certain it's always the same one – and now I'm warning him, it's gone far enough.

He'd better watch out, because if I get hold of him it'll be the Messina earthquake all over again. And now I'm going to print some notices and put them up on every street corner, so he and his gang can't miss them.'

Don Camillo shrugged.

'I'm not a printer,' he said. 'What's it got to do with me? Go and find someone with a printing press.'

'I've already done that,' replied Peppone darkly. 'But since I don't like making an ass of myself, you'd better have a look at the draft of the announcement before Barchini prints it.'

'But Barchini's no fool. If there was something wrong with it, he'd have told you.'

'You think so?' Peppone gave a bitter laugh. 'He's the next worst thing to a priest . . . I mean, he's just as reactionary, black as his miserable soul. Even if he saw that I'd written "heart" with two aitches, he wouldn't think twice about making me look small.'

'But you've got your men,' returned Don Camillo.

'Do you really think I'm going to stoop so low as to let my inferiors correct me? Besides, it would be a joke. They don't have half the alphabet between them.'

'Let's see it then,' said Don Camillo. And Peppone gave him the proof sheet.

'Well, blunders aside, the tone does seem a bit strong.'

'Too strong?' cried Peppone. 'He's a damn lowlife, he's a hooligan, he's such a scoundrel of an *agent provocateur* that if I was to write it the way he deserves I'd need two dictionaries!'

Don Camillo picked up his pencil and carefully corrected the draft.

'Now go over the corrections in pen,' he said when he'd finished.

Peppone looked sadly at the paper covered with squiggles and crossings out.

'To think that wretch Barchini told me it was all fine . . . How much do I owe you?'

'Nothing. I'd rather you kept the whole thing under your hat. I don't like the idea of anyone knowing I do work for the Department of Propaganda.'

'I'll send you some eggs.'

Peppone left, and Don Camillo went to put his conscience to rest before the altar, before going to bed himself.

'Thank you for giving him the idea of coming to see me.'

'It's the least I could do,' replied Jesus, smiling. 'How did it go?'

'A bit tricky, but fine. He doesn't have the slightest idea that it was me yesterday evening.'

'Oh yes he does,' retorted Jesus. 'He knows perfectly well it was you. All twelve times. He even saw you on a couple of evenings. Stay alert, Don Camillo: think seven times before writing "Peppone's an ass"!'

'When I go out I'll leave my pencil behind,' promised Don Camillo solemnly.

'Amen,' concluded Jesus, smiling.

The Chase

DON CAMILLO had let himself go a bit during a little harangue from the pulpit about local matters, including some pretty sharp barbs aimed at 'that lot' (Peppone's gang), and the next evening, as he was starting to heave away at the bell ropes – after the bell-ringer had been 'called away' (no one knew where) – all hell broke loose.

Some damned soul had tied firecrackers to the clappers of the bells: no damage, but a din fit to bring on a heart attack.

Don Camillo knew when to keep his mouth shut. He celebrated evening Mass in perfect calm and the church was packed: not one of 'that lot' was absent. Peppone was in the front row with a demure expression on his face that would have driven a saint to frenzy. But Don Camillo refused to be provoked. As punch-bags go, he was in the premier division, and the congregation went away disappointed.

Having closed the main door, Don Camillo put on his overcoat, and made a quick bow to the altar before going out.

'Don Camillo,' said Christ from the cross, 'put it down.'

'I don't understand,' protested Don Camillo.

'Put it down!'

Don Camillo pulled a stick out from under his coat and placed it in front of the altar.

'That looks nasty, Don Camillo.'

'But Jesus, it's not even oak: it's poplar,' said Don Camillo in self-justification. 'A flimsy thing, you can bend it . . .'

'Go to bed, Don Camillo, and stop thinking about Peppone.'

Don Camillo shrugged, and went to bed with a fever. And when late the following evening, Peppone's wife suddenly appeared in front of him, he jumped as if a firecracker had exploded under his chair.

The woman was very agitated. 'Don Camillo,' she began, but Don Camillo interrupted her.

'Out of here, you sacrilegious creature!'

'Come on, Don Camillo, enough of all that nonsense! The villain who tried to bump off Peppone is at Castellino. They've let him out!'

Don Camillo was lighting a cigar. 'Why are you telling me this, comrade? What's it got to do with you?'

The woman started shouting. 'What it's got to do with me is that they came to tell Peppone and he's shot off to Castellino like a bat out of hell. He's taken the machine gun!'

'Ah, so it's true! You do have a secret stash of weapons in spite of the amnesty.'

'Don Camillo, keep politics out of this! Don't you see? That man will kill my husband. If you don't help me, he's done for.'

Don Camillo gave a sneaky laugh. 'That'll teach him to tie firecrackers to the clappers of the bells. I hope he rots in jail. Get out of this house!'

Three minutes later, Don Camillo, with the skirts of his cassock tied around his neck, was struggling like a man possessed along the Castellino road astride a racing bike, borrowed from the sacristan's son.

There was a brilliant moon, and a few miles from Castellino Don Camillo saw a man sitting on the parapet of the little bridge over the Fossone, so he slowed down because you need to be careful when you travel at night. He stopped ten yards from the bridge, keeping his hand within reach of a little something he happened to have in his pocket.

'Young man,' he asked, 'have you seen a fat man on a bicycle go by in the direction of Castellino?'

'No, Don Camillo,' replied the other calmly.

Don Camillo came closer.

'Have you already been to Castellino?' he enquired.

'No, I thought better of it. It's not worth the trouble. Did that foolish wife of mine come and bother you with this?'

'No bother at all. A little outing.'

'Oh really? What a sight, a priest on a racing bike!' said Peppone with a mocking laugh.

Don Camillo came and sat beside him.

'My son, in this world you must be ready to see priests in all the colours of the rainbow.'

An hour or so later, Don Camillo returned home and made a brief report to the Almighty.

'It all went well, just the way you suggested.'

'Well done, Don Camillo. But remind me, did I also suggest that you should grab his feet and tip him into the stream?'

Don Camillo shrugged.

'I don't remember exactly. What's certain is that he didn't care for seeing a priest on a racing bike, and so I made sure he couldn't.'

'I understand. And is he back now?'

'He'll be here in a bit. Seeing him fall into the Fossone, it occurred to me that, being all wet, he'd find his bike a bit of a nuisance, so I thought I should come back with both of them.'

'That was a very kind thought, Don Camillo,' agreed Jesus solemnly.

Peppone turned up at the presbytery door towards dawn. He was soaking wet, and Don Camillo asked if it was raining.

'Fog,' replied Peppone through gritted teeth. 'Can I have my bike?'

'Of course. It's right here.'

Peppone looked at the bicycle.

'You didn't happen to notice by any chance if there was a machine gun tied to the crossbar?'

Don Camillo spread his arms and smiled.

'A machine gun? What's that?'

'I've only made one mistake in my life,' said Peppone at the door. 'Tying firecrackers to the clappers of the bells. It should have been half a ton of dynamite.'

'*Errare humanum est*,' observed Don Camillo.

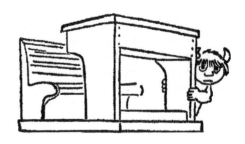

Evening Class

A GROUP OF MEN, cloaked darkly against the night, made their way stealthily through the fields. It was pitch black, but they knew every clump of earth and advanced safely. At length they came to the back of a small, isolated house half a mile from the village, and burrowed through the hedge into the garden.

A crack of light filtered through the shutters of a first floor window.

'It's going according to plan,' whispered Peppone, who was leading the little expedition. 'She's still up. So far so good! Spiccio, you knock on the door.'

A tall, bony man with a determined expression stepped forward and knocked twice.

'Who is it?' said a voice from inside.

'A few odds and ends,' the man replied.

The door opened slightly, and a little old woman appeared with snow-white hair and with a lantern in her hand. The others came out of the shadows and stood in front of the door.

'Who are all these people?' asked the old woman suspiciously.

'They're with me,' explained Spiccio. 'Old friends. We've got important things we need to talk to you about.'

The old woman led them into a small, well-kept sitting room. The men stood silent, frowning and muffled in front of the little table at which the woman had gone to sit. She put on her glasses and looked at the faces which were peering out of the black hoods.

'Hmm,' she muttered. She knew this lot from top to bottom. She was eighty-six years old and had taught the village the ABC back in the days when learning it was still big city stuff. She had taught the fathers, the sons, and the sons' sons. Her cane had come down upon the most important people in the village. Some while ago she had retired and gone to live alone in this remote cottage. Here she could leave her front door wide open because 'Signora Cristina' was a national monument, and no one would dare to touch a hair on her head.

'So . . . what is it?' she asked them.

'Something's happened,' explained Spiccio. 'There've been local elections and the Reds won.'

'Nasty people, the Reds,' commented Signora Cristina.

'*We* are the Reds who won,' added Spiccio.

'Nasty people just the same,' insisted the Signora. 'In 1901 that cretin of a father of yours wanted to take the Crucifix out of the school!'

'That was then,' said Spiccio. 'It's different now.'

'Just as well,' muttered the old woman. 'And so . . .?'

'So the fact is we won . . . but there are two minority members, two of the Blacks.'

'Blackshirts?'

'Yes, two reactionaries. Spilletti and the *cavaliere* Bignini....'

Signora Cristina laughed derisively. 'You may be Reds, but in the Council those two Blacks will turn you yellow with jaundice. It's only to be expected. Just think of all the imbecilities you'll come up with!'

'That's why we're here,' muttered Spiccio. 'We can't go to anybody but you, because you're the only person we can trust. You've got to help us, see, and we'll pay you for it.'

'Help you?'

'The whole council's here. We can come through the fields late at night and you can give us a bit of a refresher course. You look over the papers we have to read, and explain the words we don't understand. We know what we want – we won't need so much in the way of poetry, but we will have to mind our Ps and Qs with those two skunks, or they'll make fools of us in public.'

The Signora shook her head gravely.

'If you had only paid attention when you should have done, instead of getting up to mischief . . .'

'Signora, that was thirty years ago . . .'

Signora Cristina put her glasses back on, thrust out her chest, and suddenly she was thirty years younger. And so were the others.

'To your places,' she said, and they all sat down on chairs and stools. Turning up the flame of her lamp she inspected the ten faces in turn: a wordless roll call. Every face brought a name and a recollection of a childhood.

Peppone was in a dark corner, keeping a low profile.

The Signora raised her lamp, then lowered it and pointed a bony finger.

'You!' she said sternly. 'Out!'

Spiccio tried to say something, but Signora Cristina shook her head and exclaimed, 'I won't have Peppone in my house. Not even as a photograph! You have gone too far young man. Too far too often. Be off with you, and don't show your face here again.'

Spiccio spread his arms disconsolately.

'But Signora Cristina, what are we supposed to do? *Peppone's the Mayor!*'

Signora Cristina stood up and waved a long stick threateningly.

'Mayor or no mayor, you get out of here or I'll beat the skin off your head.'

Peppone stood up.

'What did I tell you?' he said hanging his head as he went out. 'I was too naughty too often.'

'And remember, you don't set foot in here again, not even if they make you Minister for Education. Ass!' she added as she sat down again.

Don Camillo knelt before the altar in the empty church lit only by two candles, chatting with Christ on the cross.

'Far be it from me to criticise you for what you have allowed to happen,' said Don Camillo at an opportune moment, 'but I would never have permitted someone like Peppone to become Mayor, and with a Council in which only two people can actually read and write!'

'Learning is not in itself important, Don Camillo,' replied Jesus with a smile. 'Ideas are what matter. Fine speeches achieve nothing if there are no practical ideas beneath the well chosen words. Let us try him out before we pass judgement.'

'You're right of course,' agreed Don Camillo. 'I only mentioned it because if the lawyer's Party had won, I'd have an assurance that the bell tower would be renovated. But at least now, if the tower falls down, we'll have compensation in a magnificent People's Palace with dance halls, shops selling alcohol, gambling dens, a theatre for variety shows . . .'

'And a zoo full of poisonous snakes like Don Camillo,' added Jesus.

Don Camillo bowed his head, sorry to have shown himself so full of ill will. He looked up.

'You misjudge me,' he said. 'You know how much a cigar means to me. Well, look: this is the only cigar I possess. Now watch what I do to it.'

He took a cigar from his pocket, and crumbled it in his enormous hand.

'Well done,' said Jesus. 'Well done, Don Camillo. I accept your penance. But now I want to see you throw away the tobacco, because you are quite capable of putting it back in your pocket and smoking it later in your pipe.'

'But we're in church,' protested Don Camillo.

'Worry not about that, Don Camillo, throw the tobacco into that corner.'

As Don Camillo did as he was told under the delighted gaze

of Jesus there was a knock at the sacristy door, and in came
Peppone.

'Good evening, Signor Mayor,' exclaimed Don Camillo
with exaggerated deference.

'Listen,' said Peppone, 'if a Christian has doubts about
something he's done, and comes and tells you, and if you can
see that he's made a mistake or two, will you point them out
to him or just pretend they're not there?'

This annoyed Don Camillo. 'How dare you question the
integrity of one of God's priests? A priest's first duty is to make
clearly known to the penitent all the errors he has committed.'

'Good,' exclaimed Peppone. 'Are you ready to hear my
confession?'

'I am ready.'

Peppone took a thick wad of papers from his pocket and
started to read: 'Citizens, in this moment in time as we hail the
victorious affirmation of our Party manifesto . . .'

Don Camillo interrupted him with a gesture and went to
kneel before the altar.

'Jesus,' he murmured, 'I cannot be held responsible for my
actions a moment longer!'

'*I* will be responsible for them,' replied Jesus. 'Peppone has
won this round, and you must acknowledge it, and do your
duty.'

'Dear Lord,' Don Camillo insisted, 'think for a moment. Are
you asking me to support the Communist Party's propaganda
machine?'

'You are going to support grammar, syntax and spelling,
and they are things which have nothing diabolical or doctrinal
about them.'

Don Camillo put on his glasses, picked up his pencil, looked
over the speech Peppone was due to give the next day, and
got its collapsing sentences onto their feet. Then Peppone
solemnly read through what he had done.

'Good,' he said. 'The only thing I don't understand is this.
Where I said, "It is our intention to extend the school building
and rebuild the bridge over the Fossalto," you've corrected it
to: "It is our intention to extend the school building, repair
the church tower, and rebuild the bridge over the Fossalto."
Why so?'

'It's a syntactical matter,' explained Don Camillo solemnly.

'Lucky you for having studied Latin and understanding all the subtleties of language,' sighed Peppone. 'I hope it means that the tower will just as subtly fall on your head.'

Don Camillo spread his arms: 'We must bow to the will of God.'

After seeing Peppone to the door, Don Camillo returned to the high altar.

'Bravo, Don Camillo,' said Jesus with a smile. 'I judged you too harshly, and I am sorry you destroyed your last cigar. It is a penance you did not deserve to make. In all sincerity, it was very rude of that Peppone not to offer you a replacement, after all your hard work!'

'Well, as it happens,' sighed Don Camillo, pulling from his pocket a cigar, and steeling himself to crush it in his huge hand.

'No, Don Camillo,' said Jesus smiling. 'Go and smoke it in peace. You have earned it.

'But . . .'

'No, Don Camillo, you did not steal it. Peppone had two cigars in his pocket. He is a communist, so by nimbly liberating one of them, you did no more than take your fair share.'

'No one understands these things better than you,' exclaimed Don Camillo with great respect.

Trespassing

Every morning without fail, Don Camillo went and measured the famous crack in the church tower. It was the same story every time: the crack was no wider, but it wasn't any narrower either. Finally he could no longer contain himself, and he sent the sacristan over to the Council headquarters.

'Go and tell the mayor to come here right away and look at this tragedy. Tell him it's serious.'

The sacristan went and at length returned.

'Mayor Peppone said he takes your word for it that the matter is serious. Or rather he said that if you really want to show him the crack, you should take it to the Town Hall. He's available until five o'clock.'

Don Camillo didn't bat an eye: he confined himself to saying after evening service, 'Tomorrow morning, if Peppone or someone from his gang is brave enough to show their face at Mass, they will witness something sensational. Unless of course they're too scared to show up.'

The next morning there was no sign of a Red in church, but five minutes before Mass was due to start, the regular steps of a military formation could be heard echoing in the churchyard outside. In a perfect square, all the local communists, not only from the village but from all the surrounding parishes, every one of them – even Bilò the shoemaker who had a wooden leg, and Roldo from the Meadows, who had a stinking cold – was marching proudly towards the church, with Peppone in the lead calling 'left-right-left'.

They entered the church in a solid phalanx and took their places in good order, wearing fierce expressions that could have belonged to the crew of *Battleship Potemkin*.[2]

When Don Camillo came to his sermon, he chose elegantly to re-tell the story of the Good Samaritan, and concluded with a brief appeal to the faithful.

'As everyone knows, though perhaps not those who most of all should know, a dangerous fissure is threatening the stability of the church tower,' he said. 'So I appeal to you, dear faithful souls, to come to the aid of God's house. In saying, "faithful" I mean to address those honest souls who are here to draw closer to God, and certainly not those sectarians who are here to show off their readiness for war, and who wouldn't much care if the tower collapsed.'

When Mass was over, Don Camillo sat at a little table near

---

[2] The crew of the battleship Potemkin famously mutinied against their Tsarist officers before the Russian Revolution.

the presbytery door, and the congregation filed past him, but nobody went home. Having made their contribution to the collection, everyone stood in the piazza to see what would happen next. And what happened next was that Peppone arrived, followed by his platoon in a perfect square, and called out a mighty 'Halt!' in front of the table before stepping proudly forward.

'Yesterday from this tower these bells greeted the dawn of Liberation, and tomorrow from this tower these bells will greet the radiant dawn of the proletarian revolution!' said Peppone to Don Camillo, putting three big red bundles of money onto the table in front of him.

Then off he went, head held high, followed by his troop. And Roldo from the meadow was so wrecked by fever that he could hardly stay on his feet, but he too carried his head high; and as Bilò hobbled past Don Camillo, he proudly beat time with his wooden leg.

When Don Camillo brought the basket filled with money before the high altar, and mentioned that there was more than enough in it to meet the cost of repairing the tower, Jesus smiled in astonishment.

'You did well, Don Camillo.'

'Naturally,' replied Don Camillo, 'because you know human beings, but *I* know Italians.'

Up to this point, Don Camillo had indeed conducted himself well. But now he spoiled it by sending a message to Peppone telling him how much he'd admired his men's demonstration of readiness for war, but that in his opinion they should get some more training in 'the about-face' and 'the at-the-double' because they'd need them urgently on the day of the proletarian revolution.

This was out of order, and Peppone lay in wait, biding his time.

Don Camillo was a perfect gentleman, but that did not stop him possessing a mighty passion for hunting and a splendid, double-barrelled shotgun with some wonderful Walstrode cartridge belts. And beside all this, Baron Stocco's estate was only three miles from the village, which constituted a serious temptation. Not only the wildlife, but even the local hens had learned that all they had to do was take refuge behind the wire fence and they were free to laugh in the faces of anyone who wanted to wring their necks.

So it was hardly surprising if one evening Don Camillo – with his cassock stuffed into an enormous pair of breeches and a huge felt hat on his head – was to be found trespassing on the Baron's land. The flesh is weak, and weakest of all is the flesh of hunters. So it was once again hardly surprising if Don Camillo happened to fire a shot which hit a big hare, three feet or more in length. Seeing it lying there on the ground, he happened to put it in his game bag and was just on the point of beating the retreat when somebody appeared out of nowhere and Don Camillo decided, with his hat pulled down over his eyes, to butt the man in the stomach and send him flying, because it would be a poor state of affairs if the whole village knew that a gamekeeper had caught the parish priest poaching.

Unfortunately, the idea of a head-butt had occurred to the other man too, and so the two heads met half way with such a crash that the rebound threw them onto their backsides seeing stars.

'A nut as hard as that could only belong to our well-beloved Signor Mayor,' grumbled Don Camillo when the mist had cleared.

'A nut as hard as that could only belong to our well-beloved arch-priest,' replied Peppone rubbing his head.

Peppone had also been doing some illicit hunting nearby, and he too had a fine devil of a hare in his sack. He looked at Don Camillo scornfully.

'I would never have believed,' said Peppone, 'that a man who preaches respect for other people's property would break into a private estate to go poaching.'

'And I would never have believed that our leading citizen, our Comrade Mayor . . .'

'Mayor, yes, but comrade too,' Peppone interrupted him. 'Which means corrupted by infernal theories about equal distribution of goods, and therefore acting much more in accord with his principles than the Reverend Don Camillo, who instead . . .'

Someone was coming, he was already a few paces away, and it was impossible to do a runner without risking a blast from a shotgun, because this time it really was a gamekeeper.

'We've got to do something!' whispered Don Camillo. 'Think of the scandal if they find us here!'

'I couldn't care less,' replied Peppone calmly. 'I always answer for my actions.'

The footsteps came closer, and Don Camillo hid behind a big tree. Peppone didn't move. Instead, when the gamekeeper appeared with his gun in his hands, Peppone greeted him:

'Good evening.'

'What are you doing here?' asked the gamekeeper.

'Picking mushrooms.'

'With a gun?'

'It's as good a method as any.'

There's also a good method for rendering gamekeepers less dangerous. If you find yourself behind a gamekeeper, all you need to do is suddenly wrap his head in a cloak and punch him. Then all you need to do is use the said gamekeeper's momentary incapacity in order to run for the fence and jump over it. Once you're outside it, all is well.

Don Camillo and Peppone met up again, sitting behind a bush a mile from the Baron's estate.

'Don Camillo,' sighed Peppone, 'we've done a terrible thing. We've raised a hand against a guardian of law and order! That's a crime.'

Don Camillo, whose hand had done the raising, was in a cold sweat.

'My conscience is punishing me,' Peppone went on, knowing how it would torment Don Camillo. 'I'll never have a moment's peace now, thinking about this horrible deed. How will I find the courage to show my face before a minister of God to ask forgiveness for my wrong-doing? I curse the day I lent an ear to the disgraceful insinuations of Moscow and forgot the sacred principles of Christian charity.'

Don Camillo could have wept with humiliation. On the other hand, he was beside himself with the urge to knock this perversity out of Peppone with a fist. Which Peppone knew only too well, so he stopped his whining.

'Damned temptation,' cried Peppone, pulling the hare out of his game bag and flinging it far away.

'Damned indeed,' cried Don Camillo, hurling his own hare into the snow and walking off with his head bowed. Peppone followed him as far as the Acacias, and then turned to the right.

Then he stopped and said, 'Excuse me, you wouldn't happen to know of a good local priest I could go to, so I can unburden myself of this sin?'

Don Camillo clenched his fists and walked straight on.

When he had worked up the courage to present himself before the high altar, Don Camillo flung wide his arms.

'I didn't do it for myself,' he said, 'I only did it because if it was known that I go poaching, it wouldn't just harm me, but the Church itself.' But Jesus remained silent, and whenever this happened it struck Don Camillo like a fever delivered by a dose of malaria, so he put himself on bread and water for days and days until Jesus took pity on him and said, 'That is enough.'

This time, Don Camillo was on bread and water for seven days before Jesus said, 'Enough,' and on the seventh evening, when he could no longer stay on his feet without leaning against the wall, and his stomach was screaming with hunger, Peppone came to make his confession.

'I have contravened the law and Christian charity,' said Peppone.

'I know,' replied Don Camillo.

'What's more, as soon as you were out of sight, I went back and picked up both the hares and got them cooked, one *alla cacciatora* and the other in a *salmi*.'

'I thought you might,' answered Don Camillo in a whisper. And when he passed the altar, Jesus smiled at him, not so much because of those seven days of fasting as because of the fact that in replying 'I thought you might' Don Camillo hadn't wished he could wallop Peppone on the head, and had instead felt nothing but shame at how for a moment that evening, he'd been tempted to go back and do the same thing.

Jesus was moved, and whispered, 'Poor Don Camillo.'

And Don Camillo threw up his hands, as if to say he was trying his hardest, and if he sometimes got things wrong, it wasn't out of ill nature.

'I know, Don Camillo, I know,' replied Jesus. 'Now go and eat the nicely cooked hare that Peppone has brought to the presbytery for you.'

The Fire-Raiser

ONE RAINY NIGHT, the Old House suddenly caught fire and began to burn.

The Old House was an ancient abandoned shack on top of a little hill, and people were reluctant to go near it, even by day, because they said it was full of snakes and ghosts. All that remained of it was an assemblage of stones, since all of the wood – the tiny remnant left after the last occupants had removed all the fixtures and fittings – had long since been eaten away. And yet, strangely, here was the old hut burning like a bonfire.

A lot of people went along the road leading out of the village to look, and every one of them was amazed.

Don Camillo came too and mingled with the throng making their way along the cart track that led to the Old House.

'I expect it's some noble revolutionary who's filled the old ruin with straw and set it alight to celebrate an important date,' said Don Camillo loud and clear, shoving his way to the front and putting himself at the head of the crowd. 'What does the mayor say?'

Peppone didn't even turn round.

'How should I know anything about it?' he grunted.

'Well, as mayor you're supposed to know everything,' returned Don Camillo with excessive relish. 'Is it the anniversary of some historic event?'

'Don't say that, even as a joke, or tomorrow it'll go round the village that we organised this whole damned thing ourselves,' said Brusco, who was marching alongside Peppone and all the other Communist bigwigs.

The cart track was flanked by hedges, and when these came to an end the ground opened out into a broad, miserably bare plateau, with at its centre the little elevation on which stood the Old House. It was now 300 yards away, and they could see it blazing like a torch.

Peppone stopped, and the crowed fanned out to the right and left.

A gust of wind carried a cloud of smoke towards them.

'That's never straw: it's petrol.'

Comments started to fly, and a few people made a move forward but were stopped by cries of 'Don't be a fool!'

For a long time after the war had ended, troops had been based in and around the village, and this could have been a store of diesel or petrol left there by a detachment of soldiers, or hidden by someone who'd stolen it. You never know.

Don Camillo laughed at these suggestions.

'Let's not get fanciful! I don't believe a word of any of that. I'm going to see with my own eyes what's going on.'

He broke away from the crowd and set off at a brisk pace towards the hut. He'd gone a hundred yards when, in four great leaps, Peppone joined him.

'Go back. Now!'

'And what gives you the right to tell me what to do?' replied Don Camillo brusquely, tipping back his hat and putting his great fists on his hips.

'I'm ordering you as mayor! I cannot permit one of my citizens to expose himself senselessly to danger.'

'What danger?'

'Can't you smell that stink of petrol? Who knows what other diabolical stuff might be in there?'

Don Camillo looked at him suspiciously.

'And what do *you* know about it?' he asked.

'Me? I don't know anything, but it's my duty to put you on your guard because if there's petrol in there, there may be other stuff too.'

Don Camillo started to laugh again.

'I see. You know what this is really about? You've lost your nerve, and you can't bear to let your followers see their leader taking lessons in courage from a poor insignificant reactionary priest like Don Camillo.'

Peppone clenched his fists.

'My men have seen me at work in the mountains and . . .'

'And now we're working in the lowlands, Comrade Mayor. On the plain and in the mountains you need different kinds of nerve.'

Peppone spat on his hands, swelled his ample chest, and set off boldly towards the fire. Don Camillo, with his arms folded, watched him go fifty yards, and then shot after him.

'Stop!' he said, grabbing Peppone by the arm.

'Not on your life!' cried Peppone, pulling himself free. 'You can go home and water your geraniums: I'm going on. We'll soon see if it's you or me who's scared.'

Don Camillo would have liked to spit on his hands, but he remembered he was a senior priest, and confined himself to swelling his own chest, clenching his fists, and setting off again.

He and Peppone walked side by side, and the distance from the flames shrank steadily. They could now hear the fire roaring, and with each step they clenched their teeth and their fists more tightly, watching each other intently from the corner of their eyes, each hoping that the other would stop, but both determined to go one step further than the other.

Eighty, seventy, fifty yards.

'Stop!' said a voice they couldn't disobey. And the two of them stopped short at that instant, did an about-face and shot off like thunderbolts.

Ten seconds later a tremendous blast shattered the silence as the hut blew up in a great flower of flame.

They found themselves sitting on the ground half way along the road with not a soul in sight, since everyone else had bolted like hares for the village.

They took a short cut and again walked side by side in silence, until Peppone muttered, 'How much better it would have been if I'd let you go on by yourself.'

'I think so too,' replied Don Camillo. 'A wonderful opportunity lost.'

'If I'd let you go on by yourself,' Peppone added, 'I'd have had the pleasure of seeing the world's blackest reactionary go up in smoke.'

'I don't think so,' answered Don Camillo without turning his head. 'I'd have stopped at twenty yards.'

'Why's that?'

'Because I knew that in the cave under the old house there were six tanks of petrol, ninety-five machine guns, two hundred and seventy-five hand grenades, two cases of ammunition, seven sub-machine guns and 600 pounds of TNT.'

Peppone stopped and stared at him with bulging eyes.

'There's nothing strange about it,' explained Don Camillo. 'I made an inventory before I set the petrol alight.'

Peppone clenched his fists, ground his teeth and yelled, 'I ought to kill you right now!'

'I know, Peppone, but I'm hard to kill.'

They started walking again. After a bit, Peppone stopped.

'But look,' he exclaimed, 'you knew how dangerous it was, and yet you got fifty yards from the fire, and if they hadn't shouted "Stop!" you'd have carried on.'

'You're right. I knew it as well as you did,' Don Camillo replied. 'It was a test of our personal courage.'

Peppone shook his head.

'What can I say? We both know what's what. It's a pity you're not on our side.'

'And I think the same about you. It's a pity you're not on our side.'

At the presbytery, they went their separate ways, but first Peppone said, 'In the end, you've done me a favour. All that damned paraphernalia was hanging over my conscience like the sword of Damocles.'

'Go easy on the historical references, Peppone,' replied Don Camillo.

'Hang on,' continued Peppone. 'You said there were seven sub-machine guns, but there were eight. Who took one?'

'Don't worry,' replied Don Camillo. 'It was me. When the proletarian revolution breaks out, you'll have to give the presbytery a wide berth.'

'I'll see you in Hell,' muttered Peppone, walking off.

Don Camillo went to the altar and got down on his knees.

'Thank you,' he said. 'Thank you for having called out, "Stop!" There'd have been quite a mess if you hadn't!'

'On the contrary,' replied Jesus, smiling. 'Knowing what you were walking towards, to go on would have been an act of suicide, Don Camillo, and you would have turned back of your own accord.'

'I know. What it shows all too clearly is the danger of over-confidence. Sometimes pride does lead to a fall.'

'I'm more interested in that story of the sub-machine gun. Would you really have taken one of those monstrosities?'

'No,' Don Camillo answered. 'There were eight, and they all got blown up. But it's useful if that lot think there's a machine gun in here.'

'Good,' said Jesus. 'If it were true. The trouble is, you really did take that accursed weapon. Why are you such a liar, Don Camillo?'

Don Camillo spread his arms wide.

The Treasure

ONE DAY SMILZO, a young ex-Partisan who had been Peppone's despatch rider during the fighting in the mountains, turned up at the presbytery. The Council had taken him on as a messenger and he had brought a large letter, printed in gothic script on hand-made paper with the Party's letterhead:

'Your Excellency is invited to honour with his presence the ceremony for the benefit of the local community which will

be held tomorrow morning at ten o'clock in Piazza della Libertà.

Branch Secretary Mayor Giuseppe Comrade Botazzi.'

Don Camillo looked Smilzo in the eye.

'Tell Signor Mayor Giuseppe Comrade Botazzi that I have no wish to come and hear the same old nonsense attacking reactionaries and capitalists. I know it off by heart.'

'No, there won't be any political speeches,' explained Smilzo. 'It's patriotic stuff, for the benefit of the community. If you say no, it shows you don't care for democracy.'

Don Camillo solemnly shook his head.

'If that's the case,' he exclaimed, 'then I have no objection.'

'Good. The boss says you're to come in uniform, with your tools.'

'My tools?'

'Yes, your bucket and your paintbrush. There's stuff to bless.'

Smilzo always spoke like this to Don Camillo, precisely because he was a Smilzo, that is, someone whose exceptional skinniness, coupled with diabolical speed, had meant that up in the mountains he could dodge between two bullets and never get even a scratch. And so when the heavy book thrown by Don Camillo reached the place where Smilzo's head had been a moment before, Smilzo was already out of the presbytery and pedalling away on his bike.

Don Camillo stood up, fetched his book, and went to pour out his annoyance to Jesus at the altar.

'Jesus,' he said, 'is there really no way for us to find out what that lot are up to? I've never seen anything so mysterious. What do all these preparations mean? Those leaves and branches that they're sticking into the ground all along the meadow between the chemist's and the Baghettis' house . . . What kind of devilry is this?'

'My son, if it was devilry, then in the first place they would not do it openly, and in the second place they would not call on you to bless it. Be patient until tomorrow.'

That evening, Don Camillo went to take a look, but there was nothing to see except branches and decorations around the meadow, and nobody knew what was going on.

When he set off next morning followed by two altar boys, his legs were shaking. He felt something wasn't right. Something underhand was going on.

He came back shattered, with a raging fever.

'What happened?' asked Jesus from the altar.

'Something that will make your hair stand on end,' stammered Don Camillo. 'It was horrendous. A band ... hymns to Garibaldi . . . a speech by Peppone . . . and the laying of the foundation stone for the People's Palace. And I had to bless the foundation stone. Peppone was nearly exploding with satisfaction. That crook invited me to say a few words, and so I had to come up with something bland for the occasion because it *was* a Party event after all, and yet the scoundrel had presented it as a public benefit!'

Don Camillo walked up and down the empty church. Then he stopped in front of Jesus.

'It's a joke!' he exclaimed. 'Meeting rooms, reading rooms, a library, a gym, a surgery and a theatre. A skyscraper, two floors high, with a playing field attached, and a bowling green. And all for the paltry sum of ten million lire.'

'That is not bad, given what prices are like these days,' observed Jesus.

Don Camillo collapsed onto a pew.

'Lord,' he sighed disconsolately, 'why have you exposed me to such ridicule?'

'Don Camillo, you are talking nonsense!'

'No I'm not. For ten years now I've been praying to you on my knees to help me find a bit of money to set up a small library, a youth club, a playground for the younger children with a merry-go-round and swings, and maybe even a little paddling pool like the one at Castellina. Ten years of struggle, flattering and cajoling filthy landowning pigs who I feel like beating up whenever I set eyes on them; I must have organised 200 raffles and knocked at 2,000 doors, and what have I come up with? Nothing. Then along comes an excommunicated good-for-nothing, and ten million lire pour down from heaven into his pocket.'

Jesus shook his head.

'The money did not fall from heaven,' he replied. 'It was

found in the earth. I have nothing to do with this, Don Camillo. It is the fruit of his own initiative.'

Don Camillo shrugged.

'In that case it's very simple. I'm just not clever enough.'

Don Camillo went off to the presbytery to rage up and down his bedroom. Having dismissed the possibility of Peppone having acquired the ten million by highway robbery or breaking into a bank vault, he thought, 'Straight after the Liberation, when Peppone came down from the mountains and it looked as if the proletarian revolution might happen at any moment, he played on the fear of those aristocratic cowards and tapped them for money.'

Then it occurred to him that there wasn't a single aristocrat in the area back then, but there had been a division of English soldiers who turned up at the same time as Peppone's men. The English had installed themselves in the houses of the nobility, taking over from the Germans who, having been in the area for quite some time, had systematically cleaned out the houses of all their best things. So, it was inconceivable that Peppone could have acquired the ten million through plunder.

Maybe the money came from Russia? He had to laugh at that . . . As if the Russians would have Peppone on their minds.

Finally Don Camillo went and implored Jesus, 'Can't you tell me where Peppone found the money?'

'What do you think I am, Don Camillo?' replied Jesus smiling, 'A private detective? Why ask God for the truth when the truth is in you? Look for it, Don Camillo. And in the meantime, why don't you have a walk into town to take your mind off things?'

The next evening, coming home after his excursion to town, Don Camillo came before Jesus in a state of extreme agitation.

'What happened to you, Don Camillo?'

'Something insane!' exclaimed Don Camillo breathlessly. 'I met a dead man! Face to face, in the street!'

'Calm down, Don Camillo, and try to think clearly. The dead people you meet face to face in the street tend, in fact, to be alive.'

'Out of the question,' cried Don Camillo. 'This one was well and truly dead. I know because I took him to the cemetery myself.'

'If that is the case,' answered Jesus, 'I have nothing more to say. It must have been a ghost.'

Don Camillo shrugged.

'That can't be! Ghosts only exist in the heads of silly women!'

'And so?'

'Humph,' muttered Don Camillo.

He tried to collect his thoughts. The dead man had been a skinny youth, from outside the village, who had come down from the mountain with Peppone's men. He'd been wounded in the head, and was in a bad way, so they'd set up a bed for him on the ground floor of the Villa Docchi which had been the German HQ and now housed the British high command. Peppone had established his own office and HQ in the room next to the injured man.

Don Camillo remembered vividly that the villa had been surrounded by three rows of English sentries so that not even a fly could get in or out because there was still fighting going on nearby, and the English were particularly keen on saving their own skin.

This had happened in the morning: the young man was dead by evening. Peppone called Don Camillo towards midnight, but when Don Camillo got there the boy was already in his coffin. The English didn't want corpses in the house, and at nearly midday the coffin containing the poor boy left the villa, carried by Peppone and three of his most trusted men and covered by the flag of the Republic, while an armed detachment of English soldiers were at least kind enough to give him military honours.

Don Camillo remembered how moving the funeral service had been, the whole village walking behind the coffin which had been placed on a gun-carriage.

And Don Camillo himself had given the address at the cemetery before the coffin was lowered into the grave, and everyone had wept. Even Peppone, in the front row, was sobbing.

Don Camillo congratulated himself as he recalled the occasion. 'I can talk when I put my mind to it.' Then he followed the logic of his reasoning to its conclusion, 'When all's said and done, I am ready to swear that the thin young man I buried is the one I met today in town.'

He sighed.

'That's life!'

The next day Don Camillo went to see Peppone who was at work lying under a car.

'Good day, Comrade Mayor. I've come to tell you that I've spent the past two days thinking about the plans for your People's Palace.'

'What do you think of it?' sneered Peppone.

'Magnificent. It's made me decide to go ahead with the little place I've had in mind for so many years, as you know – with a pool, a garden, a playground, a little theatre, and so on. I'll lay the first stone this coming Sunday. I'd appreciate it very much if you'd come, as mayor.'

'Gladly. One courtesy deserves another.'

'Fine. In the meantime, try to rein in your own building project a bit. It's too big for my taste.'

Peppone looked at him in astonishment.

'Don Camillo, have you lost your mind?'

'No more than I did that time when I held a funeral service with a patriotic address beside a coffin which can't have been properly closed because yesterday I saw the corpse going for a stroll in town.'

Peppone ground his teeth.

'What are you implying?'

'Nothing: just that the casket over which the English presented arms and which I blessed, was full of stuff that you had found in the Villa Docchi, which had previously been the German HQ. And that the dead man was alive and hiding in the attic.'

'Oh, here we go again!' yelled Peppone. 'Same old story. You're trying to blacken the name of the partisan movement!'

'Leave the partisans out of it, Peppone. You won't pull the wool over my eyes.'

And off he went, leaving Peppone to mutter threats under his breath.

That same evening Don Camillo saw him coming towards the presbytery accompanied by Brusco and two other bigwigs – the very men who had carried the coffin.

'You can drop all your insinuations,' said Peppone darkly. 'It was all stuff robbed from the Germans – silverware, photographic equipment, tools, gold, et cetera. If we hadn't taken it, the English would have. It was the only way to get the stuff out. I've got receipts and witness statements here: nobody's touched a lira. Ten million were obtained and ten million will be spent for the benefit of the people.'

The hot-headed Brusco started shouting that this was the truth and that some people needed sorting out, and he knew just how to do it.

'Me too,' replied Don Camillo calmly. And he lowered the newspaper which he had been holding spread out in front of him, and now the others could see that under his right armpit Don Camillo was holding that famous machine gun which had once belonged to Peppone.

Brusco turned pale and took a step backwards.

'Don Camillo,' said Peppone spreading his arms. 'I don't see any reason for us to argue.'

'Nor do I,' answered Don Camillo. 'All the more because I agree with you completely: the proceeds are ten million, and ten million must go to the people. Seven to your People's Palace and three to my playroom and garden for the children of the people. *Sinite parvulos venire ad me*:[3] I'm just asking for my share.'

The other four discussed this in low voices, and then Peppone said, 'If you didn't have that damned thing in your hands, my answer would be that this is the lowest piece of extortion the universe has ever seen.'

The following Sunday Mayor Peppone, with all his council officers, attended the laying of the first stone for Don Camillo's playroom and garden. He even made a little speech. But he managed to whisper to Don Camillo: 'It would have been a better idea to tie that foundation stone around your neck and throw you into the Po.'

That evening Don Camillo went to give the news to Jesus above the altar.

'What do you think?' he asked.

'I think what Peppone thought: "If you didn't have that damned thing in your hands I'd say that this is the lowest piece of extortion the world has ever seen."'

---

[3] 'Suffer the little children to come unto me.'

'But all I've got in my hands is the cheque which Peppone gave me,' protested Don Camillo.

'Exactly,' whispered Jesus. 'With those three million lire, Don Camillo, you will do so many splendid things, that I cannot possibly rebuke you.'

Don Camillo bowed and went to bed, where he dreamed of a garden filled with children, a garden with a merry-go-round and swings, and Peppone's youngest child on a swing, singing like a fledgling bird.

Trial of Strength

An important person was due to arrive from the city, and people came running from all the neighbouring districts. So Peppone arranged for the rally to take place in the main piazza, erecting a fine platform draped in red, and acquiring one of those little trucks with four big loudspeakers on top and all the electrical equipment inside for amplifying a voice.

The piazza was packed that Sunday afternoon, and the church's courtyard which adjoined it was also filled with people.

Don Camillo had sealed all the doors and taken refuge in the sacristy so as not to see anyone or hear anything, and to keep his blood from boiling. He was quietly dozing when suddenly a voice like the wrath of God made him jump out of his skin – '*Comrades!*'

So loud was it that the walls of the church may as well not have existed.

He went to pour out his indignation at the high altar.

'They must have stuck one of their damned loudspeakers right up against us,' he exclaimed. 'It is a violation of privacy pure and simple.'

'What do you expect, Don Camillo?' answered Jesus. 'It is progress.'

But after a general introduction the speaker warmed to his subject and, being an extremist, was coming out with some pretty incendiary things.

'*We need to keep within the law, and so we shall. Even if we have to take up machine guns and send all the enemies of the people to the wall . . .*'

Don Camillo stamped his foot like an impatient horse.

'Jesus can you hear this stuff?'

'I can hear it, Don Camillo. I can hear it only too well.'

'Then why don't you send a thunderbolt right into the middle of that rabble?'

'Let us keep within the law, Don Camillo. If you can only show someone he is wrong by gunning him down, then what, may I ask, was the point of allowing myself to be crucified?'

Don Camillo spread his arms.

'You are right. There is nothing to be done except wait for them to crucify us too!'

Jesus smiled.

'If you thought first and spoke afterwards instead of speaking first and thinking afterwards, you wouldn't have to regret the foolish thing you just said.'

Don Camillo bowed his head.

'. . . *as for those who, hiding themselves in the shadow of the Crucifix, attempt to cause division among the working masses with their weasel words . . .*' The voice from the loudspeaker, carried by the wind, filled the church and made the red, yellow and blue glass in the gothic windows shake.

Don Camillo seized a great bronze candelabra and, wielding it like a club, advanced with clenched teeth towards the door.

'Don Camillo, stop there!' shouted Jesus. 'You are not leaving here until everyone has gone away.'

'All right,' said Don Camillo putting the candelabra back in its place. 'I shall obey.'

He walked up and down the church and then stopped in front of the altar.

'But while I'm in here, may I do what I want?'

'Naturally, Don Camillo. You are in your own home and may do whatever you like. Anything short of standing by the window firing shots at people.'

Three minutes later, leaping like a grasshopper in the belfry, Don Camillo was cheerfully delivering the most infernal *carillon* that had ever been heard in the village.

The speaker had to break off. Turning to the village big-wigs who were standing behind him on the platform, he cried indignantly, 'You've got to *do* something.'

Peppone solemnly nodded in agreement.

'Yes indeed,' he said. 'There are two ways of stopping him: one – lay a mine under the church tower and blow it up, or alternatively, two – bring it down with a salvo of cannon fire.'

The speaker told him to stop talking nonsense. For goodness' sake, it was simply a matter of breaking down the door into the tower and going up!

'Well, yes and no,' explained Peppone calmly. 'The way up is by ladders which run from landing to landing. Now, comrade, can you see that stuff sticking out of the big window to the left of the belfry? They are all the ladders that the bell-ringer has pulled up after him. Once he's closed the trapdoor on the last landing, he is cut off from the rest of the world.'

'We could try shooting through the window of the bell-tower,' suggested Smilzo.

'Yes,' agreed Peppone. 'But we'd need a guarantee that he'd come out at the first shot. Otherwise, he'll start shooting back, and then there'll really be trouble.'

Then the bells fell silent and the speaker resumed his speech. Everything went well until he said something that Don Camillo didn't like, at which the bells rang out in refutation, then broke off, then started again whenever the speaker erred from the strait and narrow. And so it went on until the peroration, which was confined simply to a piece of moving and patriotic uplift, thanks to the efforts of the Ministry of Popular Culture in the bell-tower.

That evening Peppone met Don Camillo.

'Watch out, Don Camillo. Your provocative operation could end badly.'

'There is no provocation involved,' replied Don Camillo calmly. 'You sound your trumpets and we ring our bells. That, comrade, is democracy. But if one of us has to ask permission to make a noise, that is dictatorship.'

Peppone took the point impassively, but one morning Don Camillo got up to find a merry-go-round, swings, three shooting booths, a switchback, electric cars, a wall of death, and any number of other fairground amusements right in front of the church, a couple of feet from the boundary between his courtyard and the piazza.

The proprietors of the fairground showed him the licence signed by the mayor, and Don Camillo could do no more than retreat into the presbytery.

That evening all hell broke loose: barrel organs, loudspeakers, gunshots, yells, songs, bells, whistles, roars and bellows.

Don Camillo went and protested to Jesus. 'This is disrespectful to the house of God!'

'Is there anything immoral going on, anything scandalous?' enquired Jesus.

'No . . . merry-go-rounds, swings, dodgems, kids' stuff mostly.'

'Then it is consistent with democracy.'

'And this damned racket?' asked Don Camillo.

'The racket is perfectly reasonable too, as long as it stays within the law. Outside the church courtyard, my son, the mayor is in charge.'

The presbytery stood thirty yards from the church, with its longer side next to the piazza. And right under the window that looked onto the piazza, they'd set up a machine which immediately aroused Don Camillo's curiosity. A short column about three feet high with a kind of mushroom covered in leather fixed to the top. Behind it there was another column, narrower and taller, with a large dial marked from 1 to 1000. It was a test-your-strength machine. You hit the head of the mushroom with your fist and the needle showed how much force you'd exerted. Don Camillo, peering through a gap in the blinds, started to enjoy himself. By eleven o'clock in the evening, the highest score was 750, and that had been achieved by Badile, the Gretti family's dairyman, who had fists like sacks of potatoes. Then unexpectedly, surrounded by his top brass, Comrade Peppone turned up.

People came running to watch, and everyone started shouting, 'Come on, Peppone. Give it a go!' And so Peppone took off his jacket, rolled up his sleeves, and planted himself in front of the machine, measuring the distance with his fist. Silence fell, and even Don Camillo's heart started pounding.

The fist flashed through the air and slammed onto the mushroom.

'Nine hundred and fifty!' yelled the showman. 'I've only seen that score achieved once before, by a docker in Genoa in 1939!' The crowd yelled with excitement.

Peppone put his jacket back on and looked straight up at the window where Don Camillo was lurking.

'If anyone's interested,' said Peppone loudly, 'they might want to take note that the air's pretty rarefied up there at an altitude of 950!'

Everyone looked at Don Camillo's window and jeered. Don Camillo went to bed, his legs shaking. Next evening, there he was again, skulking behind the window, waiting feverishly for eleven o'clock. Again, along came Peppone with his top brass, took off his jacket, rolled up his sleeves and fired a blow onto the mushroom.

'Nine hundred and fifty-one!' yelled the crowd. And they all looked up at Don Camillo's window, jeering. Peppone looked up too.

'If anyone's interested,' he said loudly, 'they might want to take note that the air's pretty rarefied up there at an altitude of 951!'

Don Camillo went to bed with a fever. The next day he went to kneel before the high altar.

'Jesus,' he sighed, 'that man's pushing me to the limit!'

'Be strong and resist, Don Camillo.'

In the evening, Don Camillo went over to the window like a man on his way to the gallows. The word had gone around, and the whole village had come to see the show. And when Peppone appeared, a murmur ran through the crowd: 'There he is!'

Peppone looked up scornfully, took off his jacket, raised his fist, and everyone was speechless.

'Nine hundred and fifty-two!'

With what seemed like thousands of eyes fixed on his window, out went the light of reason, and out charged Don Camillo.

'If anyone's interested . . .' Peppone began, but didn't have time to finish his sentence about how rarefied the air was at 952: there in front of him was Don Camillo.

The crowd murmured and then fell silent.

Don Camillo swelled his chest, settled himself firmly into position, threw off his hat, and crossed himself. Then he lifted his formidable fist and fired a blow at the mushroom.

'One thousand!' yelled the crowd.

'If anyone's interested, they might want to know that the air's pretty rarefied up there at an altitude of 1000!'

Peppone had turned pale and his top brass were exchanging looks half disappointed, half offended. Other people jeered contentedly. Peppone looked Don Camillo in the eye, took off his jacket again, placed himself in front of the machine and raised his fist.

'Jesus,' whispered Don Camillo hastily.

Peppone's fist flashed through the air.

'One thousand!' yelled the crowd. And Peppone's top brass jumped for joy.

'At 1000 the air's pretty rarefied for everyone,' observed Sghembo. 'Better stay on the ground.'

Peppone went triumphantly one way and Don Camillo went triumphantly the other way.

'Jesus,' said Don Camillo when he was again at the altar, 'thank you. I was beside myself with anxiety.'

'In case you didn't score a thousand?'

'No, in case that blockhead didn't. It would have weighed on my conscience.'

'I knew that, and so I helped him,' replied Jesus with a smile. 'And what is more, as soon as Peppone saw you, he was beside himself with anxiety in case you did not reach 952.'

'What will be, will be,' muttered Don Camillo, who sometimes enjoyed playing the dyed-in-the-wool sceptic.

A Punitive Expedition

A GROUP OF UNEMPLOYED day labourers assembled in the piazza and started to make a racket because they wanted work from the Council. But the Council had no money, and so Mayor Peppone appeared on the balcony of the Town Hall to call for calm and to tell them he would think of something.

'Take cars, motorbikes, trucks and pony-traps, and bring all the employers here to me in one hour!' Peppone ordered the top men gathered in his office.

In fact it took three hours, but finally all the richest landowners and tenant farmers in the district were assembled in the Council chamber, pale and stunned, while the crowd clamoured down below.

Peppone wasted no time.

'I'll get straight to the point,' he said brusquely. 'Hungry people want bread not fine words: either you cough up a thousand lire per hectare so that we can put people to work on public projects, or else I – as mayor and leader of the working masses – will wash my hands of what happens to you.'

Brusco went onto the balcony and explained to the people gathered below that the mayor had said such and such, and that he would pass on the response of the landowners later. The people answered with a yell that turned Peppone's captives even paler.

The discussion was brief, and a good half of the employers signed a commitment on the spot to contribute so much per hectare, and it seemed as if they were all going to sign until, when they came to old Verola, the tenant of Campolungo, the deal ground to a halt.

'I won't sign, not even if you kill me,' said Verola. 'When the law says I have to, then I'll pay up, but I'm not giving you any money now.'

'Then we'll come and get it,' cried Brusco.

'Yes, do,' muttered old Verola, who – counting his sons, his sons' sons, his sons-in-law and his nephews – had as many as fifteen good shots at Campolungo. 'Do come. You know the way.'

Those who had already signed were gnawing their hands in fury, while the others said, 'If Verola doesn't sign, then neither will we.'

Brusco passed this on to the people in the piazza, and the people in the piazza yelled that if Verola wasn't thrown out to them, then they'd come up and get him. But Peppone came onto the balcony and told them not to do anything stupid.

'We can keep going nicely for two months with the 'donations' we've got already. Meanwhile, without breaking the law – and we've never done that before – we'll find a way of convincing Verola and the others.'

Everything went smoothly, and Peppone personally took Verola home in his car to try and convince him, but the old man's only response, when he got out of the car by the little bridge at Campolungo, was to say, 'When you get to be seventy, there's only one thing that frightens you; the thought of living even longer.'

After a month, they were back where they started and people were even more enraged than ever, and then one night . . . it happened.

Don Camillo was warned about it first thing the next morning, and went straight to Campolungo on his bicycle. He found all the Verolas in a field, standing in a line with their arms crossed, looking at the ground in stony silence.

Don Camillo came up, and the breath was knocked out of him: half a row of vines had been cut down, and the stems left scattered on the grass like black snakes. And someone had pinned a notice on an elm: '*First warning.*'

Sooner cut off a countryman's leg than cut down one of his vines: you'll hurt him less. Don Camillo came home as shocked as if he'd seen half a row of murder victims.

'Jesus,' he said, 'there's only one thing for it: find them and hang them.'

'Don Camillo,' replied Jesus, 'just tell me this: when you have a headache, do you cut your head off to make it better?'

'But it's all right to crush poisonous snakes!' cried Don Camillo.

'When my Father created the world, he made a clear distinction between animals and men, which means that all those who belong to the category of men are always men, whatever they do, and are therefore treated like men. Otherwise, instead of coming down to earth to redeem them by putting myself on the cross, wouldn't it have been simpler just to wipe them out?'

That Sunday Don Camillo spoke in church about the murdered vines as if they'd belonged to his father, who had himself been a countryman.

He spoke with great feeling and waxed lyrical. But when he happened to notice Peppone among the faithful, he couldn't help but take a sarcastic turn: 'Let's be thankful to the Eternal Maker of the universe, who placed the sun too high in the sky for us to touch it: otherwise someone would already have put it out to spite a political opponent who sold sunglasses. Listen to the words of your political leaders, everyone: they are the ones with real wisdom: they'll teach you that if a shoemaker's prices are too high, you should punish him by cutting off your own feet.'

And he kept staring at Peppone as if the sermon was for him alone.

In the early evening, Peppone appeared at the presbytery. He was not in a good mood.

'Was it me you were so angry with this morning?'

'I'm just angry with those who put certain theories into people's minds,' answered Don Camillo.

Peppone clenched his fists.

'Don Camillo, I hope you don't think it was me who told them to go and cut down Verola's vines!'

Don Camillo shook his head.

'No. You're violent, but you're not a villain. But it's you who set these people off.'

'I try to restrain them, but sometimes they get away from me.'

Don Camillo got up and stood right in front of Peppone with his legs apart.

'Peppone,' he said, 'you know who cut down those vines!'

'I know nothing!' exclaimed Peppone.

'You know who it was, Peppone, and unless you're the world's worst crook or the world's worst imbecile, you know equally well that it's your duty to denounce them.'

'I know nothing,' Peppone insisted.

'You have to speak out, not just because of the moral and physical damage caused by cutting down thirty vines. It's like a hole in a sweater: you either mend it straight away or tomorrow you've got no sweater. If you know, and you don't get involved, you're like the man who sees a cigarette butt burning in the hayloft and doesn't put it out. The house is destroyed in no time, and all because of you. Not because of whoever threw away the cigarette butt, even if they did it deliberately.'

Peppone insisted that he knew nothing, but Don Camillo kept on at him until he ran out of breath and had to give up the struggle.

'I won't talk, not even on pain of death! My Party contains the flower of fine gentlemanly conduct, and just because of three rogue . . .'

'I get the picture,' Don Camillo broke in. 'If something like this happens again tomorrow, the rest will get so bold and worked up that the next thing you know there'll be gunshots.'

Don Camillo spent a long while walking up and down, and when he finally stopped said, 'Do you at least admit that those villains deserve to be punished? Do you admit that it has to be done in such a way that there's no repetition of the crime they've committed?'

'I'd be a swine if I didn't admit that.'

'Good,' said Don Camillo. 'Wait here.'

Twenty minutes later Don Camillo came back in moleskin

hunter's garb, with high boots on his feet, and a shapeless old hat on his head.

'Let's go,' he said, wrapping himself in a cloak.

'Where to?'

'To where the first of them lives. I'll explain as we go.'

It was a dark, windy evening with not a soul to be seen on the roads. When they came close to an isolated house, Don Camillo muffled himself up to his eyes in his scarf and hid in the ditch, while Peppone walked on ahead, knocked, entered the house and after a while came out accompanied by a man. At the right moment, Don Camillo jumped up out of the ditch.

'Hands up,' he said brandishing the machine gun. The other two raised their arms. Don Camillo shoved a torch in their faces.

'You, clear off and don't turn around,' he said to Peppone. And Peppone cleared off.

Don Camillo pushed the other man into the middle of a field, made him lie down with his face to the ground and, holding the machine gun in his left hand, painted ten lashes on his backside with enough force to skin a hippo.

'First warning,' he explained. 'Understand?'

The other man nodded.

Don Camillo met up with Peppone, who was waiting for him at the place they'd agreed.

The second man was easier to snare because, while Don Camillo was hiding with Peppone behind an outhouse to put a different plan in motion, he came out to fill a bucket and Don Camillo caught him on the hop. When the job was done, this second man likewise took note that this was the first warning and said he understood.

Don Camillo's arm was aching because he'd approached his task conscientiously, and so he sat behind a thicket to smoke half a Tuscan cigar with Peppone.

But then duty called, and he stubbed out his cigar on the bark of a tree.

'And now for the third,' he said getting up.

'I am the third,' replied Peppone.

Don Camillo's heart missed a beat.

'You are the third?' he stammered. 'But why?'

'If you, who are so thick with the Eternal Father, don't know, how do you expect me to?' cried Peppone.

Then he threw off his cloak, spat on his hands and furiously put his arms round the trunk of a tree.

'Thrash me, you damned priest!' he shouted through clenched teeth. 'Thrash me, or I'll thrash you!'

Don Camillo shook his head and walked away without a word.

'Jesus,' said Don Camillo in consternation when he was once again before the altar, 'I would never have imagined that Peppone . . .'

Jesus interrupted him. 'Don Camillo, what you did this evening was horrific. I cannot countenance one of my ministers setting out on punitive expeditions.'

'Jesus, forgive your unworthy son,' whispered Don Camillo. 'Forgive me as the Eternal Father forgave you when you flogged the moneylenders who were polluting the Temple.'

'Don Camillo,' said Jesus mollified, 'I hope you are not about to accuse me of having behaved like one of Mussolini's fascist thugs.'

Don Camillo started walking up and down the empty church in grim mood. He felt offended, humiliated, unable to bear the fact that Peppone could have cut down anyone's vines.

'Don Camillo,' Jesus called out to him. 'Why are you fretting like this? Peppone has confessed and repented. You are the one at fault if you fail to absolve him. Do your duty, Don Camillo.'

Alone in his empty workshop, with his head under the bonnet of a truck, Peppone was furiously tightening a bolt when Don Camillo came in. Peppone stayed bent over the engine while Don Camillo decorated his bottom with ten lashes.

'*Ego te absolvo*,'[4] said Don Camillo, 'planting a kick on his backside for good measure. 'And that's for calling me a damned priest.'

---

[4] 'I absolve you.'

'I'll get you back,' said Peppone through clenched teeth, with his head still under the bonnet of the truck.

'The future is in the hands of God,' sighed Don Camillo.

On his way out he threw his whip into the distance, and that night he dreamed it had taken root where it landed, instantly growing branches and flowers and vine leaves, and then becoming laden with bunches of golden grapes.

The Bomb

THESE WERE the days when politicians were at each other's throats in Parliament and in the newspapers over the Constitution's famous *Article 4* – later to become *Article 7*. And since this enshrined the Catholic Church's desire for sovereign independence from the State, Don Camillo had no hesitation in throwing himself into the affair up to his neck.

Whenever he was sure about the justice of a cause, Don Camillo drove into it like a tank, and given that Peppone was turning this into the Party matter that would finally decide who held power in the village, relations between the priest and the Reds were extremely tense. The air bristled with unease.

'We want the day on which the Article is voted *down* to be one of universal rejoicing,' Peppone had said to his people during a meeting. 'And we intend that even our most reverend arch-priest will take part in the festivities . . .'

He had given instructions for a magnificent Don Camillo to be created out of rags and straw, with 'Article 4' written in large letters across its belly, to be carried in great pomp, accompanied by music, to the cemetery.

Naturally Don Camillo had heard about this straightaway, and having already decided to open a Catholic women's club in the Branch HQ once the legislation had been *passed*, promptly sent someone to ask Comrade Peppone if he might be prepared to give up the premises at once, rather than waiting for the approval of the Article.

The next morning Brusco appeared in the courtyard of the church with five or six other members of the gang, and they started a loud discussion full of gesticulations, pointing at different parts of the presbytery.

'Look, I think we should use the whole of the ground floor as the dance hall, and set up the buffet on the floor above.'

'Or if you like, we could open a doorway in the dividing wall and connect the ground floor with St Antonio's chapel, pull down a wall to separate it from the church, and set up the buffet in the chapel.'

'Too complicated. More importantly, where are we going to put the arch-priest? In the cellar?'

'That's too damp for the poor old thing. The attic would be better . . .'

'We could just hang him from the street lamp . . .'

'No, no, there are still three or four Catholics in the village, and we need to keep them happy too. Let them have their priest. After all, what harm does the poor creature do?'

Don Camillo was listening at a first floor window, hidden behind the blinds, and his heart was pounding like an old armoured car going uphill. In the end he couldn't stand it any longer and, opening the shutters, he leaned out with his shotgun cocked in his left hand and a box of cartridges in his right.

'Hey, Brusco,' said Don Camillo, 'since you're an authority on the subject, what gauge of cartridge would you use for going after snipe?'

'It depends,' said Brusco, as he and his companions slipped away.

This is how things stood when, unexpectedly, the daily paper brought the news that Article 7 had been passed, *and* with the support of the far left.

Don Camillo, at once pleased that Article 7 had been passed, and furious that the Reds would get the praise for voting it in, ran straight to the high altar brandishing a copy of the newspaper. But Jesus didn't let him speak.

'I know all about it, Don Camillo,' He said. 'Now put on your cloak and go for a nice walk in the countryside. Come back this evening, and make sure you don't go through the village, and especially not past *that lot's* HQ.'

'Do you think I'm scared?' protested Don Camillo.

'On the contrary, Don Camillo, it is because I dislike the idea of you going up to Peppone and asking him what time he's holding the funeral for Article 7, and if he has decided to set up the buffet on the ground floor or the first floor of the presbytery.'

Don Camillo flung out his arms.

'Jesus,' he said, 'you're putting me on trial for what I *might* do. That wasn't even remotely on my mind . . . Besides, you need to take into account that Signor Peppone . . .'

'I have taken everything into account, Don Camillo, and I have concluded that the only thing you should do is go for a walk in the fields.'

Don Camillo came back as evening was drawing in.

'Bravo,' said Jesus when he saw him approach. 'How was your walk?'

'Excellent,' replied Don Camillo. 'I'm very grateful for your advice. I've had a wonderful day with a great weight off my heart and my spirit is as light as a butterfly's shadow. One feels so much better when one's in contact with nature. It makes our resentments, our hatreds, our small-minded jealousies seem so paltry!'

'Exactly so, Don Camillo,' agreed Jesus gravely. 'Exactly so.'

'I hope you won't mind,' said Don Camillo, 'if I pop out to the tobacconist's for a moment to buy a cigar. Please excuse my impertinence, but I feel as though I've deserved one.'

'Unquestionably you deserve one, Don Camillo. Go by all means. But I would be grateful if you would light that candle for me before you go out . . . that one on the left. It makes me sad to see it unlit.'

'The least I can do!' exclaimed Don Camillo, rummaging in his pockets for some matches.

'Waste no matches!' said Jesus sternly. 'Take a piece of paper and light it at the candle just behind you.'

'Well now, it might be a bit difficult to find a piece of paper
. . .'

'But Don Camillo,' exclaimed Jesus smiling, 'you are losing
your memory. Do you not recall that letter in your pocket, the
one you meant to tear up? Burn it now, and kill two birds with
one stone.'

'Oh . . . yes,' acknowledged Don Camillo through gritted
teeth. And pulling a letter out of his pocket, he placed it over the
candle flame, where it quickly caught fire, a letter addressed to
Peppone, in which Don Camillo had written that now the Reds
of the far left had unanimously approved Article 7, Comrade
Peppone might like to nominate an executive committee for
the church, with a remit to manage the sins of the parish
and to determine, in consultation with the incumbent, Don
Camillo, the penances to be assigned to the sinners as occasion
required. And that he, Don Camillo, was ready to consider
any further enquiry from Comrade Peppone, and would be
delighted if he or Comrade Brusco would agree to take on the
preaching of some sermons to the faithful during the sacred
festival of Easter. He, Don Camillo, to return the courtesy,
would explain to the comrades the secret, profound, religious,
indeed Christian, meaning of Marxist theory.

'Now you may go, Don Camillo,' said Jesus when the
letter had been reduced to ashes. 'This way you will not run
the risk of inadvertently buying a stamp while you are in the
tobacconist's, and then sticking it on the envelope and posting
the letter.'

Instead Don Camillo went to bed, grumbling that life hadn't
been as bad as this even under the Ministry of Popular Culture.

It was now Easter: all the bosses, both from the village and
the outlying districts, were gathered in the Party HQ, where
Peppone was sweating like a soul in torment as he tried to
explain why the comrades in Parliament had done exactly the
right thing in voting to pass Article 7. 'First of all, so as not to
disturb the religious tranquillity of the people, as our Leader
has said, and he knows very well what he's talking about, and
doesn't need us to teach him. Second, to stop the reactionaries

exploiting the situation to whine about the unhappy fate of the poor old Pope who we nasty people want to send wandering through the world – as the Party Secretary says, and he's got his head screwed on, and a head full of brains, what's more. Third, the end justifies the means, as I say, and I'm not stupid, and I'm telling you that everything's grist to our mill if we're going to get into power. And when we're in power, the reactionary clergy of Article 7 will get a taste of Article 8.'

With that, Peppone ended his speech and, seizing an iron ring, a paperweight which was lying on his desk, he twisted it with his meaty hands into a figure 8. Everyone got the point, and yelled enthusiastically.

Peppone mopped his brow: following up the joke about Article 8 with the iron ring had gone down splendidly. Article 8 would make all religions equal before the Law – a mortal blow to the Catholic Church

With satisfaction he concluded, 'For now we have complete calm. But let's be clear that, Article 7 or no Article 7, we shall continue on our chosen path without deviating one millionth of an inch, and we shall not tolerate even the slightest interference from outside! Not the slightest!'

At that precise moment the door of the meeting room opened, and in came Don Camillo with an aspergillum in his hand, followed by two altar boys carrying a pail of holy water and an egg-basket.

An icy silence filled the room. Without a word, Don Camillo stepped forward and sprinkled holy water over all those who were present. Then he gave the aspergillum to an altar boy and went round the room pressing a holy figure into each person's hand.

'No, a picture of Santa Lucia for you,' said Don Camillo when he came to Peppone. 'That will help you see clearly, comrade.'

Then, with a little bow, he sprayed holy water copiously over the big portrait of the Party Leader and went out, closing the door behind him. It was as if an enchanted wind had blown through the room and turned everybody to stone.

Peppone, stunned and open-mouthed, looked first at the holy picture in his hand, then at the door, and finally exploded with an almost inhuman yell: 'Hold me back, or I'll kill him!'

They held him back, and so Don Camillo was able to return home safely, brimming with joy, his chest swelling up like a balloon.

Although it was Holy Week and the image of Christ crucified above the altar was covered with a triangle of velvet, Jesus still saw the priest when he came into the church.

'Don Camillo!' he said severely.

'Jesus,' Don Camillo calmly responded, 'if I bless hens and calves, why shouldn't I bless Peppone and his men? Or am I mistaken about that?'

'No, Don Camillo, you are right. But you are a scoundrel, all the same.'

On Easter morning, Don Camillo left the house early and there, right outside his door, was a colossal chocolate egg with a pretty red silk ribbon around it. Or rather, a formidable egg which looked very much like chocolate, but was really a 200 pound bomb painted brown and with its fins sawn off.

The war had not passed Don Camillo's village by; aircraft had visited it on more than one occasion and dropped their bombs. And because the planes had been bombing from low altitude, quite a few of these damnable things had never exploded, just lay half buried in the ground, sometimes even on the surface. When it was all over, two bomb disposal engineers had arrived from somewhere to blow up those bombs that were far enough from human habitation, and had disarmed the ones they couldn't blow up because they were too near houses. These they had gathered up, ready for removal later. But one had fallen onto the old mill, smashing the roof and getting stuck between the wall and a cross-beam. They'd left it there because the house was uninhabited and there wasn't any further danger since the detonator had been removed. That was the bomb, with its fins cut off, which persons unknown had turned into an Easter egg.

'Unknown' only in a manner of speaking, because under the words "*Happy Eester*" they had written, "*With thanks for your much apreecaited visit*." And then there was the red ribbon.

The whole business had been carefully planned, because when Don Camillo looked up from the strange egg, he found the courtyard full of people: wretches who had all assembled especially to enjoy the expression on the priest's face.

Don Camillo flew into a rage and kicked the bomb, which was naturally not in the least perturbed.

'It's massive,' someone shouted.

'You'll need a crane,' yelled another.

Sniggering could be heard.

'Try blessing it. Who knows, it might go away by itself!' shouted a third.

Don Camillo turned and found himself face to face with Peppone, who was in the front row with all his top brass, watching with arms folded, sneering.

Don Camillo turned pale and his legs started to shake.

Slowly he bent down and took hold of the bomb, gripping it with a hand at either end.

A chill came over the scene. Everyone held their breath as they watched Don Camillo, wide-eyed, almost in terror.

'Jesus,' whispered Don Camillo in anguish.

'You can do it, Don Camillo!' came the quiet response from the high altar.

The bones of that great machine of flesh were creaking. Slowly and implacably, Don Camillo stood up with the enormous block of iron fixed tight in his hands. He stood still for a moment, eyeing the crowd, and then started to move, every step weighing a ton. He went out of the courtyard and step by step, as slow and inexorable as fate, Don Camillo crossed the piazza. And the crowd followed him, speechless and astonished.

He reached the opposite side of the piazza where the Party had its Branch headquarters, and there he stopped. And the crowd stopped too.

'Jesus,' whispered Don Camillo in anguish.

'Come on, Don Camillo!' came the anxious response from the high altar of the church far away on the other side of the square. 'You can do it!'

Don Camillo crouched down and then, with a jerk, lifted the huge block of metal to his chest.

Another jerk and the bomb started slowly to rise. Everyone watched amazed. Don Camillo straightening and stretching his arms, lifted the bomb above his head, and then the bomb tipped forward and embedded itself in the ground, right in front of the Party's door.

'Returned to sender!' he said in a loud voice, turning to the crowd. 'Easter is spelled EA, not EE. Correct it and send it again.'

The crowd divided, and Don Camillo returned to the presbytery in triumph.

Peppone did not send the bomb back. Three of his men loaded it onto a cart and threw it into an old quarry a long way from the village.

The bomb rolled down the slope, but never reached the bottom because it got stuck in a bush, and stayed there upright. From above you could still read, "*Happy Eester*".

By chance, three days later, a goat came to the quarry and started to nibble the grass around the bush. It touched the bomb, which started rolling again, and after two yards it struck a rock and exploded with a terrifying roar. In the village, which was a long way off, the windows of thirty houses were blown in.

Peppone arrived breathless at the presbytery shortly afterwards and found Don Camillo going upstairs.

'And I . . .' gurgled Peppone, 'I spent a whole evening hammering away at it to chisel off the fins . . . !'

'And I . . .' replied Don Camillo with a groan . . . But he couldn't say any more because he was imagining the scene in the piazza.

'I'm going to bed . . .' gasped Peppone.

'That's where I was going too,' gasped Don Camillo.

He had the Crucifix from the high altar brought into his bedroom.

'I'm sorry to disturb you,' whispered Don Camillo, who had developed a high fever. 'I just wanted to thank you, in the name of the whole village.'

'Don't mention it, Don Camillo,' replied Jesus smiling. 'Don't mention it.'

The Egg and the Hen

Among peppone's men there was one they called Fulmine. He was an enormous brute, elephantine, and a bit soft in the head. Fulmine belonged to the 'political team' commanded by Bigio, for which he served as the armoured car: in other words, whenever some opponent was holding a rally that needed to be broken up, Fulmine would put himself at the head of the team, and since nobody could stop his solemn, inexorable advance, Bigio and the others would walk behind him, and in this way quickly reach the platform, where their whistles and boos could silence the speaker in a few minutes.

One afternoon Peppone was in the Branch HQ together with all the district chiefs, when in came Fulmine: you needed heavy artillery to stop him once he was in motion, and so everyone got out of his way and let him keep going until he arrived at Peppone's desk.

'What do you want?' asked Peppone irritably.

'I beat my wife with a stick yesterday,' explained Fulmine, bowing his head in shame. 'But it was *her* fault.'

'Why are you telling *me*?' yelled Peppone. 'Go and tell the priest!'

'I've already done that,' answered Fulmine. 'But Don

Camillo said things are different now because of Article 7, and he can't absolve me, and I need you to absolve me because you're head of this Branch.'

Peppone banged a fist onto the table to stop the others' sniggering.

'Go back to Don Camillo,' he yelled, 'and tell him to go to hell.'

'I will, Boss,' said Fulmine, 'but you've got to absolve me first.'

Peppone started bellowing, but Fulmine shook his great head.

'I'm not moving till you've absolved me,' he whined. 'If you don't absolve me, then two hours from now I'll start smashing everything up, because it means you're angry with me.'

You had two options when dealing with Fulmine: kill him or give in to him.

'I absolve you,' shouted Peppone.

'No,' muttered Fulmine, 'you've got to do it in Latin, like the priest does, or it doesn't work.'

'*Ego ti absolvio*![5] said Peppone, almost bursting with fury.

'Any penance to do?' enquired Fulmine.

'No, nothing.'

'Fine,' said Fulmine delightedly as he set off. 'Now I'm going straight back to Don Camillo to tell him to go to hell. If he makes a fuss I'll knock him out.'

'If he makes a fuss, don't do anything, or he'll give you a good hiding,' yelled Peppone.

'All right,' agreed Fulmine. 'But if you order me to knock him out, that's just what I'll do, even if I end up getting beaten up myself.'

That evening Don Camillo waited for Peppone to turn up in a rage, but Peppone never showed his face. He appeared the evening after, together with his top brass, and they all sat on benches in front of the presbytery, chattering about something in the newspaper. Don Camillo was a bit like Fulmine in some ways, and he took the bait like a newly-hatched fish. He

---

[5] Peppone gets the Latin wrong. It should be: *Ego te absolve*. His phrase suggests something more like: 'I fear for acquittal'.

appeared at the presbytery door with his hands behind his back and a cigar in his mouth.

'Good evening, Reverend!' they greeted him with great cordiality, touching the peaks of their caps.

'Have you seen this, Reverend?' said Brusco, tapping the newspaper. 'An extraordinary thing!'

It was the story of the famous hen in Ancona which, having been blessed by the parish priest, laid a remarkable egg stamped in relief with a sacred image.

'The hand of God is in this, no doubt about it!' exclaimed Peppone seriously. 'This is a miracle, pure and simple.'

'Go easy on the miracles, boys. Before we declare something a miracle, we need to investigate it, and make sure we aren't dealing with a straightforward natural phenomenon.'

Peppone solemnly agreed, nodding his huge head.

'Understood, understood. But in my opinion, you'd be better off making an egg like that at election time. It's too early in the cycle just now.'

Brusco started to laugh.

'What an innocent you are! It's all a matter of organisation. Once you have your printing press sorted out, you can get miraculous eggs laid to order!'

'Good evening,' said Don Camillo to cut the discussion short.

The next day, as he passed the Branch offices, Don Camillo glanced at the notice board and saw the cutting with the Ancona story pinned up, together with the photograph of the egg and underneath a sign reading:

'*On the orders of the Christian Democrats' official press, Catholic hens are producing electoral propaganda. What an admirable example of Party discipline!*'

The following evening he was at the window when Peppone and his top brass appeared outside the presbytery.

'It's really miraculous!' exclaimed Peppone waving a newspaper. 'Look, it says here that another hen, in Milan, has laid an egg just like the one at Ancona! Come and see, Reverend!'

Don Camillo came down, looked at the photo of the egg and the hen, and read the article.

'What a brilliant idea we missed!' sighed Peppone. 'If only we'd thought of it first . . . Just think: "*A hen joins the Party, and the next day brings forth an egg stamped with the hammer and sickle!*"'

They all sighed. But Peppone had an afterthought and shook his head.

'No,' he said. 'We couldn't have done it. The other side have got religion to sort things out for them, but we can't work miracles!'

'Some people are born lucky, and some aren't!' exclaimed Brusco. 'What can you do about it?'

Don Camillo stayed out of the discussion. He said goodbye and left, while Peppone and his comrades ran to stick the cutting with the story of the Milanese egg onto the bulletin board, adding a commentary headlined, "*Another propagandist hen!*"

Later, unable to make head or tail of this, Don Camillo went to consult Jesus at the high altar.

'Jesus,' he said, 'what's going on?'

'You know, Don Camillo. You have read about it in the newspaper.'

'Yes, I've read about it, but what I know is precisely nothing,' replied Don Camillo. 'In newspapers they write whatever they like. A miracle like this seems impossible to me.'

'Don Camillo, do you not believe that the Eternal Father could do such a thing?'

'No,' said Don Camillo firmly. 'Imagine the Eternal Father wasting his time drawing pictures on hens' eggs!'

Jesus sighed: 'You are a man without faith . . .'

'Oh no,' protested Don Camillo. 'That's not true at all!'

'Let me finish, Don Camillo. I was saying that you are a man without faith *in hens.*'

Don Camillo was still puzzled. He shrugged, crossed himself and went out.

Next morning after Mass, he went into the hen house because he fancied a new-laid egg. Blackie had just laid one. He picked it out of the nest, still warm, and took it to the kitchen. And then he thought he must be seeing things.

The egg was identical to the ones photographed in the paper, an exact copy, with a picture of a shining Host clearly drawn on it in relief.

Don Camillo was now completely bewildered. He put the egg into a glass, sat down to gaze at it, and stayed there contemplating it for an hour. Then he stood up abruptly, went and hid the egg in a wardrobe and bellowed for the bell-ringer's son.

'Run over to Peppone's and tell him to come here straightaway with his top men because I need to speak to him about something serious. It's extremely urgent, a matter of life and death!'

Half an hour later Peppone arrived, followed by his men, and stood on the doorstep, suspicious.

'Come in,' said Don Camillo. 'Bolt the door and sit down.'

They sat in silence and looked at him. Don Camillo took a little Crucifix from the wall and put it onto the red tablecloth.

'Gentlemen,' he said, 'if I swear to you on this Crucifix that I'm telling the truth, are you ready to believe me?'

They were sitting in a semicircle with Peppone in the middle. All the others turned to Peppone.

'Yes,' said Peppone.

'Yes,' answered the others.

Don Camillo rummaged in the cabinet, then put his right hand on the Crucifix: 'I swear that I took this egg from the nest of my hen, Blackie, an hour ago, and that nobody can have put it there because it was freshly laid and I undid the padlock myself, using the key that's here with the others, in a bunch that I carry in my pocket.'

He handed the egg to Peppone.

'Pass it around,' he said.

They stood up and passed the egg from one to the other, holding it up to the light and scratching at the raised image with a fingernail. Finally Peppone, who had turned pale, gently put the egg back onto the red tablecloth.

'What will you write on your dim-witted bulletin now that I've shown you all this egg, and you've all touched it?' asked Don Camillo. 'And when I've had the most important professors come from the city to analyse it, and certify with official stamps that it's not a trick?'

Don Camillo had lifted his arm, and the egg, catching the sunlight, gleamed like silver in the palm of his big hand.

Peppone shrugged.

'In the presence of such a miracle,' he mumbled, 'what can we say?'

Don Camillo stretched his arm out, and spoke in a solemn voice: 'God, who made heaven and earth, and everything which is in the universe – including you four ragamuffins – doesn't need to do a deal with a hen,' he said slowly.

With that, he clenched his fist, and crushed the egg.

'And to show people God's greatness,' Don Camillo went on, 'I don't need any help from a stupid hen either.'.

He shot from the room like an arrow, and came back carrying Blackie the hen by the neck.

'There!' he said, wringing her neck. 'Take that, you sacrilegious hen that saw fit to meddle in the sacred matters of religion!'

Don Camillo, thoroughly worked up by now, threw the hen into a corner and advanced towards Peppone with clenched fists.

'Just a minute, Don Camillo,' stammered Peppone, 'That egg was nothing to do with me . . .'

At length the four left the presbytery and crossed the sunlit piazza.

'Huh!' said Brusco at one point, stopping. 'I don't know how to put it because I'm not learned, but that bloke . . . well, even if he pounded me over the head, I wouldn't get angry with him.'

'Hmph,' grunted Peppone, who really knew what it was like to be pounded by Don Camillo till he couldn't see straight, and who deep down wasn't angry either.

Meanwhile Don Camillo had gone to report to Jesus at the altar.

'Well,' he asked, 'did I do right or wrong?'

'You did right,' answered Jesus, 'you did right, Don Camillo. Though maybe you went a bit far taking it out on a poor innocent hen.'

'Jesus,' Don Camillo sighed, 'for two months I've been dying to put her in the pot.'

Jesus smiled.

'You had every reason to, poor Don Camillo.'

Crime and Punishment

ONE MORNING Don Camillo went out into the courtyard to find that overnight someone had painted 'Don Camelo' on the presbytery wall in red letters a foot or so high.

He laboured with a paintbrush and a bucket of whitewash to cover up the words, but they were written in an aniline dye, and a coat of whitewash is meat and drink to aniline; it comes through even if you paint it three fingers deep. So Don Camillo grabbed a rasp and spent half a day scraping it all off.

He then presented himself to Jesus at the altar, white as a miller but in the blackest of moods.

'If I find out who did it,' he said, 'I'll beat him till my stick turns to tow.'

'Do not make a song and dance about it, Don Camillo,' Jesus counselled him. 'Boys will be boys. When all is said and done they have caused you no harm.'

'But it's not nice calling a priest a camel, an ugly beast of burden,' complained Don Camillo. 'And what's more, as a nickname it's right on target, and if it gets around, people will be calling me that behind my back for the rest of my life.'

Jesus smiled. 'You have broad shoulders, Don Camillo,' he said consolingly. 'I didn't have your shoulders, and I had to carry the cross, but I have never beaten anyone.'

Don Camillo conceded that Jesus was right. But he was by no means convinced, and that evening, instead of going to bed, he crouched in a well-concealed corner and waited patiently. Towards two o'clock, a fellow appeared with a bucket, put it down and cautiously proceeded to pass his paintbrush over the presbytery wall. Don Camillo didn't even let him complete the letter 'D', before emptying the bucket over his head and sending him on his way with a thunderous kick up the backside.

Aniline dye is an infuriating substance to deal with, and Gigotto (one of Peppone's stars), who had undergone the aniline shower, shut himself away for three days, rubbing his face raw with every detergent known to man. When in the end he had to leave the house and go back to work, everyone knew what had happened. In no time at all they stuck the nickname 'Redskin' on him.

Don Camillo fanned the flames, as did anger, so that poor Gigotto's red-raw face turned distinctly green about the gills until one evening when Don Camillo came home from seeing the doctor, he realised – too late – that someone had painted something nasty onto his door handle: at which, without so much as a by-your-leave, he charged into the pub and, with a smack that would have made an elephant see stars, he stuck whatever had been on his door handle all over Gigotto's face.

Naturally these things have a way of getting political, and since Gigotto had five or six companions with him, Don Camillo was obliged to start swinging a bench, as a result of which, a person or persons unknown serenaded him that night with a firecracker outside the presbytery door.

Back in the pub, the six who'd been walloped by Don Camillo with the bench were beside themselves with fury, and howled like souls in torment. It would only have taken one more little spark to set off a raging inferno, and people were starting to get concerned.

So it was that one fine morning, Don Camillo found himself summoned to the city as a matter of urgency, because the Bishop wanted to talk to him.

The Bishop was old and stooped, and he had to lift his head in order to look Don Camillo in the face.

'Don Camillo,' said the Bishop. 'You are ill. You need a few months' peace and quiet in a pretty village in the mountains. Yes, you do . . . The priest at Puntarossa has died, and you can achieve two things with one journey: reorganise the parish for me, and restore yourself to health. Then you'll come back as fresh as a rose. A young fellow called Don Pietro will stand in for you, and you can be sure he won't cause you the slightest trouble. Are you happy with this, Don Camillo?'

'No, Monsignor, but I shall go whenever Monsignor wishes.'

'Bravo,' said the Bishop. 'Your obedience is yet more praiseworthy because you are accepting without demur a task which displeases you.'

'Monsignor, will it not trouble you if people in the village say I've run away because I'm scared?'

'No,' the old gentleman replied smiling. 'Nobody in the world could ever think that Don Camillo is scared. Go with God, Don Camillo, and leave benches alone. They are never a Christian matter.'

The village quickly came to know about this, and Peppone himself brought the news to an extraordinary meeting.

'Don Camillo is going away,' Peppone announced. 'He's been punished with a transfer to the middle of nowhere, up in the mountains. He leaves tomorrow at three.'

'Hooray!' yelled the assembly. 'Let's hope he snuffs it up there.'

'In the end it's better this way,' cried Peppone. 'He'd started to think he was the Pope and the King rolled into one, and if he'd stayed we'd have had to give him an even tougher sorting out. Think of the trouble we've been spared!'

'Send him off with his tail between his legs!' yelled Brusco. 'Make it clear to everyone that it'll be bad for their health if they show their faces round here tomorrow between two o'clock and three thirty.'

When it was time to leave, Don Camillo packed his suitcase and went to say goodbye to Jesus at the altar.

'I'm sorry I can't take you with me,' sighed Don Camillo.

'I shall accompany you all the same,' answered Jesus. 'Go in peace.'

'Have I really behaved so outrageously that I have to be exiled like this?'

'Yes.'

'So now I've got everybody against me,' sighed Don Camillo.

'Absolutely everybody,' replied Jesus. 'Even Don Camillo is against you, and disapproves of what you have done.'

'That's true too,' acknowledged Don Camillo. 'I should beat myself up.'

'Leave your hands where they are, Don Camillo. And have a good journey.'

If, in the lottery of life in the city, fear reaches ninety, in the countryside it can rise to 180, and when it came to two o'clock the streets of Don Camillo's village were deserted. He climbed into the carriage and as he watched his bell-tower disappear behind a clump of trees, a wave of bitterness swept over him.

'Not even a dog has remembered me,' sighed Don Camillo. 'It's obvious that I've not done my duty . . . It's obvious that I'm a bad lot.'

The local train stopped at every single station, which meant it even stopped at Boschetto, a tiny hamlet of four houses four miles from Don Camillo's village. It was there that completely without warning, Don Camillo found his compartment invaded and himself pushed to the window, where he was confronted by a sea of people applauding and throwing flowers.

The farm manager from Stradalunga explained: 'Peppone's men said if anyone from the village showed their face when you left, they'd get beaten to a pulp. So, to avoid trouble, we all came here to say goodbye.'

Don Camillo was overwhelmed and felt a roaring in his ears, and when the train started to move again he found the compartment filled with flowers, bottles, parcels, bundles and packages, and hens tied by their feet squawking in the luggage rack.

But there was still one thorn in his heart.

'What of the others . . . they must really hate me to death! Wasn't it enough for them to have me driven out?'

A quarter of an hour later the train stopped at Boscoplanche, the last district in the municipality. Here Don Camillo heard his name being called and when he went to the window he found himself face to face with Mayor Peppone and the whole Council.

And Mayor Peppone made the following speech:

'Before you leave the Council's jurisdiction, we would like to say goodbye to you on behalf of the community and to wish you a speedy return to health, *the which* (*sic*) will enable you to return soon to your spiritual mission.'

Then, as the train started to move again, Peppone took off his hat with a ceremonious gesture, and so did Don Camillo, who stayed holding his in the air like some statue of the Risorgimento.

The church of Puntarossa was built on the mountain peak and looked like a picture postcard, and when Don Camillo arrived he took deep breaths of pine-scented air and exclaimed in satisfaction:

'I'll be fine after a bit of rest up here, *the which* will indeed enable me to return soon to my spiritual mission.'

He was perfectly serious. Peppone's 'the which' seemed to him worth more than all the speeches of Cicero put together.

Return to the Fold

THE PRIEST given responsibility for managing the parish during Don Camillo's political convalescence was a little man, young and sensitive, who understood his business perfectly and spoke with elegance, using nicely formed and inoffensive expressions which seemed newly harvested from a fine vineyard of vocabulary. Naturally, while fully aware that his role was provisional, the little priest had brought to the church some few novelties of the kind which a man needs if his stay in another man's house is to be bearable.

We're not making any specific comparisons here: but it's like staying in a hotel where, even if you know it's only for one night, you cannot do less than move the bedside table from the left side of the bed to the right and take the chair on the right over to the left; because every one of us has a completely personal conception of the aesthetic, and of the equilibrium between colours and forms, and therefore we suffer whenever we don't do all we can to re-establish an equilibrium when it has been disturbed.

The fact is that on the first Sunday when the little priest officiated, people noted two important innovations: the big ceremonial candelabra decorated with little flowers, which used to stand on the left-side of the altar on the second step of the sanctuary had been moved to the right, in front of a painting depicting a saint, a painting which had never been there before.

The whole village was present, curious to see the new priest, and Peppone and the other Red bosses were in the front row.

'You see that?' sniggered Brusco to Peppone, pointing to the displaced candle. 'A new development!'

'Hmph,' grunted Peppone, who was extremely nervous. And he went on feeling nervous until the little priest came down to the altar rail to deliver the customary sermon, by which time he could no longer contain himself, and before the priest could utter a word, Peppone broke away from the rest of the group, marched determinedly to the right of the altar, seized the big candelabra, carried it across to the left, and placed it in its old position on the second step in front of the altar rail.

Then he went back to the middle of the front row and, spreading his legs and folding his arms, looked the little priest fiercely in the eye.

'Well done!' murmured the entire congregation, reactionaries included.

The little priest, who had watched Peppone open-mouthed, turned pale, stammered his way through the sermon as best he could, and then returned to the altar to conclude the Mass.

When he left the church, he found Peppone and all the top brass waiting for him. And the courtyard was full of silent, surly people.

'Perhaps you could tell us, Don . . . Don whatever-your-name-is,' asked Peppone, pouring his words down from on high, 'Who might that new face be, the one you've hung on the pillar to the right of the altar?'

'Santa Rita da Cascia . . .' stammered the little priest.

'In this village we don't have anything to do with Santa Rita da Cascia, or any other stuff of that kind,' affirmed Peppone. 'Here we do things the way we've always done them.'

The little priest spread his arms.

'I think I'm within my rights . . .' he started to protest, but Peppone cut him off.

'Ah, that's what you think, is it? Then let's get one thing clear: there's no place here for priests like you.'

The little priest was finding it hard to breathe.

'I don't know what I've done to make you . . .'

'I'll tell you what you've done!' exclaimed Peppone. 'You have broken the law. You have tried to overthrow the established order by means of which the real incumbent of the parish has carried out the will of the people!'

'Well said!' agreed the crowd, reactionaries included.

The little priest tried to smile.

'If the picture is the only thing that's wrong, we'll put everything back as it was, and then all shall be well. Don't you think?'

'No!' replied Peppone, tipping back his hat and planting his enormous fists on his hips.

'But why not, may I ask?'

Peppone's reserves of diplomacy were starting to run dry.

'Well,' he said, 'if you want to know the truth, it won't work because if I punch you, I'll send you flying for fifteen yards, but when I punch the real incumbent, he doesn't move an inch!'

Peppone didn't think it would be helpful to explain that if

he punched Don Camillo once, Don Camillo would give him eight punches back. But though he let that pass, his meaning was clear to everyone. And even clearer to the little priest, who looked at him in terror.

'I'm sorry,' he whispered, 'but why do you want to hit me?'

Peppone lost patience.

'Who said anyone wants to hit you? Now you're denigrating the Party of the Left! I simply made a comparison to clarify my point! Do you honestly think I'd waste my time giving a couple of slaps to an economy-size priest like you?'

On hearing himself reduced to 'economy-size', the little priest proudly reared up to his full height of five feet seven inches and swelled the veins in his neck.

'Economy-size or not,' he cried shrilly, 'I have been sent here by the authority of the Church, and here I will stay for as long as the Church wishes me to. I don't take my orders from you! Santa Rita stays where she is, and as for that candelabra, watch what I'm going to do!'

He went into the church, determinedly took hold of the candelabra which was heavier than he was, and after an appalling struggle succeeded in replacing it in front of the new picture.

'There,' he said triumphantly.

'Right!' responded Peppone, who had watched the scene from the church door. He turned towards the silent, angry crowd waiting in the packed courtyard, and yelled:

'The people will make their wishes known! Everyone to the Town Hall for a demonstration, in protest!'

'Hooray!' yelled the people.

Peppone cut through the crowd and placed himself at their head, and the throng organised themselves into a procession to follow him, yelling and waving sticks.

When they reached the Town Hall, the yelling grew louder. And Peppone yelled with the rest, raising his fist at the balcony of the council chamber.

'Peppone!' shouted Brusco in his ear, 'cut out the screaming, for God's sake! Have you forgotten you're the mayor?'

'Holy . . .' exclaimed Peppone. 'I could forget my own name in the infernal racket these hooligans are making . . . I no longer know which way's up!'

He ran into the Town Hall and appeared on the balcony, and the crowd cheered, reactionaries included.

'Comrades . . . Citizens!' shouted Peppone. 'We will not tolerate this abuse of power, which offends our dignity as free men! We will remain orderly and stay within the law as far as possible, but if necessary we are prepared to reach our goal by means of cannonades! In the meantime I propose that a committee under my leadership goes to the Church authorities and democratically presents them with the wish of the people!'

'Hooray!' yelled the crowd, who didn't give a damn about their wishes being reduced to the singular. 'Three cheers for Mayor Peppone!'

When Peppone, followed by the committee, found himself in the presence of the Bishop, he struggled to get his speech under way, but when finally he lurched into gear he said, 'Your Excellency, the fellow you've sent us isn't worthy of the traditions befitting a provincial capital.'

The Bishop lifted his head to look up at the summit of Mount Peppone.

'So, tell me . . . What has he done?'

Peppone shrugged.

'For the love of God . . . Done? He hasn't done anything terrible . . . In fact, he hasn't done anything at all . . . When all's said and . . . The trouble is . . . Eminence . . . a little nobody . . . I mean, a little priest like that belongs in an oratory . . . That chap . . . pardon me, but when he's all dressed up, he looks like a coat-hanger with three overcoats and a cloak on it.'

The Bishop gravely shook his head.

With great charm, he said, 'Do you measure the value of priests with a ruler and scales?'

'No, Your Excellency,' answered Peppone. 'We aren't savages! But the fact is, the eye has an opinion too, after all, and in matters of religion it's the same as with doctors, where the way you feel about the person counts for as much as the treatment they give you and how much you trust their judgement.'

The old bishop sighed.

'I see, I see . . . Yes, I understand perfectly. But, my dear children, you have an arch-priest built like a monument, and it was you yourselves who came to ask me to get him out from under your feet!'

Peppone frowned.

'Monsignor,' he explained solemnly, 'what we are dealing with here is a *casus bello*, a *casus sui generi* as they say,[6] because that bloke was a one-man crime syndicate in the way he pushed things to the limit, and over the edge too, with his dictatorial and provocative ways.'

'I know, my son, I know,' said the Bishop. 'You told me all about it last time, and as you see, I have sent him away. Precisely because I realised that we were not dealing with an honest man . . .'

'Just a minute,' Brusco interrupted. 'I'm sorry, but we never said he wasn't honest!'

'Perhaps not dishonest,' the Bishop continued, 'but Don Camillo is an unworthy priest, inasmuch as . . .'

'Excuse me,' Peppone interrupted him, 'we've never said that he fails in his duty as a priest. We were talking about his serious defects and faults as a man.'

'Exactly,' concluded the Bishop. 'And since, unfortunately, the man and the priest are one and the same, and since Don Camillo poses a threat to his fellow men, we are thinking of making his transfer permanent. We shall leave him up there in Puntarossa with the goats. That is, if we leave him anywhere, because it has not yet been decided whether we will permit him to continue practising or whether we will suspend him *a divinis*. We shall see.'

Peppone had a brief consultation with his committee, and then turned back to the Bishop:

'Monsignor,' he said quietly – and he was pale and sweating from the effort it cost him to speak quietly – 'if the Church authorities have their special reasons for acting in this way, they are of course entirely free to do so. But it is my duty to warn you that until the real incumbent of our parish returns, nobody will go to church.'

The old bishop spread his arms.

---

[6] In cod Latin Peppone is characterising Don Camillo as a provocateur with a unique ability to start a bust-up.

'My children,' he exclaimed, 'do you realise the seriousness of what you are saying? This is coercion.'

'Not at all,' responded Peppone. 'We aren't coercing anyone, because they will all stay at home of their own accord, and there's no law that obliges them to go to church. It's a simple exercise in democratic freedom, because we are the only ones who can judge whether our priest is any good or not. After all, we've had him in our hair for twenty years.'

'*Vox populi vox Dei*,' sighed the old bishop. 'May God's will be done. By all means take back your bad lot. But don't come complaining to me that he's a bully!'

Peppone laughed.

'Your Eminence! Tough guys like Don Camillo don't impress us with their showing-off. What we did last time was just a socio-political precaution; to stop Redskin dropping a bomb on his head.'

'I'll red-skin *you*!' retorted Gigotto in annoyance. 'I didn't want to drop bombs on him. I just let off a banger outside his house to show him I wasn't going to put up with being knocked on the head with a bench, even if he *is* the reverend arch-priest.'

'Ah, so it was you, my son, who let off the banger?' asked the old bishop casually.

'Well, Your Excellency,' stammered Gigotto, 'you know how it is. You're bound to act a bit stupid when you get a bench on your head.'

'I understand perfectly,' replied the Bishop, who being old, knew how to see the best in people.

Don Camillo came back ten days later.

'How are you?' Peppone asked him when they met on the road from the station. 'Did you have a good holiday?'

'Well, there's not much fun to be had up there,' answered Don Camillo. 'Luckily I had a pack of cards with me, and I relieved my boredom by playing patience.'

He took a pack of cards out of his pocket.

'Look,' he said. 'They're no use to me now.'

And gently, with a smile, as if he were breaking a crust of bread, his big hands tore the pack of cards in two.

'I'm growing old, Signor Mayor,' sighed Don Camillo.

'Damn you and whoever brought you back here!' muttered Peppone, going off with a scowl on his face.

Don Camillo had lots of things to tell Jesus. When they'd finished chatting, he thought it was time to put a question to Him.

'What was my replacement like?' he asked with feigned indifference.

'A fine boy, well bred, kind-hearted. He would not show off by tearing up a pack of cards instead of thanking somebody who has done him a favour.'

'But Jesus,' said Don Camillo with his arms outspread, 'I don't suppose they did him any favours. And in any case, some people need to be thanked my way. I bet you Peppone is right now saying to his gang, "You know what? He tore up a pack of cards, cr-i-i-i-i-c, just like that, the son of a b....!" And what's more, he's enjoying every moment of it. Want to bet?'

'No,' replied Jesus, sighing. 'No . . . because at this very moment Peppone *is* indeed saying exactly that.'

The Defeat

THE 'WAR TO THE KNIFE' feud,[7] which had been going on for nearly a year between Don Camillo and Peppone, was

---

[7] Guareschi uses hyperbole to demonstrate the universal reference of the feud between Don Camillo and Peppone. Famously, in 1809 at the second Siege of Saragossa, General José Rebolledo de Palafox responded to the French demand for the city's surrender – 'Peace and Surrender' ('Paz y capitulación') – with the retort, 'Guerra y cuchillo!', a call for freedom and independence meaning 'War and knife', but often mistranslated as 'War to the knife'.

finally won when Don Camillo succeeded in completing his Community Recreation Centre before the People's Palace even had its window frames in place.

The Centre turned out to be a very fine set-up, with a reception room for shows, conferences, and that kind of thing; a little library with a study centre; a covered area for training sessions and winter games; and beside all this, a magnificent enclosure containing a sports field, a running track, a swimming pool, and a children's playground with a merry-go-round and swings, et cetera. Things for the most part were still in an embryonic state, but in all aspects of life what matters most is to make a start.

Don Camillo had arranged a splendid programme for the inauguration ceremony: choral singing, athletic tournaments, and a football match. For the last of these, he had put together a simply formidable team, and such was the passion he gave to the task that by the end of eight months' training, if you tallied up the kicks that Don Camillo had given his eleven players, they came to more than all the kicks the eleven players had managed to give to one single football.

Peppone was fully aware of this and found it a hard morsel to swallow. He couldn't bear to see a political party, which represented the people, coming second in a race organised by Don Camillo on behalf of the people. And when Don Camillo sent word to Peppone that, in order to demonstrate 'his sympathy for the most ignorant social strata of the village,' he would generously permit the Party's Dynamos to test themselves against his own Gagliarda, Peppone turned pale and sent for the eleven boys from the Sports Section's football team, lined them up against a wall, standing at attention, and harangued them as follows: 'You're going to play the priest's team. You'd better win or I'll smash your faces in, every one of you! These are the orders of the Party, for the honour of the downtrodden masses!'

'We'll win!' replied the eleven, sweating with fear.

When he heard about this, Don Camillo gathered the Gagliarda together and got straight to the heart of the matter.

'We don't live among coarse and savage people the way the other lot do,' he reassured his team with a smile. 'We talk things over sensibly, like gentlemen. And with God's help we'll stuff them six nil. I don't make threats. All I say is that the honour of the parish is in your hands. Or rather, in your feet. Every one of you must do his duty as a good citizen. And of course, if it turns out that some wretch doesn't give his all to the cause, right down to the last drop, well, I won't make a song and dance about it and smash his face in like Peppone. No, I'll pulverise his backside with my boot!'

The whole village was at the inauguration ceremony, with Peppone at the forefront with his whole retinue gaudily arrayed in red kerchiefs. In his capacity as *Mayor of the whole community* he was delighted by the project, and as *representative, above all, of the people* he gladly affirmed his confidence that the project would not be used for the unworthy purposes of political propaganda, as some malicious voices were whispering.

During the choral performance, Peppone found a moment to observe to Brusco that, when you came to think about it, singing was a sport too, in that it develops the lungs. And Brusco's loftily off-hand response was that in his opinion the event would have been still more efficacious in its impact on the physical improvement of young Catholics, if the boys and girls had accompanied their singing with actions capable of developing not only the lungs but also the arm muscles.

During the basketball match, Peppone expressed his sincere conviction that the game of quoits also had an unquestionable athletic value, a grace and refinement all its own, and he was astounded that the programme hadn't included a quoits tournament.

Since these observations were expressed with such discretion that they could be clearly heard at a distance of 750 yards, the veins in Don Camillo's neck were standing out like rods of acacia wood. And so he waited for the football match in a state of indescribable anxiety, for that was when he would have his say.

And now it was time to begin the match. Eleven Gagliarda in white shirts with a big 'G' on their chests. Eleven Dynamos with hammer, sickle and star entwined in an elegant 'D'.

The people didn't give a damn about the symbols, and greeted the teams with 'Hooray for Peppone!' or 'Hooray for Don Camillo!' respectively.

Peppone and Don Camillo looked at each other and each bowed his head very slightly, with the utmost dignity.

The neutral referee was Binella the clockmaker, who had been apolitical from birth. After ten minutes' play, the marshal of the *carabinieri* came up to Peppone, pale as a corpse, and was followed by two equally white-faced soldiers.

'Signor Mayor,' he stammered, 'do you think this might be a good moment to telephone for reinforcements from the city?'

'You can call up a whole division, if you want, but if those butchers don't pack in the rough stuff, no one will stop them making a pile of dead bodies three stories high! Not even His Majesty the King! All right?' yelled Peppone, who was so wound up that he'd forgotten the Republic even existed.

The marshal turned to Don Camillo, who was only a few feet away, and stammered, 'Do you think . . .' but Don Camillo didn't let him finish.

'All I think,' he yelled, 'is that not even a personal intervention from the USA will keep us all from swimming in blood if those damned Bolsheviks don't stop smashing my men's shins!'

'Very well,' said the marshal. And he went and barricaded himself in his headquarters with his two men even though he knew only too well that, after the match was over, the festivities would conclude with people trying to burn down the barracks of the *carabinieri*.

The Gagliarda scored first, and the goal was greeted by a yell that shook the bell-tower. Peppone, looking distraught, turned to Don Camillo with fists raised ready to jump on him. Don Camillo squared up to him in response. They were a hair's breadth from a collision, but Don Camillo saw from the corner of his eye that the crowd had suddenly become motionless, and all eyes were fixed on Peppone and him.

'If we start fighting, it'll end up as a bloodbath,' said Don Camillo through clenched teeth.

'All right. I'll stop for the sake of the people,' replied Peppone, relaxing his stance.

'And I'll stop for the sake of Christianity,' said Don Camillo.

Peace was restored. But at half time, as Peppone gathered the Dynamos, he let fly at his opponents – 'Fascists!' he remonstrated in a voice filled with disgust. Then he grabbed his centre forward, Smilzo, by the collar.

'You dirty traitor, just remember how I saved your skin three times when we were in the mountains. If you don't score in the first five minutes, you won't have a skin worth saving!'

When the second half started, Smilzo tried a shot at goal every time he had the ball. He used his head, his feet, his knees, his backside, even his teeth; he burst a lung, he ruptured his spleen, but in the fourth minute he sent the ball into the back of the net.

Then he flung himself on the ground and didn't move again. Don Camillo went to the far side of the field to avoid getting himself into anything compromising. The Gagliarda's goalkeeper was feverish with fear.

The Reds packed their defence and there was no way through. Thirty seconds before the end, the referee blew up for a foul. Penalty against the Gagliarda.

The ball flew through the air. Not even Zamora could have kept it out from that angle. Goal.

That was the end of the match: and all Peppone's men cared about was gathering up their men and getting them back to the Party HQ. As for the referee, he was apolitical: in other words, he was on his own.

Don Camillo was beside himself. He ran to the church and knelt in front of the altar.

'Lord,' he said, 'why didn't you help me? I lost.'

'Why should I help you and not the others? Twenty-two legs on your team, twenty-two on the other one. The legs are equal, Don Camillo. And they are no concern of mine. I concern myself with souls. *Da mihi animas, cetera tolle* ["Give me the souls and take the rest."] I leave bodies to the earth. Don Camillo, can it be that you have lost the use of your brain?'

'It's a struggle sometimes, but I always find it again,' answered Don Camillo. 'I wasn't claiming that you are personally responsible for my team's legs. Especially since they're better than the other lot's legs. I'm saying you did nothing to stop the dishonesty of one man from penalising my team for a foul they didn't commit.'

'The priest can make a mistake when saying Mass, Don Camillo: why not admit that other people can make mistakes without meaning any harm by it?'

'I admit that mistakes can be made in all areas of life. But not when it comes to refereeing a sporting event! When there's a ball in the middle of . . .'

'Don Camillo is reasoning not just worse than Peppone,' Jesus continued, 'but worse than Fulmine, who never reasons at all.'

'That's true,' Don Camillo admitted. 'But Binella's still a scoundrel.'

He broke off because a tremendous uproar could be heard approaching the church, and almost immediately a man came in, breathless and overwhelmed with terror.

'Save me!' he sobbed. 'They're trying to kill me!'

The crowd was at the door and on the point of entering the church. Don Camillo snatched up a candelabra weighing 100 pounds and brandished it threateningly.

'In the name of God,' he shouted, 'get back or I'll smash your heads in! Remember, whoever seeks sanctuary here is sacred and untouchable!'

The people stopped.

'You herd of wild beasts, you should be ashamed of yourselves! You back to your stables and pray that God forgives your bestial behaviour!'

The people bowed their heads in silent confusion, and started to move away.

'Cross yourselves!' Don Camillo commanded, looking like Sampson, tall as a mountain as he brandished the candelabra in his cyclopean hand.

Everyone crossed themselves.

'Between you and the object of your beastly hatred stands the cross, which each one of you has traced with your hand. Violation of this sacred barrier is sacrilege. *Vade retro!*' He went back into the church and bolted the door: but there was no need.

The man had flopped onto a pew and was still out of breath. 'Thank you, Don Camillo,' he whispered.

Don Camillo didn't reply. He walked up and down, and then stopped in front of the man.

'Binella,' said Don Camillo trembling. 'Here before God and me, you cannot lie! There was no foul! How much did that rogue Peppone give you to blow for a foul if the scores were level?'

'Two thousand five hundred lire.'

'Aaargh!' roared Don Camillo, putting his fists under his nose.

'But . . .' groaned Binella.

'Out!' yelled Don Camillo, pointing to the door.

When he was alone, he went to see Jesus.

'Didn't I tell you that fellow is corrupt? Am I right to be angry or not?'

'No, Don Camillo,' Jesus replied. 'It is your fault for offering Binella 2000 lire for the same service. When Peppone offered him 500 more, that was the proposition he accepted.'

Don Camillo flung out his arms.

'But Jesus,' he said, 'if we follow that line of thought, we'll end up saying that I'm the one to blame!'

'Exactly so, Don Camillo. Because you, a minister of the Church, first proposed the deal to him, he considered that it must be legitimate, and weighing one legitimate transaction with another, he chose the more profitable one.'

Don Camillo hung his head.

'Do you mean that if the poor man now gets beaten up by my supporters, it will be my fault?'

'In a way, yes, because it was you who first led the man into temptation. But your fault would have been greater if Binella had accepted your offer and awarded the penalty to you, because then the Reds would have beaten him up, and you would not have been able to stop them.'

Don Camillo thought it over for a moment.

'So the conclusion is,' he said, 'it was better that the others won.'

'Exactly so, Don Camillo.'

'Then, Jesus, I thank you for making me lose. And if I tell you that I calmly accept the defeat as a punishment for my dishonesty, you must believe that I am truly penitent. Because not to get angry after seeing a team like that lose – and I don't mean to boast, but it's a team that could play in the Second

Division – a team that could eat Dynamos for breakfast, believe me, it's enough to break one's heart . . . It cries out to God for vengeance!'

'Don Camillo!' Jesus admonished him, smiling.

'You'll never understand,' sighed Don Camillo. 'Sport is something entirely special. You're either in or out. Can you see what I mean?'

'Only too well, my poor Don Camillo. I understand you so well that . . . Tell me, when are you going to have the rematch?'

Don Camillo leapt to his feet with a heart full of joy.

'Six nil!' he shouted. 'Six thunderbolts you won't even see as they flash by! Now watch me score into the confessional!'

He threw his hat into the air and volleyed it straight through the little window of the confessional box.

'Goal!' said Jesus smiling.

The Avenger

SMILZO APPEARED on his racing bike and did an 'American stop' – a fancy manoeuvre which consists of jumping backwards off the saddle and sitting astride the wheel.

Don Camillo was sitting on a bench in front of the presbytery, reading the paper. Looking up, he asked nonchalantly, 'Are those trousers hand-me-downs from Stalin?'

Smilzo handed him a letter, touched the peak of his cap with his forefinger, got back on his bike and just as he was about to round the corner of the presbytery, turned for a moment and shouted, 'No, I got them from the Pope!' Then he stood up on the pedals and hurtled off down the road.

Don Camillo had been waiting for this letter: it was an

invitation to the opening ceremony for the People's Palace, together with the programme of celebrations. Speeches, reports, a marching band, refreshments, and in the afternoon a 'Great boxing encounter between the local Branch heavyweight champion, Comrade Mirko Bagotti, and the heavyweight champion of the Regional Federation, Comrade Anteo Gorlini.'

Don Camillo went to bring Jesus the news at the altar.

'Jesus,' he exclaimed after reading out the programme, 'this is sheer dishonesty! If Peppone wasn't the world's biggest oaf, he wouldn't have put a brawl in the programme, but the rematch between the Dynamos and the Gagliarda. So I'm going . . .'

Jesus interrupted him. 'And you do not have the slightest intention of going to Peppone's office and giving him a piece of your mind; because in fact you are quite mistaken. It was logical that Peppone would try to do something different from you. And secondly, it was logical for him not to risk inaugurating his House with a defeat. Even if his champion is guaranteed to lose, it's nothing serious: they are both comrades, so it stays in the family. But a defeat inflicted by your team would be damaging to his party's prestige. So you must admit, Don Camillo, that Peppone could not put on a match against your team.'

'But I put on a match against his team,' exclaimed Don Camillo, 'and I lost!'

'But Don Camillo,' responded Jesus gently, 'you do not represent a party. Your boys weren't defending the honour of the Church. They were simply defending the honour of a sports team which, by a happy coincidence, comes under the aegis of the parish church. Or perhaps you think that that Sunday game was a defeat for the Christian religion?'

Don Camillo laughed.

'Jesus,' he protested, 'you wrong me if you think that's what was on my mind. I only said that, from the sporting point of view, Peppone is an oaf. So you'll forgive me if I jeer when his famous champion gets such a hammering that by the third round he doesn't even know his own name.'

'Yes, I will forgive you, Don Camillo. But I will not forgive you if you enjoy the spectacle of two men trying to bash each other's brains out.'

Don Camillo spread his arms.

'I have never done so, and I'd never accept an invitation to legitimise such displays of brutality with my presence, since they only serve to strengthen that cult of violence which is already so rooted in the spirit of the masses. I agree with you entirely, and condemn any sport in which dexterity takes second place to brute strength.'

'Bravo, Don Camillo,' said Jesus. 'If a man wants to flex his muscles, there is no reason at all to do so by beating up the man next to him. It is enough if he protects his hands with properly padded gloves and pounds a sack of sawdust or a ball hanging up somewhere.'

'Quite so,' said Don Camillo, hastily crossing himself and rushing towards the door.

'Just to satisfy my curiosity, Don Camillo,' called Jesus, 'what do you call that leather ball that you have fixed on an elastic cord to the roof and floor of the attic?'

'I think it's called a punch-ball,' muttered Don Camillo, stopping.

'And what does that mean?'

'I don't know any English,' replied Don Camillo, slipping away.

Don Camillo presented himself at the opening ceremony of the People's Palace, and Peppone personally accompanied him as he toured the premises: the whole enterprise was of high quality.

'What do you think?' asked Peppone, swelling with joy.

'Charming!' answered Don Camillo with a smile. 'To be honest, it really doesn't look like something that could have been designed by anyone as second-rate as Brusco.'

'Too right,' muttered Peppone, who had spent the earth getting the best architect in the city to design his project.

'It wasn't a bad idea to have the windows horizontal instead of vertical,' observed Don Camillo. 'You can keep the ceilings lower without causing a clash in the design. Very good. Where would the magazine be?'

'It's in the assembly hall,' explained Peppone.

'Ah! And you've set up the armoury and the cells for dangerous opponents in the cellar?'

'No,' replied Peppone. 'We don't have any dangerous opponents, so all that stuff can stay out in the open. As for an armoury, we were thinking we'd make use of yours if need arises.'

'Excellent idea,' replied Don Camillo suavely. 'After all, you've seen for yourself how carefully I'm looking after the machine-gun you entrusted to me, Signor Peppone.'

They had arrived in front of a large painting of a man with an enormous drooping moustache, small eyes, and a pipe.

'Would this be one of your heroic dead?' enquired Don Camillo in a tone of regret.

'That would be one of our heroic living who, when he arrives, will make you sit on the lightning conductor at the top of the bell-tower,' explained Peppone, who was nearing the end of his tether.

'That's too high a position for a humble arch-priest. The highest position in the village should go to the mayor, and I henceforth place it entirely at your service.'

'Will we have the honour of your company at the boxing match today, Signor Arch-priest?'

'Thank you, but give my place to Fulmine, who is in a better position than I am to appreciate the delicate beauty and deep educational and spiritual significance of the spectacle. But I shall be on standby in the presbytery in case your champion needs Extreme Unction. All you have to do is send Smilzo to me, and I'll be there in two minutes.'

That afternoon Don Camillo stayed chatting for an hour or so with Jesus, and then asked to be excused: 'I'm feeling sleepy, so I'll spend a little time in bed. And thank you for having made it rain cats and dogs. I think it'll be very good for the wheat.'

'And more importantly, you think it will stop people who live some distance away from attending Peppone's show,' added Jesus. 'Is that not the case?'

Don Camillo shook his head.

Though the rain was indeed coming down in cats and dogs, it hadn't by any means spoiled Peppone's celebrations: people had come from all the districts in his Council's jurisdiction, and from neighbouring districts too, and the big gymnasium in the People's Palace was full to bursting. The regional champion was widely known, and Bagotti had an undoubted local following; and to some extent this was a contest between town and country, which added to the interest.

Peppone, in the front row right under the ring, was triumphant at the flow of people. Moreover, he was sure that Bagotti would only lose on points: and in these circumstances, that counts as a victory.

At exactly four o'clock, after thunderous applause and enough yelling to bring down the ceiling, the gong sounded for the start of round one, and the crowd began to work themselves up into a frenzy.

Peppone was awash with sweat and looked as if he'd swallowed dynamite.

The second round began well for Bagotti, who went onto the attack: but all at once he dropped like a stone. And the referee started counting the seconds.

'No!' yelled Peppone leaping up and standing on his seat. 'That was below the belt!'

The champion of the Federation turned to Peppone, smiling sarcastically. He shook his head and touched his chin with his fist.

'No!' yelled Peppone in exasperation, while the crowd went wild. 'They saw it all! First you hit him below the belt, and when he bent forward in pain, you whacked him on the chin! It doesn't count!'

The regional champion shrugged and sneered. By now the referee had counted ten, and taken the winner's hand to raise it, but then the tragedy happened.

Peppone threw off his hat and, bounding up into the ring, came towards the champion with his fists clenched.

'I'll show you!' yelled Peppone.

'Smash him, Peppone!' yelled the frenzied crowd.

The boxer put up his guard, while Peppone bore down on

him like a Panzer tank and launched a blow. But Peppone was too enraged to think clearly, so the other man dodged him easily and flashed a jab against his jaw. It was a simple matter to keep on hitting the target because Peppone was standing still, completely undefended. It was like punching a sack of sawdust.

Peppone fell like a stone, and an icy wind of dismay blew through the crowd, freezing the cries in people's throats.

But there and then, even as the regional champion looks at the giant stretched out on the mat and smiles in commiseration, the crowd raises a tremendous roar, for a man jumps into the ring. He doesn't even bother to take off his drenched raincoat and hat. He grabs two gloves from the bench in one corner of the ring, slips them on without tying them, squares up to the champion, and throws a punch.

Naturally the federal champion parries the blow, but fails to retaliate because his opponent defends himself so well. However, the action suffers only a three-second delay. The champion is bouncing around his opponent, who just keeps turning slowly and unhurriedly, and suddenly the time comes and the champion fires a formidable shot at the man, who, scarcely moving, parries the punch with his left hand and with his right hammers an atrocious blow to the jaw that knocks the champion into a *wagon-lit* [a railroad sleeper car]: in other words, he's fast asleep by the time he hits the canvas.

Everyone went crazy!

It was the bell-ringer who brought the news to the presbytery, and Don Camillo had to jump out of bed and open the door to him because the sacristan seemed beside himself with excitement, and would have burst if he hadn't told the whole story from A to Z.

Don Camillo went to report it all to Jesus.

'So how did it go?' asked Jesus.

'A shameful uproar, a display of disorder and immorality you couldn't imagine!'

'Rather like the attempted lynching of your referee?' asked Jesus casually.

Don Camillo laughed.

'Nothing to do with the referee. In the second round Peppone's champion collapsed like a sack of potatoes. And then Peppone himself jumped into the ring and started exchanging punches with the winner. Now of course Peppone is as strong as an ox, but he's such a blockhead that he advances with his platoons side by side like the Zulus and the Russians, so the other man hurls a jab right onto his chin, and there's Peppone on the deck, dead as a doornail.'

'So his Branch has suffered two defeats.'

'Yes, two for his Branch and one for the Regional Federation,' chuckled Don Camillo. 'But that's not the end of the story because, no sooner has Peppone collapsed, than in jumps another chap, presumably someone from a town nearby: quite a sight, with a beard and a moustache, and he also squares up to the regional champion and whacks him with a jaw-breaker.'

'But of course,' Jesus interrupts, 'the champion dodges the blow and retaliates: and so to complete the brutal spectacle the man with the beard ends up on the floor too.'

'No! The man's as indestructible as a bank vault, so the champion starts dancing around, trying to take him by surprise. And there it comes – wham! – a right jab, so I parry it with my left and thump him with my right. Boom! Out of the ring!'

'How do you come into it?'

'I don't understand.'

'You said, "I parry it with my left and thump him with my right."'

'I haven't any idea at all why I could have said that.'

Jesus shook his head.

'Could it perhaps have been because you were the man who knocked out the champion?'

'It doesn't seem likely,' answered Don Camillo solemnly. 'I don't have a beard or a moustache.'

'And yet a man could disguise himself, so that people would not see the arch-priest showing an interest in the spectacle of two men attacking each other in public with their fists.'

Don Camillo shrugged.

'Jesus, I admit it's possible, but you have to take into account the fact that even arch-priests are made of flesh and blood.'

Jesus sighed.

'We do take this into account. But what we also take into account is that, whether or not they are made of flesh and blood, arch-priests must not forget that they are also made of brain. Because if the flesh and blood arch-priest puts on a disguise so that he can go to a boxing match, the arch-priest with a brain should stop him from putting on a show of violence.'

Don Camillo shook his head.

'You're right. But it would be a good idea to take into account that arch-priests are made of something else besides flesh, blood and brain. And when this something else sees a mayor knocked to the floor in front of all his officials by a rotten skunk from the city who wins by hitting his opponent below the belt (a trick that cries out to God for vengeance), this something else takes hold of the arch-priest made of flesh, blood and brain, and compels him to jump into the ring.'

Jesus nodded.

'You mean I should allow for the fact that arch-priests are also made of heart?'

'For the love of heaven,' exclaimed Don Camillo, 'I'll never presume to give you advice. Only perhaps remind you that nobody knows the identity of the man with the beard.'

'Well, that includes me,' answered Jesus with a sigh. 'But more importantly, do you yet have any idea what punch-ball means?'

'My understanding of the English language has not increased, Lord,' replied Don Camillo.

'Then let us make do with this conclusion,' said Jesus smiling. 'That there are times when education does more harm than good. Goodbye for now, Regional Champion.'

Nocturne with Bells

FOR SOME TIME, Don Camillo had felt he was being watched. Whenever he turned suddenly while walking along the road or through the fields, although he couldn't see anyone, he was sure that if he looked behind the hedge or in a bush he'd find two eyes, and more.

On a couple of occasions, when he went out in the evening, he had detected a rustling behind his front door and glimpsed a shadow.

'Let it be,' Jesus had answered when Don Camillo asked him for advice. 'Two eyes have never hurt anyone.'

'It would be good to know if the two eyes are going around by themselves or in company with a third: a nine-calibre one for example,' sighed Don Camillo. 'That detail is not without importance.'

'Nothing can damage a clear conscience, Don Camillo.'

'I know that, Jesus,' sighed Don Camillo. 'The trouble is that people who do this sort of thing don't shoot you in the conscience but in the back.'

Don Camillo did nothing, however, and time passed, until one evening when he was alone reading in the presbytery, he suddenly 'felt' the eyes upon him.

And there *were* three of them. Looking up slowly, Don Camillo first saw the black eye of a pistol and then the eyes of Biondo.

'Should I put my hands up?' asked Don Camillo calmly.

'I don't mean you any harm,' replied Biondo, putting the pistol back in his jacket pocket. 'I was afraid you'd be startled by seeing me all of a sudden and start shouting.'

'I see,' answered Don Camillo. 'Didn't it occur to you that you could have saved yourself all that bother by just knocking on the door?'

Biondo didn't answer and went to lean on the window sill. Then all of a sudden he turned and sat by Don Camillo's table.

His hair was a mess, his eyes were sunken, and his forehead was bathed in sweat.

'Don Camillo,' he said through clenched teeth, 'the bloke in the house by the dyke. It was me that did him in.'

Don Camillo lit himself a cigar.

'By the dyke?' he said calmly. 'That's old news. Political stuff really. It comes under the amnesty. What are you worried about? You're not in trouble with the law.'

Biondo shrugged.

'I don't give a damn about the amnesty,' he said angrily. 'Every night, when I turn out the light, he's there, I can feel him standing by my bed. I don't get it! What's going on?'

Don Camillo blew his cigar smoke into the air.

'Nothing,' he said smiling. 'Listen: try sleeping with the light on.'

Biondo jumped to his feet.

'You can make fun of that cretin, Peppone!' he shouted, 'but not of me!'

Don Camillo shook his head.

'In the first place, Peppone is by no means a cretin, and in the second place there's nothing else I can do for you.'

'If it just means buying some candles or making a donation to the church, I'll pay!' shouted Biondo. 'But you've got to absolve me. Never mind the law.'

'I agree with you, my son,' said Don Camillo gently. 'The trouble is that they haven't made an amnesty for consciences, which means we carry on here with the same old method. And so in order to be absolved you need to repent, and to show that you have repented, and to do so in a way that earns forgiveness. It's a long job.'

Biondo sneered.

'Repent? Repent bumping that bloke off? I'm just sorry I only got rid of one!'

'It's an area in which I'm utterly incompetent. Besides, if your conscience is telling you that what you did was good, then all is well,' said Don Camillo, opening a book and putting it in front of Biondo. 'We have some very precise rules, and political movements aren't exempt. See there? Number five: thou shalt not kill. Number seven: thou shalt not steal.'

'What's that one got to do with it?' asked Biondo in a mysterious tone.

'Nothing,' Don Camillo reassured him. 'I just thought you'd told me that you did the man in for his money, and used politics as your excuse.'

'I never said that!' shouted Biondo, pulling out his pistol and pointing it at Don Camillo's face. 'I never said that, but it's true. Yes, it's true, and if you dare tell anyone, I'll blow you away!'

Biondo seemed calmer now. He opened his hand and looked at the pistol.

'What a genius!' he exclaimed, laughing. 'I didn't even notice that the safety catch was on.'

He flipped off the safety and cocked the gun.

'Don Camillo,' said Biondo in a strange voice. 'I've had enough of seeing that bloke by my bed. You've got two choices: either you absolve me, or I shoot you.'

The pistol shook slightly in his hand. Don Camillo turned pale and looked Biondo right in the eye.

'Jesus,' said Don Camillo silently, 'this is a rabid dog. He'll shoot. An absolution granted in these circumstances is invalid. What should I do?'

'If you are scared, absolve him,' came the voice of Jesus.

Don Camillo crossed his arms on his chest.

'No,' he said.

Biondo ground his teeth.

'Don Camillo, grant me absolution or I'll fire!'

'No.'

Biondo pulled the trigger, and the hammer fell. But there was no shot.

Then Don Camillo fired his own shot, and it landed right on target because punches delivered by Don Camillo never missed.

Then he charged up into the bell-tower and, though it was eleven at night, rang a festive peal for twenty minutes. And everyone said that Don Camillo had gone mad – everyone except Jesus above the altar who shook His head and smiled, and Biondo, who was running through the fields like a madman, and was about to throw himself into the black water of the river when the sound of the bells reached him, and he stopped.

And Biondo turned back because he had heard a Voice that was quite new to him. And this was the real miracle because a pistol that misfires is a fact of life, but a priest who peals bells of celebration at eleven o'clock at night is truly something out of this world.

Men and Beasts

LA GRANDE was a great estate with a hundred cattle in its stable, a modern cheese dairy, an orchard, and so on. It belonged to old Pasotti, who lived by himself at the Abbey, and had an army of retainers under his command.

One day these retainers rose up in protest at working conditions and, led by Peppone, went *en masse* to the Abbey, where old Pasotti granted them a hearing from a window. 'Damn the lot of you!' he shouted, sticking out his head. 'Can't decent citizens be left in peace any more in this filthy country?"

'Decent citizens can, yes,' answered Peppone, 'but not exploiters who deny workers what is theirs by right.'

'As far as I'm concerned, a right is decided by the law,' Pasotti retorted. 'And I'm within the law.'

So Peppone said that, since Pasotti had not conceded the improvements demanded, the workers of La Grande would withhold their labour.

'And we'll feed you to your hundred cows!' concluded Peppone.

'Very well,' replied Pasotti. And closing the window, he went to resume his interrupted nap.

And so began the strike at La Grande, organised by Peppone personally with surveillance teams, rotating guard duties, despatch riders and picket lines. The doors and windows of the stable were nailed shut and sealed.

On the first day, the cows lowed because they hadn't been milked. The second day they lowed because they hadn't been milked and because they were hungry, and on the third day thirst was added to the list, and the lowing could be heard miles from the village. Then Pasotti's old housekeeper came out of the staff entrance to the Abbey and explained to the men on the picket line that she was going to the chemist's in the village to buy some disinfectant.

'The master said he doesn't want to catch cholera from the stink the cows will make once they've all starved to death.'

This made the oldest retainers shake their heads, because they had worked with Pasotti for fifty years and they knew he had a will of cast iron. But Peppone intervened with the full backing of his top brass, and said if anyone dared to go near the stable he would be treated as a traitor to his country.

Towards evening on the fourth day Giacomo, an old dairyman at the Great Estate, came to the presbytery.

'There's a cow in labour, crying fit to break your heart, and she'll die for sure if they don't go and help her: but anyone who goes near the stable will get his legs broken.'

Don Camillo went and clutched the altar rail.

'Jesus,' he said to the crucified Christ, 'hold me back or I'll re-enact the March on Rome!'

'Stay calm, Don Camillo,' Jesus gently cautioned him. 'You will never achieve anything by violence. You must calm people with reason, not enrage them by acts of violence.'

'True,' sighed Don Camillo. 'I should persuade those people to try and think. But it'll be a pity if, while I'm busy persuading, the cows drop dead.'

Jesus smiled: 'If we use violence that calls up further violence, and succeed in saving the hundred beasts but lose a man, or if by using persuasion we lose a hundred beasts but avoid the loss of the man, which would you say is better: violence or persuasion?'

The outraged Don Camillo, who still hadn't given up the idea of the March on Rome, shook his head.

'Jesus, you're changing the terms of the argument: it's not a question of a hundred beasts. We're talking about our common heritage. The death of a hundred animals doesn't simply represent a loss for that bone-head Pasotti, it represents a loss for everyone, the good and the bad. And it may have repercussions which exacerbate existing quarrels and create a conflict in which not just one man dies, but twenty.'

Jesus disagreed.

'If the use of your reason prevents one death today, why couldn't your reason prevent more deaths tomorrow? Have you lost your faith, Don Camillo?'

Don Camillo was so on edge that he went out for a walk in the fields, and in time – quite by chance, naturally – the sound of the lowing of La Grande's hundred cows came to his ears. Then he heard the muttering of the men in the picket line, and ten minutes later he found himself crawling through the canal's great cement irrigation tube, which passes under the wire fence and fortunately happened to be dry.

'Now,' thought Don Camillo, 'all I need is for someone to be waiting for me at the end of the tube to give me a kick in the head, and that really will make my day.'

But there was no one there and so Don Camillo was able to walk cautiously along the whole length of the canal bed towards the dairy.

'Stop there,' said a voice a little later, and with one bound Don Camillo was out of the canal and behind the broad trunk of a tree.

'Stop there or I'll shoot!' said the voice again from behind a broad tree trunk on the other side of the canal.

It was an evening of coincidences, for by dint of fate, Don Camillo found that he had a great big steel contraption in his hands. So he pulled back one of its movable parts and answered, 'You watch out, Peppone, because I'll fire too.'

'Ah,' the other man muttered, 'I just knew I'd end up with you under my feet!'

'Let's call a truce,' said Don Camillo. 'A man who breaks his word is the Devil incarnate. Now I'm going to count, and when I say "three" we both jump into the ditch.'

'Only a priest could be that suspicious,' replied Peppone. And on 'three' they both jumped and there they were, sitting on the bed of the canal.

The lowing of the cows from the stable was now a hellish sound, enough to bring you out in a cold sweat.

'I don't know how you can like that kind of music!' muttered Don Camillo. 'What a pity it will stop when the cows are dead. You're right to stand firm though, since you're the one who'll have to explain to the workers why the granaries and haylofts are burning, and their homes too. Just think how furious poor Pasotti will be when he's forced to take refuge in some Swiss chalet and spend the few millions he's got deposited up there.'

'Let's see if he can get to Switzerland first,' replied Peppone in a menacing tone.

'True!' exclaimed Don Camillo, 'You're right. It's time to ditch that old fifth commandment business: you know, the one about not killing. And the next time someone's up before the Eternal Father, he'll say loud and clear: "Don't make a fuss, dear Signor Eternal Father, or Peppone will call a general strike and make everyone down tools." By the way, Peppone, how do you plan to get the Cherubim to down tools? Have you given any thought to that?'

Peppone bellowed louder than the cow in labour, which was screaming fit to break your heart.

'You aren't a priest!' he said through gritted teeth. 'You're the commandant of the GPU!'

'The Gestapo,' Don Camillo corrected him. 'The Soviet Secret Police are your lot.'

'You go around people's houses at night like a bandit with a machine gun in your mitts!'

'And what about you?' Don Camillo calmly objected.

'I'm serving the people!'

'And I'm serving God!'

Peppone kicked a stone.

'It's no good talking to priests! You say two words and they turn everything into politics!'

'Peppone,' Don Camillo gently began, but the other wouldn't let him go on.

'Don't start going on about national heritage and all the rest of it, or by the living God I'll shoot you!' he shouted.

Don Camillo shook his head. 'It's no good talking to Reds. You say two words and they turn the whole thing into politics!'

The cow in labour gave another piercing cry.

At that moment somebody very close to the ditch said, 'Who's there?' It was Brusco, Magro and Bigio.

'Make a tour along the road to the mill,' ordered Peppone.

'Right,' answered Brusco. 'Who were you talking to?'

'Your damned soul!' shouted Peppone in a rage.

'The cow in labour is screaming,' muttered Brusco.

'Go and tell the priest!' yelled Peppone. 'Cut her throat! I serve the interests of the people, not cows!'

'Don't get angry, boss,' Brusco stammered as he went off with his team.

'All right, Peppone,' whispered Don Camillo, 'now let's go and serve the interests of the people.'

'What are you planning?'

Don Camillo walked quietly along the canal towards the dairy, and Peppone told him to stop or he'd empty a cartridge into his back.

'Peppone is a stubborn beast, stubborn as a mule,' said Don Camillo calmly, 'but he doesn't shoot poor priests in the back when they're doing what God commands them to do.'

Peppone swore, at which Don Camillo turned round abruptly and said, 'Stop playing the fool or I'll fire a shot right on your nose, like the one I fired at your famous Regional Champion . . .'

'There's nothing you can tell me about that: I knew it had to be you. But this isn't the same thing at all.'

Don Camillo walked calmly on, while the other followed

muttering and threatening to shoot him. When they reached the stable, a voice called out, 'Stop there!'

'Go to hell!' answered Peppone. 'It's me. Go and check the cheese dairy.'

Don Camillo didn't even bother to glance at the sealed stable door. He climbed the ladder to the hayloft above the stable and softly called, 'Giacomo.'

The old dairyman who had come to the presbytery a little earlier to tell Don Camillo about the cow in labour, appeared out of the hay. Don Camillo switched on a torch and lifted a bale of hay to one side, revealing a trapdoor.

'Go down,' he said to the old man.

The old man went through the trapdoor and stayed down there for some time.

'She's given birth,' he whispered as he reappeared. 'I've done a thousand of these and I know more about it than a vet.'

'Now go home,' Don Camillo told the old man, and the old man went.

Then Don Camillo reopened the trapdoor and rolled a bale of hay through it.

'What are you up to now?' said Peppone, who had remained hidden till that moment.

'Help me throw bales down and I'll tell you.'

Grumbling, Peppone set to work throwing down bale after bale, and then followed Don Camillo down into the stable.

Don Camillo carried a bale to the manger on the right hand side of the stable, broke its lashings, shook the hay loose and threw it in front of the cows.

'You see to the manger on the left,' he said to Peppone.

'I'd sooner cut my throat!' shouted Peppone, taking a bale and carrying it to the manger on the left.

They worked like an army of cattlemen on the milking. Then there was the job of watering the cows, and since this was a modern stable with mangers at either side and water troughs arranged along the walls, they first had to get 100 cows to do an about-turn, and then wear their arms out beating the cows on the horns to pull them away from the water before they drank themselves to death.

When they had finished, it was still pitch dark in the stable, because the wooden windows had been nailed shut from outside.

'It's three in the afternoon,' said Don Camillo, looking at his watch. 'We'll have to wait till evening to get out of here.'

Peppone started chewing his hands in rage, but then accepted that he had no choice but to stay calm.

When evening came, Peppone and Don Camillo were playing cards in a corner of the stable by the light of a petrol lamp.

'I'm so hungry I could swallow a bishop whole!' Peppone exclaimed in fury.

'That's hard stuff to digest, Citizen Mayor,' answered Don Camillo calmly, though he himself had grown faint with hunger and could have eaten a cardinal. 'Don't tell me you're hungry till you've gone without food for three days like these animals.'

Before leaving, they threw yet more hay into the mangers, which Peppone tried to resist, saying it was a betrayal of the people, but Don Camillo was unyielding.

And so that night the stable was silent as a grave, and old Pasotti, not hearing the cows lowing any more, was terrified by the thought that they were now on the brink of death and no longer had the strength to cry out. And in the morning he went down to negotiate with Peppone, and after some yielding on both sides, things started to work again.

That afternoon, Peppone turned up at the presbytery.

'Well!' said Don Camillo with the utmost sweetness, 'you revolutionaries should always pay attention to the advice of old arch-priests. You really should, my dear children.'

Peppone stood with his arms folded, contemplating this astounding piece of shamelessness.

'Reverend,' said Peppone. 'My machine gun!'

'Your machine gun?' replied Don Camillo. 'I don't understand. You had your machine gun.'

'Yes, I had it, but when we came out of the stable you shamelessly took advantage of the confusion in my head to relieve me of it.'

'Oh yes, maybe it's coming back to me,' replied Don Camillo with exquisite candour. 'My apologies, Peppone. I'm afraid that at my great age I don't seem to be able to remember where I put it.'

'Reverend,' exclaimed Peppone, 'that's the second one you've nicked off me.'

'Well, don't worry, my son. You'll get another. Who knows how many you still have scattered here and there about the house?'

'You're one of those priests who force honest Christians to turn Muslim, over and over again.'

'Maybe,' answered Don Camillo, 'but you're in no such danger. You're not an honest Christian.'

Peppone threw his hat onto the floor.

'If you were an honest Christian,' Don Camillo went on, 'you'd thank me for what I've done for you and the people.'

Peppone picked up his hat, stuck it on his head and started to leave. At the door he turned:

'You can con me out of two, or even 200,000 machine guns. When the uprising comes I'll still get hold of a 75-calibre weapon to fire on this house of the devil!'

'And I'll get hold of an 81-calibre mortar for returning fire,' replied Don Camillo easily.

As he passed the church, since the door was open and the altar was visible, Peppone furiously removed his hat, and then put it straight back on in case anybody saw him.

But Jesus had seen him and told Don Camillo so when he came into the church. 'Peppone saluted me as he went by,' said Jesus happily.

'Take care, Jesus,' replied Don Camillo. 'There've been others who did more than just salute you. They kissed you, and then sold you for thirty pieces of silver. That man who's just saluted you told me three minutes ago that when the uprising comes, he'll get a 75-calibre gun to fire at the house of God.'

'And what did you say to him?'

'That I'd get an 81-calibre mortar and return fire on the People's Palace.'

'I see. The trouble is, Don Camillo, that you really do have an 81-calibre mortar.'

Don Camillo spread his arms.

'Jesus,' he said, 'I've got a few odds and ends, the kind

of thing you never manage to throw away because they're souvenirs. We men are all a bit sentimental. And isn't it better for that sort of stuff to be in my house rather than in someone else's?'

'Don Camillo is always right,' Jesus replied with a smile. 'As long as he does not get above himself.'

'No fear of that; I've got the best advisor in the universe,' answered Don Camillo.

Which left Jesus lost for words.

The Procession

Every year, as part of the village festival, the Crucifix above the altar was carried in procession as far as the river bank, where the water was blessed to make sure the river behaved itself and didn't get up to any funny business.

It seemed that on this occasion everything would go as smoothly as usual, and Don Camillo was putting the finishing touches to the programme of events, when Brusco appeared at the presbytery and said, 'The Branch Secretary has sent me to inform you that the whole section, complete with red flag, is going to take part in the procession.'

'I thank Secretary Peppone,' replied Don Camillo, 'and I shall be delighted for the whole section to be present, if they will be so kind as to leave their flag at home. There's no place for political flags in a sacred procession. Those are my orders.'

Brusco left and a little while later Peppone arrived, red-faced, with his eyes bulging out of his head.

'We're Christians like everyone else!' shouted Peppone,

coming into the presbytery without even knocking. 'What makes us different from other people?'

'The fact that you don't take off your hat when you come into other people's houses,' replied Don Camillo calmly.

Peppone furiously removed his hat.

'Now you're equal to the other Christians,' said Don Camillo.

'Why can't we take our flag on the procession?' shouted Peppone. 'What's wrong with it? Is it a thieves' and murderers' flag?'

'No, Comrade Peppone,' Don Camillo explained, lighting his cigar. 'It's a party flag, and it can't be there. This is a religious event, not a political one.'

'Then Catholic Action can't have their flag there either!'

'Why not? Catholic Action isn't a political party. Indeed, I'm its secretary. In fact, I advise you and your comrades to join.'

Peppone sneered.

'If you want to save your wretched black soul, you should join our Party!'

Don Camillo shrugged.

'This is what we should do,' he answered smiling. 'Let's stay as we are, and be friends like before.'

'You and I were never friends,' asserted Peppone.

'Not even when we were in the mountains together?'

'No! That was just a strategic alliance. For the triumph of the cause you sometimes have to make alliances even with priests.'

'Fine,' said Don Camillo calmly. 'But leave the flag at home if you want to come on the procession.'

Peppone gnashed his teeth.

'If you think you can play *Il Duce*, Reverend, you are mistaken!' exclaimed Peppone. 'Either our flag comes on the procession, or there won't be a procession at all!'

Don Camillo was unimpressed. 'He'll get over it,' he said to himself. And indeed for the three days preceding the Sunday of the festival, not a whisper was heard on the subject. But on the Sunday itself, an hour before Mass, some frightened people turned up at the presbytery. Peppone's men had gone to every house early that morning and warned people to stay away from the procession if they valued their health.

'They've said nothing to me,' replied Don Camillo. 'So it's no concern of mine.'

The procession was supposed to start at the end of Mass, and while Don Camillo was putting on his robes for the occasion, a group of parishioners came to see him.

'What shall we do?' they asked.

'We'll go on the procession,' replied Don Camillo calmly.

'But that lot are quite capable of throwing bombs at the procession,' objected the parishioners. 'You can't expose your congregation to such danger. We think you should postpone the procession, notify the police, and only hold the procession once enough *carabinieri* have come from the city to ensure people's safety.'

'You have a point,' observed Don Camillo. 'In the meantime, perhaps you could explain to the martyrs of our religion how wrong they were to act as they did, and tell them that instead of going out to spread the message of Christianity when it was forbidden, they should have waited for the *carabinieri* to turn up.'

Then Don Camillo showed them the door and the parishioners went away grumbling. A little later, in through the same door came a group of old men and women.

'We're coming, Don Camillo,' they said.

'No, you're going home right now!' replied Don Camillo. 'God will take note of your pious intentions. This is one of those situations in which old people, women and children should definitely stay at home.'

A small group of people had stayed outside the church, but when they heard gunshots coming from the village (it was only Brusco rattling off his machine-gun into the air by way of demonstration), even this small group of diehards slipped away; and so when Don Camillo appeared at the church door he found the courtyard deserted, bare as a billiard table.

'Well, Don Camillo, shall we go?' asked Jesus from the altar. 'The river must look magnificent in all this sun. I am really looking forward to seeing it.'

'Yes, let's go,' answered Don Camillo. 'But as you'll see, there'll only be me in the procession this time. I hope that will be sufficient for you . . .'

'When Don Camillo is present, that is already more than enough people,' said Jesus smiling.

Don Camillo speedily fitted himself into the leather harness with the pouch for the foot of the cross, took down the enormous Crucifix from the altar, slipped it into the pouch, and finally sighed:

'They could have made this cross just a little bit lighter.'

'You are telling me?' replied Jesus with a smile. 'I had to carry it all the way up that hill, and I did not have the shoulders you have got.'

A few minutes later, Don Camillo, carefully carrying the enormous Crucifix, solemnly passed through the church door.

The village was deserted: in their fear everyone had gone to ground, and they were now peeping out through the gaps in their shutters.

'It must have been like this for those friars who used to go around with a black cross through the streets of cities depopulated by the plague,' thought Don Camillo. Then he began to sing a psalm in his great baritone voice, which seemed greater still in the silence.

He crossed the piazza and began walking down the high street, and here too all was silent and deserted.

A little dog came out of a side street and quietly started walking alongside Don Camillo.

'Get away!' muttered Don Camillo.

'Let it be,' whispered Jesus from above his head. 'It means that Peppone will not be able to say that not even a dog joined the procession.'

The street curved at the end of the village, and after the last houses a path led to the river bank. As soon as he'd rounded the bend, Don Camillo was surprised to find his way barred.

Two hundred men had blocked the entire road and were standing there silently with their arms folded and their legs apart, and in front of them was Peppone with his hands on his hips.

Don Camillo wished he could have been an armoured car. But he couldn't be anything other than Don Camillo, and when he was a few feet away from Peppone, he stopped.

Then he drew the enormous Crucifix from its leather sheath and raised it, brandishing it like a club.

'Jesus,' he said, 'hold on tight, in case I need to bring you down on them fast!'

But there was no need because quickly understanding the situation, the men withdrew towards the two pavements either side of the road, and a passage magically opened before him.

Only Peppone was left in the middle of the street, with his hands on his hips, firmly fixed with his legs apart. Don Camillo slid the foot of the Crucifix into its leather pouch and walked straight towards him.

And then Peppone moved out of the way.

'I'm not stepping aside for you, I'm stepping aside for Him,' said Peppone pointing to the Crucifix.

'Then take your hat off!' replied Don Camillo without even looking at him.

Peppone took off his hat, and Don Camillo passed solemnly between Peppone's men.

When he was on the river bank, he stopped.

'Jesus,' said Don Camillo in a loud voice, 'if the houses of the few decent citizens in this corrupt community could float like Noah's ark, I'd pray for a flood so big it would burst the river bank and submerge the whole neighbourhood. But since the few decent citizens live in the same brick houses as all the good-for-nothings, and it wouldn't be fair to make good people suffer for the wrongdoing of rogues such as Mayor Peppone and his band of godless brigands, I pray that you will keep this land safe from the waters and grant it all prosperity.'

'Amen,' said the voice of Peppone behind Don Camillo.

And from behind Don Camillo, Peppone's men, who had followed the Crucifix, also chorused, 'Amen.'

Don Camillo made his way back, arrived at the church courtyard, turned so that Jesus could give the last blessing to the distant river, and found himself standing in front of the little dog, Peppone, Peppone's men, and the whole community, even the pharmacist who didn't believe in God. But then – my goodness! – he'd never come across a priest like Don Camillo, one who could actually make the Eternal Father likable to an unbeliever.

The Rally

PEPPONE GAVE a start when he saw it – a poster on the street corner announcing that some fellow from the city was going to hold a rally in the piazza at the invitation of the local Liberal Party.

'Are we going to allow this kind of provocation in the Red Fortress?' he demanded. 'We'll show them who's in charge around here!'

He summoned his top brass, and the unheard-of event was studied and analysed. A proposal to burn down the Liberal Party's office forthwith was rejected. The idea of banning the rally also came to nothing.

'That's the trouble with democracy!' Peppone seethed. 'Any scoundrel can allow himself the luxury of speaking in a town square!'

They decided to stay within the bounds of law and order with a general mobilisation of all their forces, surveillance squads to prevent ambushes, occupation of strategic points, a garrison at the HQ, and despatch riders standing by to call reinforcements from neighbouring districts.

'The mere fact that they're holding a public rally here shows they think they can beat us,' he said. 'They won't catch us off guard, not for an instant.'

The lookouts along the roads leading to the village were under orders to report any suspicious movement, but when they got to work on Saturday morning, they didn't see so much as a cat all day. During the night, Smilzo spotted a suspect cyclist but it turned out to be no more than the usual drunk. The rally was meant to take place on Sunday afternoon, and yet by three o'clock there had been no sightings.

'They'll come on the 3.35 train,' said Peppone. And he arranged the perfect reception committee around the station.

But when the train came in, the only person who got off was a skinny little man with a light cloth suitcase.

'You see? They knew something was up,' Peppone decided, 'and didn't feel they had sufficient numbers to strike the first blow.'

At that moment the little man came up, greeted them civilly, and asked Peppone if he'd be kind enough to show him the way to the office of the Liberal Party.

Peppone looked at him in astonishment.

'The office of the Liberal Party?'

'Yes,' said the man, 'I'm due to give a little speech in twenty minutes, and I don't want to be late.'

Everyone looked at Peppone, and Peppone scratched his head.

'Well, it's quite difficult to explain because the town centre is a mile or so away.'

The little man reacted with dismay.

'Will it be possible to find a vehicle to take me there?'

'I've got my truck outside,' muttered Peppone. 'Do you want a lift?'

The little man thanked him. Then when he got outside and saw the truck filled with grim-faced people in red kerchiefs and all those Party badges, he looked at Peppone.

'I'm the boss,' said Peppone. 'Come in the front with me.'

Halfway there, Peppone stopped the vehicle and looked the little man in the face. He was a thin gentleman of middle age, with very refined features.

'So you're a Liberal?' he asked.

'Yes,' came the reply.

'And aren't you afraid at finding yourself here in the middle of fifty communists?'

'No,' answered the man calmly.

A threatening murmur arose from the men in the truck.

'What's in your case? TNT?' asked Peppone.

The man laughed and lifted the lid.

'Pyjamas, slippers and a toothbrush,' he said.

Peppone crumpled his hat and beat his thighs.

'This is crazy!' he shouted. 'Would you please be so good as to tell me why you aren't frightened?'

'Precisely because I'm not alone and there are fifty of you,' the little man calmly explained.

'Never mind the fifty others!' yelled Peppone. 'Don't you think I'd be capable of throwing you all the way into that canal by myself, with one hand?'

'No, I don't think so,' the man calmly replied.

'Then you're mad, or just stupid, or deliberately out to con us.'

The man laughed.

'It's much simpler than that, Signore. I'm a respectable person.'

Peppone gave a start.

'No, my dear Signore! If you were a respectable person, you wouldn't be an enemy of the people! a slave of reaction! a tool of capitalism!'

'I'm nobody's enemy and nobody's slave. I'm just someone who thinks differently from you.'

Peppone put the truck in gear and roared off like a rocket.

'Did you make your will before coming here?' he sneered as they drove along.

'No,' replied the man easily. 'My only wealth is my work, and if I die I can't leave it to anyone.'

Before entering the village Peppone stopped a moment to talk to Smilzo, his motorcycle courier. Then by way of some side streets they arrived outside the office of the Liberal Party.

Doors and windows closed.

'Nobody there,' said Peppone darkly.

'They'll all be in the piazza for sure,' replied the little man. 'It's already late.'

'Yes of course, that must be it,' answered Peppone, winking at Brusco.

When they arrived at the piazza, Peppone and his men got out of the truck, surrounded the man, and cut their way through the crowd until they reached the platform. The speaker climbed up onto it and found himself in front of 2000 men in red kerchiefs.

He turned to Peppone, who had followed him onto the rostrum.

'Excuse me,' he said, 'but might I perhaps have come to the wrong rally?'

'No,' Peppone reassured him. 'The fact is that there are only twenty-three Liberals, and they don't really stand out in a crowd.'

'Which shows that Liberals have more faith in the democratic propriety of the Communists than you do,' replied the man.

Peppone seethed silently for a moment and then turned to the microphone.

'Comrades!' he shouted, 'I'd like to introduce this gentleman who is going to give a speech, after which you're all going to join the Liberal Party.'

An enormous laugh greeted these words, and when there was a bit of silence the man spoke.

'I thank your leader for his kindness,' he said, 'but it's my duty to make clear that the outcome he's suggested doesn't match my wishes at all, because if, at the end of my speech, you were all to go and join the Liberal Party, I would be compelled to go and join the Communist Party, and that would be against my principles.'

He was unable to continue because at that moment a tomato whistled through the air and hit him in the face.

The crowd started to snigger and Peppone turned pale.

'Anyone who laughs is no better than a swine!' he yelled into the microphone. And the crowd fell silent.

The man stood firm and tried to wipe his face clean with his hand. Peppone was a man of instinct, and often capable of fine gestures without realising it. He took his handkerchief out of his breast pocket, then put it back and unknotted the big red kerchief from around his neck and offered it to the man.

'I wore this when I was in the mountains,' he said. 'Wipe yourself with it.'

'Bravo Peppone!' yelled a thunderous voice from a first floor window in a nearby house.

'I don't need the approval of the clergy,' responded Peppone indignantly, while Don Camillo bit his tongue in fury at having allowed himself to call out.

The man shook his head, bowed, and came to the microphone.

'Too much history is enclosed in that kerchief to let it to be stained by a vulgar incident which belongs to the less heroic story of everyday life,' he said. 'An ordinary hankie is enough to wipe away this mess.'

Peppone blushed and bowed in return, which moved a lot of people, and a tremendous round of applause broke out, while the young vandal who'd thrown the tomato was kicked all the way out of the piazza.

The man spoke calmly, gently, with no harshness, smoothing over every rough edge, avoiding any slightly difficult subject because he realised that no one would retaliate if he let himself go, and he thought it would be unworthy of him to capitalise on that.

At the end they applauded and made way for him as he came down from the rostrum.

Crossing the piazza he found himself under the arcade at the front of the Town Hall, and stayed there in some confusion with his little case in his hand because he didn't know what to do or which way to go, when Don Camillo appeared and turned to Peppone, who was two paces behind the little man.

'You and your godless party moved fast, didn't they, to ally themselves with the diehard anti-clericals in the Liberal Party!' exclaimed Don Camillo loudly.

'What?' said Peppone, turning in amazement to the little man. 'You're against the clergy?'

'But . . .' the man stammered.

'Silence!' Don Camillo broke in. 'You should be ashamed of yourself for wanting a "free Church in a free State"!'

The man was about to protest, but Peppone wouldn't let him even start:

'Bravo!' he yelled. 'Give me your hand! Even reactionary liberals are my friends if they're anti-clergy too!'

'Hear hear!' responded Peppone's men.

'You're my guest!' said Peppone to the man.

'Don't think of it,' retorted Don Camillo. 'This gentleman is *my* guest. I'm not a lout who throws tomatoes in my opponent's face.'

Peppone squared up threateningly in front of Don Camillo.

'I said he's *my* guest,' he said in a grim voice.

'And I said it too,' replied Don Camillo, 'which means we can decide it with a punch-up if you like, and you can take the punches that should have gone to those dimwit Dynamos of yours.'

Peppone clenched his fists.

'Come on,' said Brusco to him. 'Do you get into fights with priests in the main square now?'

At length it was decided they would settle on a meeting on neutral ground. All three went for a late lunch outside the village at Gigiòto's, a completely apolitical landlord, and so finally the contest over democracy ended democratically in a draw.

On the River Bank

BETWEEN ONE and three o'clock on an August afternoon the heat in the villages of the Plain, swathed in maize and hemp, is something you can see and touch. It's as if there is a great rippling veil of boiling glass before your face, all but an inch from your nose.

Cross a bridge and look down into the canal, and you'll see how the bed is dry and cracked, with a dead fish here and there. And when you look from the road on the dyke into a graveyard you seem to hear the bones of the dead crackling under the beating sun.

A few high-wheeled carts filled with sand make their way slowly along the main road, and the carter sleeps open-mouthed on top of his load, with his belly exposed and his back scorching, or, sitting on the shaft, with a little hook he fishes out pieces of a half watermelon placed on his lap like a basin.

Then, when you reach the main dyke . . . there is the river: vast, deserted, silent and motionless; not so much a river as a graveyard of dead water.

At one-thirty on just such an August afternoon, Don Camillo was walking towards the main dyke wearing a big white handkerchief between his head and his hat. Seeing him alone like this on the white road under the sun, you couldn't imagine anything blacker, or anything more like a priest.

'If there's a single person within ten miles who isn't asleep, I'll eat my head,' said Don Camillo to himself.

Then he climbed over the dyke and went to sit in the shade of an acacia thicket where he could see the water glistening through gaps in the leaves. He undressed, carefully folded his clothes up into a bundle which he hid in the branches of a small tree, and wearing only his underpants went and flung himself into the water.

It was wonderfully peaceful: no one would have seen him; beside it being the deadest time of day, he had chosen the most out of the way place possible. In any case, he was being discreet and after half an hour, he came out of the water, slipped into the acacias, came to the little tree . . . and his clothes were no longer there.

At which Don Camillo's heart missed a beat.

This couldn't be a theft: who'd take a fancy to a priest's faded old cassock? Someone was clearly up to mischief. And sure enough, barely another moment passed before voices could be heard coming towards the dyke. When Don Camillo realised that they belonged to a large gang of boys and girls, and that Smilzo was their leader, the whole stunt became clear to him, and he felt like pulling up an acacia and stabbing them all with it. Of course there was no doubt what those wretches were after: let's flush out Don Camillo and enjoy the show!

So Don Camillo threw himself back into the river, and swam

under water until he reached an islet in midstream where he could clamber ashore and disappear among the reeds.

But even though they wouldn't have been able to see him, since he had emerged on the far side of the islet, they spotted the ripples he left behind: so they spread themselves along the bank and waited, singing and laughing. Don Camillo was under siege.

How weak a strong man is when he feels ridiculous!

Don Camillo lay down among the reeds and waited: he could see without being seen, and so he was able to watch Peppone arriving, followed by Brusco, Bigio and all the top brass. Smilzo was recounting the story with expansive gestures, and everyone was laughing. Then yet more people arrived and to Don Camillo it felt as if the Reds were settling scores, both old and new, and that this time they'd found the best possible method because when a man is rendered ridiculous he can no long inspire fear, even if his fists weigh a ton, and even if he's the representative of the Eternal Father. But this was all a grievous misunderstanding because Don Camillo had never meant to frighten anyone – only the Devil. And now politics had somehow contrived to distort the situation so that the Reds considered their parish priest an enemy, believing it was the fault of the priests if things didn't go as they should. When things don't go well, finding a way of making them go better always seems less important than finding someone to take the blame.

'Jesus,' said Don Camillo, 'I feel ashamed addressing you in my underpants, but the situation is serious, and if it isn't a mortal sin for a poor priest dying in the heat to take a plunge in the water, help me because I can't do this on my own.'

They had brought flasks, cards and an accordion, and the river bank now looked like a beach. You could see they hadn't any intention of lifting the blockade. On the contrary, they had tightened it by occupying 500 yards of the shore upstream, apart from the notorious part around the ford – 200 yards of river bank full of bushes and weeds – where no one had set foot since 1945.

As they retreated, the Germans had destroyed the bridges and planted mines along a broad section of the shore where it was fordable, and so this part, and the opposite shore, were thickly sown with mines laid to such malign effect that after a couple of disastrous attempts, the bomb disposal team had decided to seal off the area with stakes and barbed wire.

There were none of Peppone's Reds there, but they didn't need to be because only a lunatic would consider coming ashore in that bed of mines. So there was nothing Don Camillo could do, because if he tried to leave the water beyond the upstream blockade he'd end up right in the middle of the village, and if he tried to go beyond the downstream blockade he'd get stuck in the tangled undergrowth of the minefield. And for a parish priest in his underpants either choice was a luxury he couldn't afford.

Don Camillo didn't move. He stayed there, lying on the damp ground, and confined himself to chewing a reed and working out a complicated line of thought.

'Well, a respectable man can still be respectable in his underpants,' he concluded. 'The important thing is for him to act respectably, and then his clothes don't count for anything.'

Now evening was drawing in, and on the river bank they were lighting torches and lanterns: it looked like a fashionable beach soirée. When the green of the grass had turned to black, Don Camillo slipped into the water and cautiously swam upstream until he reached the shallows near the ford. Then he headed directly towards the shore. They couldn't see him because he was walking rather than swimming, and putting his mouth out of the water every so often to breathe.

Now he was at the bank, but it was difficult to get out of the water undiscovered. Once he was in the bushes he'd easily be able to reach the dyke, and if he ran safely over that he could drop down into the vines and maize, and then get to the presbytery garden without any trouble.

He took hold of a bush and slowly lifted himself up, but when he'd almost made it onto the bank, the bush gave way and Don Camillo fell back into the water. People heard the splash and pricked up their ears. But with a bound Don Camillo reached dry land and disappeared among the bushes.

There were shouts and everyone gathered from one side or the other while the moon rose to illuminate the spectacle.

Peppone came to the front and yelled, 'Don Camillo! Don Camillo!'

There was no reply and a silent chill fell over everyone.

'Don Camillo!' yelled Peppone again. 'For God's sake, don't move! You're in the minefield!'

'I know,' came the calm voice of Don Camillo from a bush in the middle of the murderous patch of scrub.

Smilzo stepped forward with a bundle in his hand.

'Don Camillo!' he yelled. 'Don't move! All it would take is for you to touch a mine with a tip of your toe and you'll go sky high!'

'I know,' answered Don Camillo's calm voice.

Smilzo's face was covered in sweat.

'Don Camillo!' he yelled. 'It was a stupid joke. Stay there. I've got your clothes.'

'My clothes? Thank you, Smilzo. I'm right here if you feel like bringing them to me.'

A branch thrashed at the top of the middle bush. Smilzo's mouth fell open. He turned and looked at the others.

In the silence an ironic chuckle could be heard from Don Camillo.

Peppone snatched the bundle from Smilzo's hands.

'I'll bring them to you, Don Camillo,' said Peppone advancing slowly towards the stakes and barbed wire. And was already about to climb over the wire, when Smilzo leaped up to him and pulled him back.

'No, Boss,' said Smilzo taking the bundle and entering the enclosure. 'The one who did the damage ought to pay.'

Everyone drew back, their foreheads dripping with sweat, their hands anxiously over their mouths.

Smilzo moved slowly through the undergrowth, placing his feet with great care, and the silence weighed like lead.

'Here,' said Smilzo faintly when he reached the middle bush.

'Good,' muttered Don Camillo. 'Come right in. You are authorised to see Don Camillo in his underpants.'

Smilzo went in.

'Well? What do you make of an arch-priest in his pants?' asked Don Camillo.

'I don't know,' stammered Smilzo. 'Everything looks black

with red dots spinning around. The moon's spinning too.' He was gasping for breath. 'I've nicked a few bits and pieces,' he went on, 'and I've knocked a few people about, but I've never done any harm to anyone.'

'*Ego te absolvo*,' replied Don Camillo making the sign of the cross on Smilzo's forehead.

They walked slowly towards the dyke and everyone held their breath as they waited for the blast.

After climbing the barbed wire they reached the road, Don Camillo in front and Smilzo behind, his mind in a fog, still on tiptoe as if he hadn't left the minefield, until he suddenly slumped to the ground. Peppone, who was walking twenty yards behind them at the head of the crowd, bent down for a second without taking his eyes from Don Camillo's back, grabbed Smilzo by the collar of his jacket, and dragged him along like a bundle of rags. At the church door Don Camillo turned for a moment, took his leave of the assembled company with a dignified bow, and went inside.

The others dispersed silently, leaving only Peppone in the courtyard, standing with his legs apart, staring fixedly at the closed door, and still holding onto the unconscious Smilzo by his collar. Then he shook his head and went off too, slowly dragging his bundle behind him.

'Jesus,' whispered Don Camillo to the crucified Christ, 'protecting the dignity of a parish priest in his underpants is also a way of serving the Church.'

Jesus made no reply.

'Jesus,' whispered Don Camillo again, 'did I commit a mortal sin by going for a swim?'

'No,' answered Jesus. 'You committed a mortal sin when you entrusted Smilzo with the return of your clothes.'

'I didn't think he'd do it. It was careless of me, but I didn't mean him any harm.'

A distant roar was heard from the direction of the river.

'Every so often a hare goes through the minefield and sets off a mine,' explained Don Camillo, in thought more than in words. 'And so we have to conclude that you . . .'

'Do not conclude anything, Don Camillo,' said Jesus with a smile. 'You cannot draw calm conclusions when you are in the grip of a fever.'

Meanwhile Peppone had arrived at Smilzo's door. An old man answered when he knocked, and silently took delivery of the bundle which Peppone was presenting to him. At that moment Peppone too heard the explosion, and a flood of thoughts poured through his mind. Then he took Smilzo back again for a moment and gave him a smack on the head which made the boy's hair stand on end.

'Keep going!' said Smilzo in a faint voice, as the old man took him inside.

Rough Stuff

FOR THE PAST WEEK, Don Camillo had been in a permanent state of agitation, so busy scurrying to and fro that he even forgot to eat. Then, coming back one afternoon from a neighbouring village, he'd no sooner arrived in his parish than he was compelled to alight from his bike because there were men digging a trench right across the whole street. There'd been no sign of it in the morning.

'We're laying a new waste pipe,' explained one of the workmen. 'Mayor's orders.'

So Don Camillo went straight to the Town Hall and as soon as he was in Peppone's presence he exclaimed in fury, 'We're going mad here! What are you lot up to, digging this filthy ditch? Don't you know it's Friday?'

'So what?' said Peppone in astonishment. 'Is it forbidden to dig ditches on Fridays?'

Don Camillo roared, 'But don't you realise it is only two days till Sunday?'

Peppone looked worried. He rang a bell and Brusco appeared. Peppone consulted him: 'Listen, the Reverend says that since today is Friday, there are only two days to go till Sunday. What do you think?'

Brusco gave the matter serious consideration. He picked up a pencil and did some calculations on a piece of paper.

'That is correct,' he said, 'if we take into account the fact that it's four in the afternoon, and that in eight hours it will be midnight, then it's only thirty-two hours till Sunday.'

Don Camillo had been foaming at the mouth as he watched this performance, and finally lost his temper completely.

'I see what you're up to!' he shouted. 'This has all been planned specifically so you can ruin the Bishop's visit!'

'Reverend,' answered Peppone, 'what has the drainpipe got to do with the visit of the Bishop? And excuse me, but who might this Bishop be? And what might he be wanting to do here?'

'To take your damned soul to hell!' shouted Don Camillo. 'You'll have to fill in that trench, otherwise on Sunday the Bishop won't be able to get through!'

Peppone acted dumb.

'Won't be able to get through? Well how did *you* get through? If I'm not mistaken there's a plank over the trench.'

'But the Bishop is coming by car!' exclaimed Don Camillo. 'You can't make the Bishop get out of his car!'

'I beg your pardon,' replied Peppone. 'I didn't know Bishops can't walk. If that's the case, then it's a different story. Brusco, ring the city and get them to send a crane straight away. They can put it next to the trench, and when the Bishop's car arrives they can attach it to the hoist and lift it across so the Bishop doesn't have to get out. Got that?'

'Got it, Boss. What colour would you like the crane?'

'Let's have it nickel-plated or chrome. That'll make a good impression.'

In this kind of situation, even someone without Don Camillo's fists of steel would have started lashing out. But in fact, it was in exactly this kind of situation that Don Camillo showed his capacity for remaining calm. And this was due to the formidable simplicity of his thinking: 'Whenever that fellow provokes me as blatantly and shamelessly as this, it means he wants a reaction from me. So if I punch him in the face I'll be doing him a favour. In fact, I wouldn't be hitting any old Peppone but a mayor in the course of his official duties, which would cause an appalling scandal and create general hostility towards me, and towards the Bishop.'

'It doesn't matter,' he said. 'Even bishops can walk.'

That evening, in the church, he spoke almost sorrowfully, exhorting everyone to remain calm and to do no more than pray that God would enlighten the mind of the Signor Mayor in such a way as to prevent the ceremony from being ruined by deliveries of building materials, and the procession from being messed up by forcing the faithful to cross a wobbly board one at a time. And they should pray that God would stop the board breaking as they went across it, so that a day of rejoicing would not be transformed into a day of mourning.

This incendiary sermon succeeded in terrifying all the women, who as soon as they'd left the church, gathered around Peppone's house giving him what for, until the Mayor appeared and shouted that they could all go to hell and that the trench would be covered over.

And all went well, except that on Sunday morning, the streets were full of posters saying:

'*Comrades!*

'*Using the start of work on a public utility as their pretext, the forces of reaction have stirred up an unseemly uproar which offends our democratic sensibility. On Sunday the representative of a foreign power will be a guest in our village, the same representative who indirectly gave rise to the unseemly uproar. While taking note of your resentment and indignation, we are concerned to avoid any demonstration which might complicate our relations with foreigners, and we invite you therefore, to confine yourselves categorically to receiving the representative of the foreign power with dignified indifference.*

'*Viva the democratic republic! Viva the proletariat! Viva Russia!*'

The whole thing was further livened up by a general mobilisation of all the Reds who, as was immediately obvious, had the specific task of walking up and down 'with dignified indifference,' displaying their red kerchiefs and ties.

Don Camillo, white as a sheet, slipped away into the church and was on the point of rushing off out again when Jesus called out to him. 'Don Camillo! Where are you off to in such a hurry?'

'I've got to go and meet the Bishop on the main road into the village,' Don Camillo explained. 'It's quite a way off. And besides, the road is full of people wearing red kerchiefs, and if the Bishop doesn't see me, he'll think he's in Stalingrad.'

'And those people in red kerchiefs,' enquired Jesus. 'Are they foreigners? . . . Do they belong to another religion?'

'No, they're the usual crooks you see before you in church from time to time.'

'Well if that is the case, Don Camillo, it would be best if *that thing* you have under your cassock went back into the sacristy wardrobe.'

Don Camillo pulled the machine-gun out from under his cassock and went to put it back in the sacristy.

'You may take it out again when I say so,' ordered Jesus, and Don Camillo shrugged.

'*You* tell me to get the machine-gun out?! That'll be the day! You know it will never happen. If I may be honest with you, there are a number of cases in the Old Testament . . .'

'Get out of here, reactionary!' said Jesus smiling. 'While you are wasting time chattering, your poor defenceless old Bishop is falling prey to raging Red demons!'

The poor defenceless old Bishop was indeed in the hands of the Red horde. The Christian faithful had been lining the main road since seven in the morning, forming two long and formidable walls of enthusiasm, but a few minutes before the Bishop's car was due to arrive, Peppone's lookout post sent up a flare warning him of the approach of the enemy: at which Peppone gave the order to advance, and in a lightning-swift manoeuvre every active Red leapt into action 500 yards further down, so that when the Bishop arrived he found the road awash with people in red kerchiefs, strolling about or stopping in groups to chat, showing the most sublime indifference towards the approaching car, which had to move forwards at a walking pace and keep sounding its horn to make a way through.

This was indeed the demonstration of 'dignified indifference' which the top brass had wanted, and Peppone and the others were beside themselves with delight as they mingled with the crowd.

Our famous Bishop, old as the hills, white-haired, and so stooped that when he spoke his voice seemed to come from some other place and some other century, immediately recognised the 'dignified indifference' and told his driver to stop the car (which was an open-topped model), made an unsuccessful attempt to turn the door handle, making it clear that he wasn't strong enough, and Brusco who was standing there fell into the trap. By the time he realised his folly (which he did when Peppone dealt him a kick on the shin) it was too late, and he'd already opened the door.

'Thank you, my son,' said the Bishop. 'It will be better if I enter the village on foot.'

'But it's a long way,' stammered Bigio, likewise earning himself a kick on the shin.

'That doesn't matter,' replied the Bishop with a smile. 'I don't wish to disturb your political meeting in any way.'

'It isn't a political meeting,' explained Peppone darkly. 'These are workers quietly chatting about their own affairs. By all means stay in the car.'

But by then the Bishop had got out, and Brusco got a second kick because, seeing how wobbly the Bishop was, he had offered him an arm to lean on.

'Thank you, thank you, my son,' said the Bishop. And off he went, gesturing to his secretary to get out from under his feet because he wanted to walk on his own.

And so he reached the part of the village under occupation by Don Camillo's team, followed by the silent and glowering Red horde, and there in the front row alongside the Bishop was Peppone with his top brass and a bunch of his fiercest fanatics, because as Peppone had rightly said, all it would take was some cretin doing something foolish to 'the other lot' and the forces of reaction would use it to cook up the most damaging possible accusations.

'The order stays unchanged. And it isn't going to change,' he decided. 'Dignified indifference.'

As soon as he saw the Bishop arriving, Don Camillo rushed towards him.

'Monsignor,' he exclaimed in great agitation, 'forgive me, but it's not my fault! I was waiting here with the whole congregation, but at the last moment . . .'

'Don't worry,' replied the Bishop smiling. 'It is entirely *my* fault for getting out of the car and choosing to take a little walk. As we get old, we bishops all go slightly crazy.'

The faithful applauded, the band played, and the Bishop looked around him delightedly.

'It's a really fine village,' he said moving on again. 'Truly lovely. Cheerful, and excellently maintained. There must be a top-notch administration.'

'We do what we can for the benefit of the people,' answered Brusco, receiving his third kick from Peppone.

When he came to the piazza, the Bishop saw the fountain, and stopped.

'A fountain in a village of the Low Country!' he exclaimed. 'You've found drinking water!'

'You just need to know how to look for it, Your Eminence,' replied Bigio, who had gained the principal credit for the achievement. 'We sent down 300 yards of pipe and out came the water, with God's help.'

The additional gain for Bigio was a series of kicks. Then, since the fountain was in front of the People's Palace, the Bishop caught sight of the extensive new building and it aroused his interest.

'And what is this fine palazzo?'

'It's the People's Palace!' answered Peppone with enormous pride.

'Truly magnificent!' exclaimed the Bishop.

'Would you like to see it?' said Peppone on impulse before a terrible kick in the shins made him jump. And this one came from Don Camillo.

The Bishop's secretary, a thin young man with glasses and a big nose, rushed forwards to warn that this would not be appropriate, that His Eminence really shouldn't do it, but the Bishop had already set off and was soon inside the building. They showed him everything: the gymnasium, the reading room, and the study centre; and when they arrived at the library, the Bishop went up to the bookcases and read the titles on the spines of the books. In front of the 'political' bookcase, filled with books and leaflets of propaganda, he said nothing, merely sighed, but Peppone was nearby and noticed.

'It's all right, Monsignor,' he whispered. 'Nobody reads them.'

Peppone decided against a visit to the office, but he couldn't resist the temptation to show the Bishop the theatre-cum-reception hall which was his pride and joy, so that on his way out the Bishop found himself confronted with that enormous portrait of the man with small eyes and the big moustache.

'You know what politics are like, Your Eminence,' said Peppone in a low voice. 'When all's said and done, believe me, deep down he's not a bad man.'

'May the Good Lord enlighten his mind too,' replied the Bishop quietly.

With all this was going on, Don Camillo was plunged into a painfully paradoxical situation. Even as he was bubbling over with indignation at how the Bishop's kindness was being exploited by making him visit a People's Palace – and this cried out for divine vengeance! – it did matter to him that the Bishop should see how forward-thinking and well run this village was. And it also mattered to him that if the Bishop was impressed by the Reds' organisation, this would surely enhance his impression of the superior parish recreation centre and garden, and consequently his own status and significance in the eyes of the Bishop.

When the visit was finished, Don Camillo approached the Bishop.

'Monsignor,' he said in a loud voice so that Peppone could clearly hear him, 'it's a pity that Signor Peppone hasn't shown you his armoury. Apparently it's the best supplied in the province.'

Peppone was about to respond to this, but the Bishop stopped him.

'It won't be as well supplied as yours,' answered the Bishop with a smile.

'Well said!' put in Bigio.

'He's even got an 81-calibre mortar buried somewhere,' exclaimed Brusco.

The Bishop turned towards Peppone's top brass.

'Do you want it back?' he said. 'Keep a better hold on it then. Didn't I tell you before that he's a dangerous character?'

'He can't scare us,' said Peppone with a sneer.

'You keep your eye on him,' advised the Bishop.

Don Camillo shook his head.

'You're joking as always, Monsignor,' he exclaimed, 'but you have no idea what kind of people these are.'

By the door the Bishop saw the bulletin board with that notorious poster, and he stopped to read it.

'Ah,' he said, 'the representative of a foreign power is coming here! Who would that be, Don Camillo?'

'I don't get involved in politics,' replied Don Camillo. 'You'll have to ask the gentleman who put up the poster. Signor Peppone, Monsignor would like to know who is the representative of the foreign power mentioned in your poster.'

Peppone hesitated a moment and then muttered, 'Oh . . . America . . . as usual.'

'I see!' replied the Bishop. 'It's all about the Americans coming here to look for oil. Am I right?'

'Yes,' answered Peppone. 'It's a disgrace: the oil is ours!'

'I realise that,' agreed the Bishop gravely. 'But you have done well to advocate calm and to order your men to confine themselves to a show of dignified indifference. In my opinion, we have nothing to gain by spoiling our relationship with America. Don't you agree?'

Peppone flung out his arms.

'Monsignor,' he said, 'you'll understand me when I say that we put up with something as far as we can, and then the moment comes when we can't hold ourselves back any longer!'

When the Bishop arrived in front of the church, he found all the children from the parish recreation centre, nicely turned out and standing in a row to sing a song of welcome. Then an enormous bunch of flowers detached itself from the group of children and came slowly forwards until, when it was in front of the Bishop, the flowers were lifted and a little boy appeared from behind them, so tiny, so pretty, so curly-haired and so well dressed that the women went crazy over him.

There was complete silence and then the child recited a poem to the Bishop, all in one go and without a single stumble, in a clear, delicate voice like a trickle of water. And when he'd finished, the villagers yelled with enthusiasm and said it was an extraordinary achievement.

Peppone came up to Don Camillo and whispered in his ear. 'You coward! You've taken advantage of an innocent child to make me look ridiculous in front of everyone. I'll break every bone in your body. And as for the boy, I'll show you. You've contaminated him and I'm going to throw him into the Po!'

'Have a nice trip,' Don Camillo replied. 'He's your son.'

And it really was a brutal episode, because Peppone carried the boy all the way to the river bank and, with threats of monstrous violence, charged him to recite the Bishop's poem three times over in honour of that poor, weak and gullible old Bishop who, being the 'representative of a foreign power' – (the Vatican), had been received according to plan, with 'dignified indifference'.

The Bell

D ON CAMILLO – after waylaying Bigio at least three times a day for the past week whenever he came across him, and yelling at him that he and every other builder were *bandits* trying to make themselves rich on the backs of the people – had finally succeeded in agreeing a price with him and had got him to re-plaster the front of the presbytery. Now, whenever Don Camillo went to sit on the little bench in the middle of the courtyard to smoke half a cigar, the view of all that whiteness, along with the green of the newly painted shutters and the jasmine festooning the door, made a truly magnificent effect.

Yet, even as he sat quietly enjoying it all, Don Camillo could not avoid turning to look at the bell-tower and pining for Geltrude.

The Germans had taken Geltrude away, and Don Camillo had been eating his heart out over this for three years, because Geltrude had been the biggest bell and, if you wanted to buy a replacement on the same scale, only the hand of God would be able to find the money.

'Do not pine over this, Don Camillo,' Jesus said to him from the altar one day. 'A parish can be in good order even if its church tower is missing a bell. These things are not measured by volume. God has the finest of ears and can hear you perfectly well, even if you call on him with a bell the size of a hazelnut.'

'Of course,' sighed Don Camillo. 'But humans *are* hard of hearing, and it's humans above all who are called by the bells. You have to talk to humans at the top of your voice. The mass of people only listen to those who make the most noise.'

'Persevere, Don Camillo, and you shall succeed.'

'Jesus, I've tried everything. Those who'd like to give money don't have any, and the rich don't cough up a single lira, not even if you were to threaten to cut their throats. Two of my lottery tickets have come so close . . . It's such a pity! All it would take is for someone to tip me the wink, just one word, or one name, and I could have bought ten bells by now.'

Jesus smiled.

'Excuse my negligence, Don Camillo. You mean that next year I should pay proper attention to the football championship. And the lottery too, apparently.'

Don Camillo blushed.

'You're misinterpreting me,' he protested. 'When I said "someone" I wasn't remotely suggesting it should be You! I was speaking . . . generally.'

'I am glad to hear it, Don Camillo,' Jesus solemnly agreed. 'It is always prudent to speak *generally* in matters of this kind.'

A few days later, Don Camillo was called to the villa of Signora Giuseppina, the chatelaine of Boscaccio, and when he came home he was beside himself with happiness.

'Jesus!' exclaimed Don Camillo as he stopped breathlessly in front of the altar, 'tomorrow you will see a twenty-pound candle burning here in front of you. I'm going to town to buy it, and if they don't have one I'll get it made specially.'

'Who's giving you the money, Don Camillo?'

'Don't worry about that: even if I have to sell the mattress off my bed, you'll have your candle! You've done too much for me already!' Then Don Camillo calmed down. 'Signora Giuseppina is offering the church the money we need to replace Geltrude!'

'What gave her the idea?'

'She says she made a vow,' explained Don Camillo. '"If Jesus helps me bring a certain piece of business to fruition, I will present the bell to the church." The transaction has gone well and, thanks to your help, within a month Geltrude will once again lift up her voice to heaven! Now I'm going to order the candle!'

Don Camillo was rushing off at full steam when Jesus called him back.

'No candles, Don Camillo,' said Jesus sternly. '*No* candles.'

'But why not?' asked Don Camillo in astonishment.

'I cannot take any credit for this,' replied Jesus. 'I did not help Signora Giuseppina to complete her piece of business. I do not concern myself with competitions or with commerce. If I were to get involved in commercial transactions, those who made profits would have reason to bless me, but those who made losses would have reason to curse me. If you find a wallet full of money, it is not because I made you find it, any more than I made your neighbour lose it. Light your candle in front of the broker who helped Signora Giuseppina to add to her millions. I am no middleman.'

The voice of Jesus was unusually pitiless, and Don Camillo was filled with shame.

'Forgive me,' he stammered, 'I'm a poor, coarse, ignorant country priest, and my brain has nothing in it but fog.'

Jesus smiled and exclaimed, 'Do not run Don Camillo down. Don Camillo always hears my voice, and that shows his brain is not filled with fog. It is often too much learning that fills brains with fog. You are not the one who sinned. On the contrary, your gratitude moves me because you are quick to see God's benevolence in every small thing which brings you joy. And your joy is always honest, as is your joy in regaining your bell. And you are honest in wanting to thank me for enabling you to do so. It is Signora Giuseppina who is dishonest in thinking that she can buy God's complicity in her sordid financial affairs.'

Don Camillo had listened in silence with his head bowed. He looked up again.

'Thank you, Jesus. I'll go and tell that money-grubber to keep her cash!' he exclaimed. 'My bells must all be respectable. Otherwise I'd rather die without ever hearing Geltrude's voice again!'

'Don Camillo,' said Jesus, 'I know exactly how much your bell means to you because I can read your thoughts from moment to moment. And this renunciation of yours is great and noble enough to purify the bronze in a statue of the Antichrist himself. *Vade retro, Satana*! Get out of here before you force me to grant you not only your bell, but who knows what other piece of wickedness.'

Don Camillo stood up.

'So I can keep it?'

'Yes, keep it. You have earned it.'

On occasions like these, Don Camillo invariably forgot where he lived. He bowed before the altar, did an about face, resumed his gallop, slammed on the brakes, and skidded all the way to the door.

And Jesus watched him with satisfaction because this too was a way of singing the praises of the Lord.

Then a few days later, something awful happened. Don Camillo caught a boy scribbling on the white plaster of the presbytery with a piece of coal, and bore down on him like a buffalo. The boy shot off with the speed of a lizard, but Don Camillo was not in God's grace and ran after him.

'I'll catch you even if my lungs explode!' he shouted.

And so he set off on a furious pursuit across the fields, and Don Camillo's rage grew with every step. At length the boy found himself in front of an impenetrable hedge, and so he stopped and turned in dismay, putting his hands out, with no breath left to speak.

Don Camillo came to a halt with the force of an armoured car, gripped the boy's arm with his left hand and raised his right to start raining down a storm of blows, but the arm felt so thin and fragile under his fingers that he shuddered, opened his hand and let the boy's arm fall.

Now he looked at the little creature in front of him, and saw the pale face and wide eyes of Stràziami's son.

Stràziami was the most wretched among Peppone's ultra-faithful: not that he was a layabout; on the contrary he was always looking for work. The trouble was that whenever he found a job he'd work at it quietly for one day, and then on the second day he'd get into a fight with the boss, which meant he only actually worked five days a month.

'I won't do it again, Don Camillo,' said the little boy beseechingly.

'Scram!' growled Don Camillo.

Then Don Camillo sent for Stràziami, who strolled into the presbytery with his insolent hands in his pockets and his hat on his impudent head.

'What does the clergy want from the people?' he asked arrogantly.

'First of all: take off your hat or I'll knock you into a pulp; and secondly, give up the hard man act because it won't wash with me.'

Stràziami was as thin and shabby as his son, and a punch from Don Camillo would have finished him off. He threw his hat onto a chair and acted bored.

'I suppose you want to tell me that my son has dirtied Your Eminence's palace? I know all about it. He's told me already. Your Grey Eminence will be compensated. I'll give the boy a beating tonight.'

'If you lay a finger on him I'll break your neck!' yelled Don Camillo. 'What you ought to do is give him something to eat. Can't you see the poor creature is nothing but skin and bone?'

'The Eternal Father doesn't bring everyone good luck . . .,' began Stràziami sarcastically. But Don Camillo wouldn't let him go on.

'When you get a job, keep it instead of losing it after two days with your revolutionary antics.'

'You look after your own dirty business!' retorted Stràziami aggressively. Then he turned to go, and Don Camillo grabbed him by the arm. But the arm felt as skinny as his son's, and Don Camillo let him go.

Then he went and protested to Jesus.

'Jesus,' exclaimed, 'how is it possible that I keep finding sacks of bones in my hands?'

'Anything is possible in a land made wretched by so many wars and so much hatred,' answered Jesus with a sigh. 'I would prefer you to keep your hands to yourself.'

Don Camillo went to Peppone's garage and found him working with a vice.

'As Mayor, you should be doing something to help the child of that wretch Stràziami,' said Don Camillo.

'With all the funds the Council has left, I can but fan him with the back of the calendar,' replied Peppone.

'As your Party's Branch Secretary then . . . Stràziami is one of your most fanatical no-goods, if I'm not mistaken.'

'Ditto: I can but fan him with a folder off my desk.'

'Do me a favour! What about all the money you get from Russia?'

Peppone carried on polishing.

'The Red Czar's messenger has been delayed,' replied Peppone. 'Why don't you lend me some of the money they send you from America?'

Don Camillo shrugged.

'If you don't understand either as Mayor or as leader of the herd, you should at least understand as the father of a son yourself (though who knows by whom?) that you ought to help that poor wretch who messed the presbytery wall with coal. And by the way, tell Bigio that if he doesn't clean it up for me, and free of charge, I'll attack your party on the Christian Democrats' bulletin board.'

Peppone went on polishing, and then said, 'Stràziami's son isn't the only one in the neighbourhood who needs a bit of healthy air by the sea or in the mountains. If I'd found the money I'd have set up a children's holiday camp.'

'Then get out there and do it!' exclaimed Don Camillo. 'All the time you're standing here being the Mayor and polishing bolts you're not finding money. Country folk are loaded with cash.'

'Country folk don't cough up a red cent, Reverend. They'd only give money to help set up a camp for fattening their calves. Why don't you go and ask the Pope . . . or Harry Truman?'

They argued for two hours and on at least thirty occasions came within an inch of resorting to their fists. Don Camillo didn't get home until late in the evening.

'What news?' asked Jesus. 'You seem to be in a bit of a state.'

'Hardly surprising,' replied Don Camillo. 'When a poor priest has to argue for two hours with a militant proletarian mayor to get him to understand the necessity of creating a children's camp by the sea, and then has to argue for two more hours to convince a capitalist money-grubber to shell out the money we need to get the colony set up, there isn't much to be cheerful about.'

'I understand,' replied Jesus.

Don Camillo hesitated.

'Jesus,' he said finally, 'you must pardon me for involving you in this business over the money.'

'Involving me?'

'Yes, because in order to convince that skinflint to hand over a few coppers I had to tell her that last night you appeared to me in a dream and told me that it would please you more if she gave money to benefit the community rather than giving it for the purchase of a new bell.'

'Don Camillo, can you dare to look me in the face after doing that?'

'Yes,' replied Don Camillo easily. 'The end justifies the means.'

'I do not think Machiavelli is a sacred text you should rely on exclusively,' exclaimed Jesus.

'It's a blasphemy, Jesus, I know,' answered Don Camillo, 'but there are times when he's rather convenient.'

'Yes, that is true,' Jesus admitted.

And so, ten days later, when a flock of singing children passed by the church on their way to the station before travelling to the holiday camp, Don Camillo ran to see them off and to load them up with holy images. And when he came upon Stràziami's son at the end of the line, he scowled, and said menacingly, 'We have a score to settle when you get back!'

Then seeing Stràziami following some way behind the band of children, Don Camillo made a gesture of disgust. 'Family of criminals!' he muttered, turning and going back into the church.

That night he dreamed that Jesus appeared to him and said he'd prefer Signora Giuseppina's money to be used for a public service rather than for a bell.

'Done that already,' whispered Don Camillo in his sleep.

An Obstinate Old Man

In 1922 when Mussolini's Fascist squads were going around the Lower Plain in their armoured cars burning down socialist co-operatives, Maguggia was already 'old Maguggia': tall, long-bearded, and thin as a rake.

The squads came to this village too, and when the first truckload arrived without warning, everybody shut themselves away or escaped along the dykes, except for Maguggia who stayed put: so when the wreckers came into the co-operative they found him standing behind the shop counter.

'This has nothing to do with politics,' said old Maguggia to the one who seemed to be the leader. 'It's an administrative matter. I founded this co-operative, and I've always run it. The accounts have always balanced and I want them to balance right to the end. On this paper there's a note of everything that's currently in the shop. Give me a receipt and then burn whatever you like.'

They were a bunch of hard nuts, because only hard nuts can treat politics as if it was a matter of burning whole parmesan cheeses, and lard and salami and flour, using axes to smash up the copper pans in cheese dairies, and shooting pigs with muskets: which is exactly what they were doing to the socialist co-operatives of the Lower Plain. Anyway, after telling that he'd get his receipt all right, beaten into him with a stick, they scratched their heads in puzzlement, checked the parmesan cheeses and the other main items, and at the bottom of the inventory they wrote, 'Va bene'.

'Take the list to the regional authority if you want to get your reimbursement,' they told him, laughing.

'I'm in no hurry, there's plenty of time. Make yourselves comfortable,' replied old Maguggia, as he left the building.

Then he stopped at the other end of the piazza to watch the co-operative burning, and when the whole building was nothing but a few embers, he doffed his hat and went home.

Nobody bothered him, and old Maguggia lived shut away on his own little piece of land, and nobody saw him again in the village.

Until one evening in 1944 he appeared in front of Don Camillo at the presbytery.

'They proposed me as head of the regional administration,' he explained. 'I refused, and now they want to get revenge by sending my son to Germany. Can you help me?'

Don Camillo said yes.

'One moment Don Camillo,' old Maguggia interrupted him. 'Let's get one thing clear. I'm asking for help from you, Don Camillo, a man I hold in high esteem, not you Don Camillo the priest who I must hold in low esteem because of the very fact that you are a priest.'

Old Maguggia was a 'veteran socialist', one of those who can't wait to die so that they can mock the priest by refusing the comforts of religion and arranging for their funerals to be accompanied by the 'Internationale'.

Don Camillo hid his hands behind his back and silently prayed to God that he'd be able to keep them there.

'That's fine,' replied Don Camillo. 'As a man I'd happily kick you out of my house, but as a priest I must help you. However, let's be clear that I'm helping you the upright citizen, not you the anti-cleric.'

He kept Maguggia's son hidden in the belfry for six days, and then found a way to send him off to safer shores inside a wagonload of hay.

The trouble ended and time went by. One day the word went round the village that old Maguggia was very ill, so ill that he could only last a few hours. And one afternoon someone came to Don Camillo's house to tell him that old Maguggia wanted to talk to him.

Don Camillo jumped on his bike, leaned over the handlebars as if launching into the Tour of Italy, and shot off like lightning. But he found Maguggia's son standing in the doorway.

'I'm sorry Don Camillo,' said the man. 'You have to come round this way.' And he led him round to an open window at the side of the house. And inside, right under the window, was old Maguggia's bed.

'I swore that no priest would ever cross the threshold of this house,' explained old Maguggia, 'so don't take offence.'

Don Camillo was within an inch of storming off, but he stayed put.

'Can I speak to you as a man and not as a priest?' asked old Maguggia.

'Speak.'

'I want to die with no debts on my conscience,' said old Maguggia. 'I called you to thank you for saving my son's skin that time.'

'I had nothing to do with it,' replied Don Camillo. 'If your son managed to get away, you mustn't thank me, you should thank God.'

'Don Camillo, let's not make this political,' said Maguggia. 'Let me die in peace.'

'You can't die in peace if you don't die in the grace of God,' exclaimed Don Camillo in anguish. 'Why, if you have always loved others so much, do you hate yourself so much?'

Old Maguggia shook his head.

'But Don Camillo, what does it matter to you?' he asked. Then after a little while he added, 'I understand. Civil funerals trouble you because they are a moral blow to you in your capacity as parish priest. All right: I want to die peacefully with no one thinking badly of me. I reject the comforts of religion but, as a personal favour to you, I shall write in my will that I want a religious funeral.'

'As a personal favour I'd like to send you to hell! What do you take me for, a tradesman?' shouted Don Camillo.

The old man sighed, and Don Camillo calmed down.

'Maguggia,' he begged him, 'think for just a moment. Meanwhile I'll pray to God to enlighten your mind.'

'There's absolutely no point in doing that,' replied the old man. 'God has always enlightened me, otherwise I couldn't have lived in obedience to his commandments. But I won't confess because you would think that old Maguggia acted cocky with priests while he was well, and then when things turned bad he lost his nerve and gave in. I'd rather go to hell!'

Don Camillo was struggling for breath.

'But if you believe in God and hell, why don't you want to die like a good Christian?'

'So as not to give satisfaction to a priest!' was old Maguggia's obstinate reply.

Don Camillo went home in a state of great agitation and went to tell Jesus all about it at the altar.

'Is it really possible,' he concluded, 'that a decent citizen should reduce himself to dying like a dog because of such foolish pride?'

'Don Camillo,' replied Jesus sighing, 'anything is possible when politics is involved. In war a man can forgive the enemy who a little while ago was trying to kill him, and can share his bread with him, but in a political battle a man hates his opponent, and a son can kill his father and the father kill his son over a word.'

Don Camillo walked up and down, and then stopped. 'Jesus,'

he said, spreading his arms, 'if it's written that Maguggia must die like a dog, then it's pointless to go on about it: may God's will be done.'

'Do not bring politics into this, Don Camillo,' Jesus admonished him sternly.

Two days later the news spread through the village that old Maguggia had undergone an operation which had been a magnificent success. And after a month had passed, he appeared at the presbytery and stood before Don Camillo looking lively, almost sprightly.

'Things are different now,' said Maguggia. 'And because I want to thank the Eternal Father in the customary manner, I'd like to become a communicant. But since this is a matter between me and the Eternal Father and not between my party and yours, it would be a kindness if you didn't summon all the clergymen of the province to be present at the ceremony with bunting and a brass band playing.'

'Very well,' replied Don Camillo. 'Tomorrow morning at five. Only the leader of my party will be present.'

When Maguggia had gone, Jesus asked Don Camillo who the leader of his party might be.

'It's you,' said Don Camillo.

'Do not bring politics into this, Don Camillo,' Jesus admonished him with a smile. 'And think twice before you say it is the will of God that a decent citizen should be allowed to die like a dog.'

'Don't take it too seriously,' Don Camillo replied. 'People say all sorts of things!'

General Strike

DON CAMILLO was smoking his half cigar, sitting on the bench in front of the presbytery, when a cyclist hurtled up, and it was the gangly Smilzo.

He had learned a new way of braking – the 'Socialist Stop' as he called it – a highly complicated business at the end of which Smilzo either found himself standing behind the bike with the rear wheel held between his legs, or else he found himself sprawling on the ground with the bike on top of him.

Don Camillo watched Smilzo as he did his Socialist Stop, left his bike against the church wall and flung himself against the door to the tower. But the door was locked, and there was nothing to be gained by banging it.

'Where's the fire?' asked Don Camillo, standing up and going over to Smilzo.

'There isn't one. But the government's a pig and we need to summon the people.'

Don Camillo went and sat down again.

'Go summon them on your bike. It'll take you a bit longer than ringing the church bell, but you'll make less noise.'

Smilzo shrugged in resignation.

'All right,' he sighed. 'The one with the power makes the laws. Il Duce is always right.'

He got on his bike and set off back towards the Party HQ, but as soon as he'd rounded the corner of the presbytery, he slipped off his bike without warning and launched into a sprint. By the time Don Camillo noticed what was happening it was too late: Smilzo was climbing like a squirrel up the iron filament of the lightning conductor, and already half way up the tower. On reaching the belfry, he pulled up the top-floor ladder and started hammering away at the bells.

Don Camillo tranquilly considered the matter. No point in waiting till Smilzo came down. If general indignation was the order of the day, then breaking a stick on Smilzo's rump would be interpreted as an act of provocation, which was something to be avoided at all costs. So Don Camillo went back into the presbytery. But first he went round the side of the house, loosened the wing nuts on the hub of the front wheel, slid the wheel out of the fork and carried it into the house.

'Now you can do a Christian Democrat Stop,' muttered Don Camillo as he bolted the door.

After half an hour of bell-ringing, people started to arrive in the piazza, and when they were all there Peppone came out onto the balcony of the Town Hall and began to speak:

'Under an anti-democratic and reactionary government, oppression becomes law. And this law orders the unjust sentence of eviction to be carried out against Artemio Polini. But the people will defend their rights and will not allow it!'

'Hear hear!' yelled the crowd.

Peppone continued in this tone, there was a protest march, and a committee was elected which composed an ultimatum to be sent to the magistrate: 'Either suspend the execution of the sentence and begin the procedure of annulling it, or there'll be a general strike. Twenty-four hours to decide.'

People came from the city, then the committee went to the city, there were telegrams and telephone calls, and the twenty-four hours became forty-eight and then ninety-six: but you can't pull a spider out of a hole, and in the end the general strike was declared.

'Nobody is to work for any reason whatever!' affirmed Peppone finally. 'When we say "general strike" we mean abstention from all work without exception. Surveillance squads will be set up and will intervene immediately.'

'And the cows?' said Brusco. 'They have to be fed and milked. And if you milk them you can't throw away the milk. So that means the cheese dairies need to work too.'

Peppone fumed and exclaimed, 'That's the curse of communities where everything is based on agriculture! In cities you can organise a general strike in no time! Close the factories and the workshops, and that's it. Machines don't need milking. And even if a strike lasts fifteen days, all you do at the end is switch the machines back on and away they go. But if you let a cow snuff it, you can't switch it back on. At least we're lucky enough to be on a main road, so we can blockade it and slow down the traffic across the whole province. And what's more we could give the strike national importance by pulling up fifty yards of track from the railway and cutting off the line.'

Bigio shrugged.

'You pull it up and two hours later three armoured cars arrive and once they've put the rails back, you won't pull them up again.'

Peppone retorted that he didn't give a damn about the armoured cars, but his mood was gloomy nevertheless. Then he abruptly cheered up.

'Still, the general strike will matter to the people who matter: the important thing is to make sure the eviction order isn't carried out. That's the bottom line. We'll get organised into squads to defend ourselves to the bitter end, and if need be we'll shoot.'

Bigio started to laugh.

'If they want to carry out the eviction they will,' he said. 'It'll be just like the railway track. Along come five armoured cars, and you've had it.'

Peppone became even more gloomy.

'You look after the road blocks, the despatch riders and advance signalling stations at either end of the main road. Put Smilzo and Patirai in charge of the flares. Put people up on the dykes. It won't need many: armoured cars avoid water and dykes. I'll take care of the rest.'

During the next three days there were rallies and marches, but nothing out of the ordinary happened. The blockade on the main road worked perfectly: cars arrived, they stopped, the drivers swore, they turned back for five or six miles and went the long way round on secondary roads.

Don Camillo didn't put his nose out of doors even for a second, but he kept himself fully informed because old women had been mobilised, and from morning till evening there was a continuous coming and going of grandmothers and great-grandmothers, though on the whole their news was of no importance whatever. The one important piece of information came at the end of the third day, and it was brought by widow Gipelli.

'Peppone has held a big rally and I heard the whole thing,' said the woman. 'It was pitch dark, but you could tell that there was something nasty going on. He was shouting like a soul in torment. He said that over in the city they could decide whatever they want, but the eviction won't happen. He said the people will defend their rights at any cost.'

'And what did the people say?'

'They were almost all Reds, and some of them had come from other districts, and they were shouting like fiends.'

Don Camillo spread his arms.

'May God bring His light to their minds,' he sighed.

At nearly three o'clock that night Don Camillo woke up. Someone down below was throwing pebbles against his window. Don Camillo knew how the world works, so there was no question of his looking out. He went downstairs cautiously, not empty-handed, and went to peep out through a little window half hidden by the vine which trailed along the front of the presbytery, and since it was a moonlit night, he could identify the pebble-thrower. He went to open the door.

'Brusco, what's going on?'

Brusco came in and told Don Camillo not to switch on the light. It took him a couple of minutes before he could bring himself to speak. Then, in a low voice he said, 'Don Camillo, it's happening. They're coming tomorrow.'

'Who?'

'*Carabinieri* and civilian police in armoured cars, to carry out the eviction of Polini.'

'I don't see anything strange about that,' answered Don Camillo. 'It's the law. The workings of justice have established that Polini is in the wrong, and Polini must go.'

'Some justice!' exclaimed Brusco through clenched teeth. 'We call it fleecing the people.'

'I don't see why we need to have a discussion like this at three in the morning,' observed Don Camillo.

'That's not why I'm here,' replied Brusco. 'The reason is that Peppone has said the eviction won't happen, and you know that when he puts his back into something, the rest of us come out in a cold sweat.'

Don Camillo put his hands on his hips.

'Get to the point, Brusco.'

'Well,' whispered Brusco, 'the fact is . . . If a green flare and then a red one go up from the direction of the city, it'll mean the armoured cars are coming that way, and so a pillar of the Fiumetto bridge will get blown up. If there's a green flare and then a red one from the other direction of the main road, the wooden bridge over the main canal will get blown up.'

Don Camillo grabbed Brusco by the lapels.

'Peppone and I mined them two hours ago,' said Brusco, 'and Peppone is manning the detonator on the Fiumetto dyke and I'm manning the detonator on the dyke by the canal.'

'You're staying here,' exclaimed Don Camillo, 'and you don't move or I'll break your neck! No, it's better if you come with me so we can disarm the mine.'

'I've already done it,' answered Brusco. 'I'm the world's worst coward for betraying Peppone, but I think it would be worse cowardice not to betray him. He'll kill me when he finds out.'

'He won't find out,' answered Don Camillo. 'And now stay here and don't move. I have to go and sort out that lunatic. Even if I have to smash his head in.'

Brusco looked worried.

'And how will you do that? He'll know what's going on as soon as he sees you, and he'll blow up the bridge without the flares rather than give in. And besides, how will you get onto the dyke? You have to go by the bridge, and that's a hundred yards behind Bigio's blockade.'

'I'll go through the fields.'

'But he's on the dyke down there, and you'll have to cross the river.'

'God will help me.'

Don Camillo wrapped himself in a black cloak, climbed over the garden hedge, and headed off into the countryside. It was four o'clock now and starting to get light. He passed through the vineyards, and got soaked crossing the alfalfa meadows, but he arrived unseen right at the foot of the Fiumetto dyke. Peppone would be lying in wait a hundred yards from the bridge on the opposite embankment.

Don Camillo had no plan: making plans is difficult in these circumstances. You need to be on the spot to see, and then decide. He slipped under a bush, climbed cautiously up the side of the dyke and looked over. Peppone was standing on the dyke on the other side of the river, almost opposite him, and looking towards the city. Nearby was the box containing the detonator, with its handle raised. Don Camillo began to work out a plan for outflanking Peppone: the water was high and running in swirls towards the bridge, but if he went upstream shielded by the embankment of the dyke he'd find a good point from which to swim across unobserved, even if it meant staying underwater. The bridge was nearby, eighty or ninety yards away, but nothing could be done from there.

He had barely begun to move when he heard a whistle, and a green flare went up from the road towards the city. In a few moments the red flare would go up in confirmation.

'Jesus,' begged Don Camillo, 'make me a bird or a fish for ten seconds.'

He dived into the water and was carried downstream, partly by the current, partly by his own desperate strokes, partly by the Eternal Father, so that when Peppone turned round on hearing his name being called, Don Camillo was already clinging like an oyster to one of the bridge's pillars.

And at that moment, up went the red flare.

'Don Camillo, get away from there!' yelled Peppone. 'Let yourself drop! The whole thing's going to blow up!'

'We'll go up together,' answered Don Camillo.

'Get away from there!' yelled Peppone again, with his hands on the detonator's plunger. 'I'm going to blow up the bridge. You'll get buried.'

'I'll see you with the Eternal Father,' replied Don Camillo clutching the pillar ever more tightly.

The vehicles could be heard approaching. Peppone yelled again and went into a total frenzy, then he let go of the plunger and flung himself down on the dyke.

The vehicles went rumbling over the bridge.

Time passed. Peppone stood up again, but Don Camillo was still down below hanging onto the pillar.

'Get away from there, you bloody priest!' shouted Peppone angrily.

'If you don't disconnect the wires and throw the detonator into the river, I'll stay here till next year. I've grown fond of this pillar.'

Peppone pulled out the wires and threw the detonator into the water. Then Don Camillo told him to throw the wires in too, and Peppone did so.

'Now come and give me a hand,' said Don Camillo.

'Hold on tight then, while I get down to you,' answered Peppone, stretching out from a clump of acacia, and then reaching Don Camillo.

'I've been dishonoured,' said Peppone. 'I'll resign from all my positions.'

'It seems to me you'd have been more dishonoured if you'd blown up the bridge.'

'And what will the people say? I promised to stop the eviction!'

'Tell them it looked stupid to fight to liberate Italy and then to declare war on Italy.'

Peppone agreed.

'That's true after all,' he muttered. 'As Mayor I think Italy works fine. But as Branch Secretary I don't. I've weakened the prestige of my party!'

'Why? Does your party's constitution say you have to shoot the *carabinieri*? . . . Well then, tell those hard nuts that in the end the *carabinieri* are also sons of the common people who are exploited by capitalism.'

'Dead right!' agreed Peppone. 'By capitalism and by the priests! Even the *carabinieri* are the sons of the people who are exploited by capitalism and by the clerical priests!'

Don Camillo felt like a drowned rat and was in no mood for a quarrel. He merely advised Peppone not to talk nonsense.

'"Clerical priests" doesn't mean anything.'

'It does mean something,' retorted Peppone. 'You, for example, are a priest, but you're not a clerical priest.'

Then everything was sorted out, because as compensation for Polini's eviction the Council was finally granted funds to rebuild in stone the temporary wooden bridge over the main canal, and that solved the unemployment problem. ('*We thought it best to sacrifice the interests of the single tenant farmer, Artemio Polini, in favour of the interests of the masses. In any case, the debt is simply renewed, not paid: our account with the government remains open, comrades!*')

Then Don Camillo said in church that a parishioner had found a bicycle wheel and that whoever had lost it should come and collect it from the presbytery. And so along came Smilzo that same afternoon to get his wheel and a two-ton kick up the backside.

'We will settle our account later,' said Smilzo. 'When the second wave comes.'

'Just remember I'm a good swimmer,' Don Camillo replied.

City Types

THE PEOPLE Don Camillo really couldn't stand were the Reds from the city. The urban proletariat are all very well as long as they stay urban, but the minute they escape the city they feel obliged to act the part of city-dwellers, and then they're as obnoxious as smoke in the eyes.

It's worst of course when they travel around in groups, and especially in trucks, because then they start shouting, 'You dumb blockhead!' at every unfortunate individual they come across on the road, and if you're fat they call you 'Gutbucket' or 'Lardbelly'. And let's not even mention what happens when they bump into a girl.

The real show starts when they've reached their destination and got out of the truck, because then they put on their hard-man walk, rolling and swaggering along with a cigarette stuck in the corner of their mouths as if it had been shot there by a catapult, and before you know it there's an uproar like a cross between an old gangster movie and the antics of an Antipodean sailor on shore leave. Then they sprawl at tables in the inn and roll up their sleeves showing their white, flea-bitten arms, and behave like slum-dwellers banging their fists on the table and yelling from the bottom of their guts. And the whole thing is sure to end with them coming across a hen wandering in the street and showing it no mercy.

One Sunday afternoon a truck arrived crammed with Reds from the city on the pretext of escorting some Federation bigwig who was coming to make a speech to the small landowners. And when the rally was over, before going back to the office to give the bigwig a report on the present situation, Peppone told the city blokes that they were the guests of the Branch and that they should make themselves at home at the Little Mill Inn where there was a flagon of beer at their disposal.

There were about thirty of them, along with five or six girls decked out in red, the kind of girl who'd call out 'Oi, Gigiòto, give us a fag!' and the one called Gigiòto would take the cigarette out of his mouth and throw it to the girl, who'd catch it and puff at it hard until she was blowing smoke out of her mouth, nose and ears.

They sat outside the bar drinking and singing: and they didn't sing badly, especially stuff from operas. Then, when they got tired of that, they started making critical comments about passers-by. So when Don Camillo came up on his bike, the sight of the unwieldy looking thing sent them into hysterics of amusement, and they shouted, 'Look at that, a racing priest!'

Don Camillo took this calmly and sailed through the laughter like a Panzer tank over a pile of straw. Then, when he got to the end of the road, instead of turning towards his house, he went back again.

The second time he passed he was an even greater hit than before, and the gang of Reds from the city were unanimous in calling after him, 'Full speed ahead, Fatso!'

Don Camillo took this with the same imperturbability and went on his way without batting an eye. Then, naturally, having reached the end of the road, he had to stop and go back again, and this third occasion was memorable because the gang's choice of imagery slipped easily from 'fat' to 'guts' and from the generic to the particular, and to what might be inside those guts.

Anyone in Don Camillo's place would have objected to this. But Don Camillo had nerves of steel and formidable self-control.

'They're on the wrong road if they want to provoke me,' he thought. 'A priest never gets into brawls with drunks in bars. A priest doesn't stoop to the level of a drunken docker!'

So naturally he braked, threw down his bike, went up to the group, grabbed the table, pulled it out from under them, lifted it and flung it down on top of the whole crowd. Then, finding he had a bench in his hands, he started to wave it around.

At that moment Peppone arrived with a crowd behind him, so Don Camillo calmed down and was escorted back to the presbytery by the duty team because, once the bench-storm had abated and they had climbed out from under the table, the city lot had started screaming that they wanted him strung up, and the women were screaming worst of all.

'This is a fine business, Signor Priest!' said Peppone sternly when they reached the presbytery door. 'Politics has made you lose your *dominus tecum*.'

'You aren't a priest, you're a Fascist thug!' shouted the Federation bigwig, who had joined them. Then he looked at the enormous bulk of Don Camillo and the enormous shovels of his hands and corrected himself: 'You are a whole Fascist squad!'

Don Camillo went and flopped into bed. Then he closed the window. Then he closed the door and bolted it. Then he stuck his head under his pillow . . . But there was nothing to be done. Someone was calling him from downstairs, and no matter what he did he could still hear the voice.

So he went slowly downstairs and stood before Jesus at the altar.

'Have you nothing to say to me, Don Camillo?'

Don Camillo spread his arms.

'It was outside my control,' he said. 'While the rally was on, I kept out of the village to avoid any possibility of incidents. I had no idea that lot would go and sit outside the Little Mill. If I'd known, I'd have stayed at home until nightfall.'

'But when you went back for the first time, you knew they were there,' retorted Jesus. 'Why did you go back?'

'I'd left my prayer book at home . . . when I was keeping away from the rally.'

'No fibs, Don Camillo,' exclaimed Jesus severely. 'You had your prayer book in your pocket. Can you deny that?'

'I take great care of it,' protested Don Camillo. 'I had it in my pocket but I thought I'd forgotten it. When I put my hand in my pocket to take out my handkerchief and found my prayer book, I'd already passed the bar. And I had no choice but to go back again. As you know, there isn't any other road.'

'You could have gone home and stayed there, as you had done during the rally. By now you were well aware that those people were outside the bar. You had already heard what they were yelling at you. Since you could have avoided giving them an opportunity to show their bad manners, why did you not do so?'

Don Camillo shook his head.

'Jesus,' he said solemnly, 'if it is God's law that we should not take His name in vain, why has God given men the power of speech?'

Jesus smiled.

'They could have found a way to blaspheme in writing, or by using sign language,' he replied. 'But the reason is that virtue consists precisely in not sinning even though you have the means and the urge to sin.'

'So if I want to do penance by fasting for three days, I mustn't take medicine which removes the sensation of hunger because it's my duty to keep the hunger intact and overcome it.'

'Don Camillo,' said Jesus anxiously, 'where is this leading?'

'*Ergo*, if having come to the end of the road, I mean to show God that I can follow his commandment by overcoming my instincts and by forgiving those who insult me, I shouldn't avoid a test of this. On the contrary, I should face it tranquilly and go past those wretches one more time.'

Jesus shook his head.

'That is a serious fault, Don Camillo. You must not lead your neighbour into temptation, nor invite him to sin, nor provoke him.'

Don Camillo spread his arms sadly.

'Forgive me,' he sighed. 'I see my error now. Since it could constitute a temptation to others and might lead them into sin if I show myself in public wearing this costume which until recently I was proud to wear, I will either stay at home or go out dressed as a tram driver.'

Jesus was becoming a little concerned.

'These are the quibbles of a sophist. I have no wish to debate any further with someone who resorts to splitting hairs in order to justify his wrongdoing. I would rather accept that your intentions were good when you chose to pass by the third time. So how do you explain the fact that, instead of showing God that you know how to dominate your instincts and you know how to forgive those who abuse you, you got off your bike and went to work with tables and benches?'

'I committed an error of judgement and a sin of presumption. What I mean is, I mistakenly thought I could tell how much time was going by, and so when I got off my bike I was sure that at least ten minutes had passed from the moment I heard the final insult, but in reality I found myself in front of the bar after only a few seconds.'

'Let us say tenths of a second, Don Camillo.'

'Yes, Lord. My sin of presumption lay in thinking my merit was great enough that God would lighten the darkness of my mind in such a way as to permit me to master my instincts perfectly. You see, Jesus? I have too much faith in you. If you think a priest is to be condemned for excessive faith, then condemn me.'

Jesus sighed.

'Don Camillo, this is a serious situation. Without your realising it, the Devil has come to live inside you, mixing himself in your speech and blaspheming through your mouth. Try to stay on bread and water, and no cigars, for three days. You will see. The Devil will feel ill, and leave.'

'Very well,' said Don Camillo, 'and thank you for your guidance.'

'Wait till the third day before you thank me,' said Jesus with a smile.

It was the talk of the village. Then no sooner had Don Camillo finished his anti-diabolical diet (an excellent course of treatment which completely cured his sophism) than a police officer turned up at the presbytery, followed by Peppone and all his top brass.

'The forces of law and order have completed their investigation into the crime,' explained Peppone self-importantly, 'and have found that the version which you gave in your written evidence to the magistrate does not correspond to the one which the assaulted comrades have given to the Federation.'

'I told the truth and haven't added anything,' asserted Don Camillo.

The officer shook his head.

'And yet it states here that your conduct was provocative, indeed, "shamelessly provocative."'

'My conduct was the same as it always is when I go out on my bicycle,' replied Don Camillo. 'Nobody around here has ever found it provocative.'

'Huh, that depends,' said Peppone. 'Lots of people around here, when they see you cycling by, wish your front wheel would come off and you'd end up flat on your face.'

'Every village has its scoundrels,' observed Don Camillo. 'That doesn't mean a thing.'

'Secondly,' continued the officer, 'whereas your version says you were alone, the other party's version states that people came to assist you, people you had standing by, and this seems credible to me, given the consequences of the encounter.'

Don Camillo challenged this fiercely.

'I was alone. And quite apart from the waving of the bench, the table I threw on top of that riffraff was enough to dent five or six pumpkins from the city.'

'Fifteen pumpkins,' the officer corrected him. Then he asked Peppone if the table was the one they had seen a little while before. And Peppone said it was.

Then the officer said ironically, 'You should consider, Reverend, that it's a bit hard to believe a single man could play that sort of havoc with an oak table which must weigh half a ton.'

Don Camillo stuck his hat on his head.

'I don't know how heavy it is,' he said brusquely, 'but there's nothing to stop us finding out.'

Off he went, and the others followed.

When they got to the Little Mill, the officer pointed out the oak table.

'Is it this one here, Reverend?'

'This is the one,' answered Don Camillo. And taking hold of the table, God knows how, he carried it over his head on straight arms and flung it onto the lawn.

'Good throw!' everyone shouted.

Peppone stepped forward scowling, took off his jacket, seized the table, gritted his teeth, lifted it up and flung it once more onto the lawn.

A lot of people had gathered and there was an explosion of enthusiasm.

'Hooray for the Mayor!'

The officer, who had been standing with his mouth open, touched the table and found it impossible to move. Then he looked at Peppone.

'That's how we do things in our village,' exclaimed Peppone with pride.

Then the officer said, 'That's fine, that's fine,' jumped into his car and shot off like a bolt of lightning.

Peppone and Don Camillo looked each other in the eye ferociously, then each turned his back and went off without saying a word.

'I don't know what's got into them,' muttered the host of the Little Mill. 'Priests, Communists . . . why do they need to take it out on that poor table? Damn politics and whoever invented it.'

The affair ended in the only way it could: Don Camillo received a summons from the Bishop, and went trembling to the city.

The tiny old white-haired Bishop was alone in a reception room on the ground floor, barely visible in a leather-covered armchair.

'Here we are again, Don Camillo,' said the Bishop. 'It isn't enough for you to fan people with benches. Now you're wielding tables as well!'

'A moment of weakness, Monsignor,' stammered Don Camillo. 'I . . .'

'I know all about it, Don Camillo,' the Bishop interrupted him. 'I shall have no choice but to send you to some mountain top to live with the goats!'

'Monsignor, they . . .'

The Bishop stood up and, bent over his walking stick, came to stand in front of Don Camillo, and looked up towards the giant priest's own mountain top.

'"They" are of no consequence!' he exclaimed, threatening Don Camillo with his stick. 'One of God's priests, a man entrusted with the mission of preaching love and gentleness, cannot act the devil and chuck tables onto his neighbour's head. You should be ashamed!'

The Bishop walked a little way towards the window and then turned.

'And don't come here telling me you were alone! You organised the attack, you set the trap! One man on his own doesn't crack fifteen skulls.'

'No, Monsignor,' answered Don Camillo. 'I was alone, I swear. It was the table falling on the whole bunch that caused the mess. You have to understand that it was a great big heavy table, like this one.'

Don Camillo touched the huge engraved table which stood in the middle of the room, and the Bishop watched him sternly.

'*Hic Rhodus, hic salta!*' he said.[8] 'If you aren't a shameless liar, prove it. Lift it if you can.'

Don Camillo went up to the table and took hold of it. It was much heavier than the one at the inn but when Don Camillo got into gear he was more immoveable than the American army.

His bones creaked and the veins in his neck stood out like tree trunks, but he got the table off the ground, slowly lifted it over his head, and kept it there on straight arms.

The Bishop watched him and held his breath. When he saw the table high above Don Camillo's head, he banged his walking stick on the floor and said: 'Throw it!'

'But, Monsignor,' groaned Don Camillo.

'Throw it! That's an order!' cried the Bishop.

The table crashed into a corner and the house shook. It was just as well the room was on the ground floor otherwise all hell would have broken loose.

The Bishop looked at the table, went and tapped the pieces with his stick, and then turned to Don Camillo, shaking his head.

'Poor Don Camillo,' he sighed. 'What a pity . . . You'll never become a bishop.'

He sighed again, then shrugged: 'If I'd been capable of wielding a table like that, I'd probably still be a parish priest in my little village.'

The crash had brought people running to the room, and they stood in the doorway with their eyes bulging. 'What happened, Monsignor?'

'Nothing.'

They looked at the fragments of the table.

'Ah,' said the Bishop. 'Nothing. It was me. Don Camillo troubled me a little and I lost patience. It's a dreadful thing, my sons, to let oneself be overcome by anger. May the Lord forgive me. *Deo gratias!*'

The others went away and the Bishop touched the head of Don Camillo, who was now kneeling before him.

---

[8] 'Be judged by your actions, not your words', inspired by the punch line to Aesop's fable, *The Boastful Athlete*.

'Go in peace, Musketeer to the King of Heaven,' he said smiling. 'And thank you for having worked so hard to amuse a poor old man.'

Don Camillo went home and told Jesus all about it. Jesus shook his head, and sighed, 'What a bunch of lunatics!'

Rustic Philosophy

THE DAY LABOURERS and regular farm workers were on strike right in the middle of the harvest, and everything in the big farms was beginning to languish.

This was something Don Camillo couldn't allow to continue, and when the order came to reduce the cows' fodder in order to lower milk production, he went to intercept Peppone, who was to be found constantly inspecting his surveillance posts.

'Listen,' said Don Camillo, 'if a woman is breast-feeding both her child and someone else's child, and they aren't paying her very much as a wet nurse, what should she do?'

Peppone laughed. 'Tell the baby's father, "Give me more, or else breast feed the child yourself."'

'Right,' said Don Camillo. 'But this woman is a special case, and to make more money, do you know what she does? She takes medicine which little by little reduces her milk, and then she says to the baby's father: "Either pay me more, or I'll carry on doing this until I don't have a drop of milk left." And so there are two children going hungry, her baby and the other baby. Would you say this is an intelligent woman?'

Peppone grimaced and muttered, 'Let's not make this political. Comparisons are the most devious things in the world because they reduce all problems to a practical example, when what counts in life is ideology. Wet-nursing is a fine thing, but the truth is that workers should be paid according to what's fair: and when workers are fairly paid this will allow wet nurses to be well recompensed by a socially just system without the need for medicine or any other cheap tricks. And social justice, my dear Signor Priest, has got to start somewhere if we're ever going to achieve it. It's like a ball of wool: if you don't find the right place to start unwinding it, what are you going to do, wait for the Holy Ghost to show you how? You start somewhere, and then things get worked out as you go along the road.'

Don Camillo interrupted him. 'Aren't comparisons the most devious things in the world?'

Peppone shrugged. 'It depends who's making them.' Then he added, 'You see, what counts is the underlying theory.'

'Then I have this to say to you: the theory is that in times of universal famine you eat what you can, and if someone ruins the little there is, you can sing the "Internationale" all you like, but you'll drop dead because no one's going to give you anything to eat.'

'We're all going to drop dead!' exclaimed Peppone. 'All of us, sooner or later have to drop dead.'

'Then drop dead yourself!' shouted Don Camillo, stomping off. And when he got to the church he poured it all out to Jesus at the high altar.

'These people need to be taught a lesson,' he said. 'Send a cyclone to throw everything up into the air. This has become a foul world full of hatred, ignorance and wickedness. It needs a universal flood. Let's all drop dead so we can get around to having the last judgement and then everyone can present himself before the divine tribunal to receive the punishment or reward they deserve!'

Jesus smiled.

'Don Camillo, a universal flood is not what is needed. Everyone is destined to die when his turn comes and to present himself before the divine tribunal for his reward or punishment. Is it not the same thing with or without cataclysms?'

'Yes, that's true,' acknowledged Don Camillo, becoming calm again.

But he was unhappy to give up entirely on the idea of the flood, so he tried to salvage something from it.

'You could at least make it rain a bit. The land is dry and the reservoirs are all empty.'

'It will rain, Don Camillo, it will rain,' Jesus reassured him. 'There has always been rain, ever since the world began. The mechanism has been set in motion so that it will rain when the time is right. Or are you of the opinion that the Eternal One has slipped up in his management of the universe?'

Don Camillo bowed. 'Very well,' he said sighing. 'I understand what you are saying perfectly. But if a poor country priest can't even allow himself to ask his God for a few bucketfuls of rain, well . . . forgive me, but it's disheartening.'

Jesus looked grave.

'You are right a thousand times over, Don Camillo. All that remains is for you to go on strike in protest.'

Don Camillo was still unhappy and walked off with his head down, but Jesus called him back.

'Fret not, Don Camillo,' whispered Jesus. 'I know that men wasting God's grace looks to you like a mortal sin, because you know that I got down from a horse to pick up a breadcrumb. But you should forgive them because they do not mean to offend God. They search desperately for justice on earth because they no longer have faith in divine justice, and just as desperately go after worldly goods because they have no faith in the recompense to come. They only believe in what they can touch and see. The flying machines, they are the angels of this infernal hell on earth which they are trying in vain to turn into a paradise. It is a body of ideas – a culture – that leads to ignorance, because when a culture is not supported by faith, there comes a point where man sees only the mathematics of things. And the harmony of this mathematics becomes his God, and he forgets that it is God who created this mathematics and this harmony.

'But your God is not made of numbers, Don Camillo, and good angels fly in the skies of your paradise. Progress makes man's world ever smaller: one day, when cars run at 100 miles a minute, the world will seem microscopic to men, and then mankind will find itself like a sparrow on the pommel of a flagpole and will present itself to the infinite, and in the infinite it will rediscover God and faith in the true life. And mankind will hate the machines which have reduced the world to a handful of numbers and it will destroy them with its own hands. But all this will take time, Don Camillo. So do not worry, your bicycle and your scooter are in no danger for now.'

Jesus smiled, and Don Camillo thanked him for putting him on earth.

One morning 'The Flying Squad of the Proletariat' commanded by Smilzo caught sight of a man working in one of Verola's vineyards, and so they took him and virtually carried him to the piazza where the farm workers were waiting, seated on the ground.

They crowded around him: he was a man in his forties and protested vehemently.

'This is kidnapping!'

'Kidnapping?' said Peppone, who had just arrived. 'How's that? Nobody's keeping you here. Go, if you want to.'

Smilzo and the rest of the Flying Squad released the man, who looked all around him at the wall of men who were watching him, arms folded, motionless, silent and glowering.

'So what do you want from me?' exclaimed the man.

'And what about you? What do *you* want here?' replied Peppone.

The man gave no answer.

'Filthy scab!' exclaimed Peppone, grabbing him by the front of his smock and shaking him. 'Traitor!'

'I'm not betraying anyone,' answered the man. 'I need a wage, so I work.'

'These people need wages too, and they're not working!'

'That's nothing to do with me,' exclaimed the man.

'I'll make it have something to do with you,' yelled Peppone, letting him go and giving him a backhander that knocked him to the ground like a rag.

'It's got nothing to do with me,' stammered the man, getting up again with his mouth full of blood.

A kick from Bigio sent him back into Peppone's hands.

'Search him,' Peppone ordered Smilzo, and while Smilzo was sticking his hands into the man's pockets, Peppone held him by the arms like a vice and it was impossible for him to get loose.

'Throw him into the river!' yelled the crowd.

'Hang him!' yelled a scruffy woman.

'Just a minute!' said Peppone. 'First let's see what sort of scoundrel we're dealing with.'

Smilzo passed Peppone the wallet he'd found in the man's pocket and, handing the man over to Brusco, Peppone leafed through the papers and examined the cards at length. The he put everything back in the man's wallet and returned them to him.

'Let him go,' he ordered with his head down. 'There's been a misunderstanding.'

'Why?' yelled the scruffy woman.

'Because I say so,' replied Peppone angrily. And the woman shrank back.

They put the man into the Flying Squad's truck and took him back to the hole in the hedge they'd pulled him through before.

'You can go back to work,' said Peppone.

'No, no,' the man replied. 'I'm going home. There must be a train in an hour or so.'

Some minutes of silence passed during which the man washed his face in the ditch and dried himself with his handkerchief.

'I'm sorry,' said Peppone. 'But you're a professor, a man with a degree, and you can't set yourself up against the poor people who work the land.'

'A professor earns less than the lowest-paid peasant. And besides, I'm unemployed.'

Peppone shook his head.

'I know, but that's not the point. Even if the peasant and you need the same quantity of food, the peasant's hunger is different from yours. When the peasant's hungry, he's hungry the same way a horse is, and he can't master his hunger because no one has taught him how to. But you can.'

'My baby can't.'

Peppone spread his arms.

'If he's destined to do what you do, he'll learn.'

'Does that seem fair to you?'

'I don't know,' said Peppone. 'The real question is how to understand why you and we, who in the end are in the same situation, can't make common cause against those who have too much.'

'You said it yourself: because even though we need the same food, our hunger is different from yours.'

Peppone shook his head.

'If it hadn't been me who said it,' muttered Peppone, 'it would have passed for philosophy.'

They parted, each going his own way, and the matter ended there. And the problem of the middle class remained unsolved.

Juliet and Romeo

WHEN THEY SAID, 'He's from the Wasteland,' they'd said all you need to know, for when anybody from the Wasteland got involved in something, the flying of fists was enough to make your hair curl.

The Wasteland was a broad strip of land which ran from Boscaccio to the main dyke, and the farm had got that name because it looked as if it had been laid waste by Attila. It had probably once been part of the river bed and had nothing but stones underneath, so the only way to get anything out of it would have been to sow it with dynamite. Ciro had bought the land on his return from Argentina, *temporibus illis*,[9] and

---

[9] 'In those far-off days'.

although it broke his back he carried on sowing grain; but all he produced was children and so, finding himself with an army to feed, he threw the last of his Argentine earnings into the purchase of a traction engine, a threshing machine and a hay baler, and since in 1908 these were the first machines to be seen in that part of the world, not only did they keep Ciro's bones in better condition, but they enabled him to thresh for three or four of the largest farms in the neighbourhood. By 1908 they were already calling him the old man of the Wasteland, because although he was only just forty he had six children, the eldest of which was eighteen and already a big brute of a man.

At the edge of the Wasteland, just beyond Boscaccio, lay the smallholding of La Torretta, whose owner was called Filotti and who in 1908 had thirty head of cattle and five children, and was thriving because all he had to do was spit on his land and up came maize and wheat good enough to win international prizes.

If the truth be told, Filotti was tight with money, as tight as a drum, and you'd need the help of God Himself to get a penny out of him: and yet, rather than make use of the machines at the Wasteland, he paid three times as much every year to bring a traction engine from Casa di Dio. And silly things began to happen: a hen was bumped off by stoning, a dog was beaten . . . In the Lower Plain, where in summer the sun cracks people's heads and weighs down on the houses, and where in winter you cannot tell the village from the graveyard, all it takes is this kind of stupidity to set two families perpetually at war with each other.

Filotti was a man of the church who'd sooner see his whole family drop dead than miss a single Mass, while the old man of the Wasteland rested on Saturdays and worked on Sundays just to spite him, and he always had a boy on lookout duty around the house to let him know whenever Filotti happened to be near the boundary hedge. Then he'd come out and yell insults fit to strip the bark off an oak tree. Filotti took it all and swallowed his bile, storing up his revenge for the right moment. This came with the general strike of 1908 when people seemed to go crazy with militant fervour. Naturally they had it in for the priest too because he was taking the landlords' side, and they wrote on walls that if anyone dared to go to Mass they'd live to regret it.

Sunday came and Filotti, having left his family guarding the stable, slung his shotgun over his shoulder and set off calmly to Mass. He found the old priest in the presbytery.

'They've left me all on my own,' said the priest. 'They've all run away, even my housekeeper and the sacristan. They're half dead with fear.'

'That doesn't matter,' replied Filotti. 'We'll go ahead anyway.'

'And who'll help me with the Mass?'

'I'll take care of that,' answered Filotti.

And so the old priest started to celebrate Mass, and his server was Filotti who kept hold of his shotgun even as he was kneeling on the altar steps.

There wasn't a soul in church, and it was so quiet outside that everyone might have been dead.

At the Elevation when the priest lifted up the consecrated Host, the church door opened with a bang. Instinctively the priest turned around and saw people silently gathering in the courtyard.

Ciro from the Wasteland appeared in the doorway with his hat on his head and a cigar in his mouth.

The priest stood holding up the Host as if he'd been turned to stone. Ciro took a puff from his cigar, pulled his hat down over his head, thrust his hands into his pockets and came into the church.

Filotti rang the altar bell, took aim, and fired at Ciro.

Then he reloaded his gun and rang the bell again, while the priest pulled himself together and calmly proceeded with the Mass.

And in the courtyard there was nothing to be seen, not even a fly.

Ciro wasn't dead, but he was badly wounded. He stayed on the floor because he was terrified of being shot a second time. When Mass was over he stood up, walked to the doctor, got the shot removed from his thigh which had been torn to shreds, and never said a word.

One evening a month later when he was fully healed, Ciro called his four eldest sons, handed each of them a shotgun, and went out. The traction engine was running at full steam, and the four sons prepared to escort it while Ciro climbed in, opened the throttle, took hold of the wheel and set the machine moving.

Traction engines have died out because petrol-fuelled tractors have replaced them. They were wonderful, built like steamrollers but without the roller in front: slow, powerful, and silent. They were used for threshing and to break up virgin land.

And so the march began: they crossed the fields towards Filotti's house. A dog jumped out but didn't even have time to bark before a blow from a stick finished it off. A strong wind enabled the machine to come within forty yards of Filotti's house without anyone realising it. Ciro turned the vehicle around and then his eldest son took one end of the thick steel hawser from the winch, and while the old man released the lever, moved slowly and inexorably towards the dark, silent threshing floor. The others followed him with their shotguns at the ready. He reached the biggest pillar supporting the central passageway, attached the cable and ran back to his father.

'Ready.'

Ciro started the winch, released the throttle, and there was an earthquake. He rewound the cable onto the winch, sounded his whistle and drove home.

None of the Filottis died, although three of their cows did, and half the old pile came down, part of the house and part of the stable. But Filotti didn't utter a word.

A private matter. Nothing to concern the justice system.

There were no other incidents as violent as this. Whenever there was some small flare-up between the children, the heads of the two families came out of their houses and slowly made their way towards the boundary hedge, at a point where a wild pear tree stood. Their entire families followed them in silence, and then stopped silently twenty yards from the boundary while the fathers went on to the pear tree. Here they met, took off their jackets, rolled up their sleeves, and began to punch each other without exchanging a word, each punch a ton weight falling slowly and implacably like hammer blows onto an anvil. When they had thoroughly battered each other's bones, they stopped and went back to base followed by their families. As the children grew there ceased to be any occasion for such mishaps, and the two old men stopped hitting each other. Then came the war, which carried off a couple of sons from both families, then all the troubles of the years after the war, et cetera, and so about twenty years passed and it seemed as if no one was giving the feud a thought.

But in 1929 at the age of two, Mariolino, old Ciro's first grandchild, realised that a man has a moral duty to travel the world in order to get an idea of what life is about, and so off he toddled. When he'd got as far as the boundary hedge, he sat down under the pear tree. After a while he was joined by a grubby little creature of the same age, and this was a certain Gina, Filotti's first grandchild.

It happened that both of them would have liked exclusive rights to a half rotten pear that had fallen from the tree, and so they started to pull each other's hair and scratch each other's face. And then when they couldn't do any more they spat at each other and returned to base.

No explanation was needed: the whole Wasteland army was at the table and when Mariolino came in with his face in shreds, his father leaped up, but old Ciro nailed him back into his seat with a look. Then Ciro stood up and, followed at a distance by the whole tribe, made his way to the pear tree.

There he found old Filotti waiting for him. They were both in their sixties, but they hammered at each other like schoolboys. However, they discovered that it took a month or more to put themselves back together again, and in due course old Ciro, arriving at the boundary one morning, discovered that someone had sealed half of it off with a wire fence. So he sealed up the other half with wire and no one spoke about it again.

In big cities people put a lot of thought into finding new, original ways of living, and so stuff like existentialism crops up, which doesn't mean a thing though it gives you the illusion of living differently from the old systems. But in places like the Lower Plain you are born, live, love, hate and die according to the same old conventions. And people don't give a damn if they find themselves mixed up in something pinched straight out of *Romeo and Juliet* or 'Blood of Romagna' or *The Betrothed* or *Cavalleria Rusticana* and such like. So there is an everlasting repetition of banality going back to the ark, but in the end, when all's said and done, people in the Lower Plain end up underneath it all exactly the same way as literate city-dwellers, with the difference that literate city-dwellers die more angrily than country people because in the cities it isn't just dying that people don't like, but dying in some ordinary way; whereas country people simply dislike the fact that they can't any longer draw breath. Learning is the worst con in the universe because it embitters not just life, but death too!

Years and years went by. Another war, and more post-war conflagration, with the Communist Wasteland lot 'red' as fire, and the Christian Democrat Torretta lot 'black' as coal. This is how things stood when one evening a Filotti farmhand came to summon Don Camillo.

'It's urgent,' explained the farmhand. 'Come now.'

Don Camillo came and found himself in the presence of a full family congress. They were all seated around the enormous table, and old Filotti was presiding over the assembly.

'Take a seat,' he said solemnly, pointing to an empty chair on his right. 'I need your spiritual assistance.'

There was a moment of silence, then old Filotti gave a sign and in came Gina, his eldest grandchild, who was a really beautiful girl. She stood in front of her grandfather, and the old man pointed a menacing finger at her.

'So, is it true?' he asked. The girl bowed her head. 'For how long?'

'I don't remember,' stammered the girl. 'When he made a hole in the wire fence. We were little. We must have been four or five years old.'

The old man threw up his hands.

'So that scoundrel had made a hole in the hedge!' he yelled.

'Keep calm,' advised Don Camillo. 'Who is this man you're calling a scoundrel?'

'That Mariolino from the Wasteland.'

'Him?' yelled Don Camillo, leaping to his feet.

'Yes, Don Camillo. Him.'

Don Camillo went up to the girl.

'The son of the Antichrist, the damned soul of Peppone, the Red delinquent who makes speeches in the piazza stirring up the people to rebellion! Answer me, you shameless creature! How could a decent, God-fearing girl like you, even lay eyes on such a firebrand of hell?'

'We were babies,' said the girl.

'Oh yes, that hole in the hedge,' sneered old Filotti.

He stood up slowly, approached the girl and slapped her.

The girl hid her face in her hands, but after a moment she lifted her head.

'We're going to be married,' she said in a hard voice.

Late one evening about three weeks later, as Don Camillo was sitting in his armchair reading a pamphlet, he heard someone knocking quietly on the presbytery door. He went to open it and found himself face to face with a woman whose head was covered by a black scarf. He didn't recognise her in the dark passageway, but once she was in his study he saw that it was Gina Filotti.

'What brings you here at this hour?' he said in astonishment.

'I want to get married,' the girl replied.

Don Camillo thought of Lucia Mondella (the heroine of Manzoni's *The Betrothed*), and started to laugh.

'And after that, what will you do about your Don Rodrigo?' he exclaimed. 'Besides, a marriage needs two people.'

'I am here,' said a voice. And in came Mariolino of the Wasteland.

Don Camillo clenched his fists.

'What can you possibly want in the house of God's minister, you emissary of the Cominferno?'

Mariolino took hold of Gina's arm.

'Let's go,' he muttered, 'didn't I always say these clerics have their teeth poisoned by politics?'

The young man had combed his hair so that it almost covered his eyes, but when he instinctively threw his head back you could see there were stitches in his forehead.

'What happened to you?' asked Don Camillo.

Gina intervened furiously.

'They jumped on him, his whole family. They beat him on his head and broke chairs over his back because some slut spied on us when we were sending messages to each other. They're damned Bolsheviks and you should excommunicate them.'

Mariolino grabbed the girl by a shoulder and pushed her under the lamp.

'My family are damned Bolsheviks,' he said with a bitter laugh, 'but hers are holy and God-fearing people. Look here.'

Now that the girl's shawl had fallen from her head and her face was no longer in shadow, you could clearly see that her face was covered in bruises, and she looked as if she'd combed her hair with a rabid cat.

'They've kept her locked up in her room for fifteen days, and the minute they found out she was signalling to me through her window, they beat her as if she was a bundle of hemp. You Filottis are a gang of hypocritical bigots, false as Judas,' cried the boy.

'And you lot from the Wasteland are sacrilegious vandals, criminals with no God and no conscience!' retorted the girl hotly.

'Stalin will put everything right!' shouted the boy.

'Justice will put you all in jail!' shouted the girl. 'I can't wait to be married to you so I can scratch your eyes out!'

'And I can't wait till you're my wife so I can give you a good slapping,' retorted the boy.

Don Camillo stood up.

'If you two don't stop, I'll give you both a good kicking,' he said firmly.

The girl dropped into a chair, hid her face in her hands, and started to cry.

'Yes of course,' she sobbed, 'my family want to beat me, he wants to beat me, the priest wants to beat me. Everybody wants to beat me. What have I done to make everybody hate me like this?'

The boy put his hand on her shoulder.

'Don't get upset,' he said affectionately, 'aren't I in the same situation as you? Maybe I'm the one who's done something wrong.'

'No you haven't,' groaned the girl, 'you're just the victim of those crooks in your family . . .'

'Stop right there!' said Don Camillo. 'Let's not chase after that wild goose all over again. If you've come here to quarrel you can leave right now.'

'We've come here to get married,' answered the girl.

'Yes, to get married,' added the boy. 'Have you got something against that? Aren't we both Christians like anyone else? Aren't we old enough? Aren't we free to marry, or do we have to ask the Christian Democrats for permission?'

Don Camillo spread his arms.

'There's no need to boil over,' he replied calmly. 'I've never said I won't marry you. I'll marry you the same way I've married everyone whose affairs are in order and who comes here to be married. Everything will be done according to the law.'

'But we're in a hurry!' exclaimed the girl.

'And I'm here to help you out. As soon as possible after the banns are published you shall be married.'

The boy shrugged. 'The banns? If our families know we want to get married, they'll kill us on the spot. No, Reverend, this is an emergency, we need to get married right now.'

'My children, marriage is not a game. It takes ten minutes, but it lasts a lifetime. It's a serious, solemn act, no matter how modestly and simply it may be celebrated. There are rules which cannot be set aside. Be patient. Marriage isn't a zabaglione where you take two eggs, beat them together and in ten minutes it's done.'

The boy broke in, 'And what if some unfortunate man is on the point of death and wants to marry a woman, do you have to publish the banns and wait for a set time to pass? Will the Bishop keep him breathing as you count off the days?

'That would be an exceptional case,' retorted Don Camillo.

'Our case is just the same,' said the boy, 'because we're in just as much danger, and you know it, so you can marry us in *articolum mortorum* just the same as if we were in our death throes.'

Don Camillo spread his arms (as much in tacit response to the boy's misquotation – he had meant '*in articulo mortis*', meaning 'at the point of death' – as in surprise at his ingenuity).

'Oh really, *articolum mortorum*? When your combined ages add up to just forty and your health is good enough to see you both reach the age of 150?! Let us not rush. Give me time to think. Let me go and see the Bishop to find out how we can keep you safe, given the circumstances.'

'We need to get married *right now*!' asserted the girl in a decisive voice.

'But why? Isn't it the same if we postpone for a few days? No one's going to die.'

'That remains to be seen,' said the boy.

'We've run away from home,' said the girl. 'And we're not going back. But we can't leave the village if we aren't married first.'

Don Camillo shivered. That affirmation made so calmly, serenely, precisely, confidently, in the same tone as one might observe that it is impossible to walk on water or to see with one's ears, left him struggling for breath. And he looked at the two young people in admiration.

'Be patient,' he said in anguish. 'Let me think until tomorrow morning. I assure you I will sort everything out.'

'Good,' replied the boy. 'We'll come back tomorrow.'

The pair went out, and when he was alone Don Camillo clenched his fists, swelled his chest, and exclaimed, 'I'll marry them even if it means world revolution!'

Alone in his garage, Peppone was working on a tractor engine when he heard the door squeak, and looking up he found Mariolino and Gina in front of him.

As far as Peppone was concerned, a Filotti in front of him was no different from a horned viper; but Gina Filotti was even worse than the rest because her sacrilegious tongue brought the whole of womankind into disrepute.

'Have you brought her here to get her head straightened out?' enquired Peppone of Mariolino.

Peppone knew perfectly well that the couple were engaged, and he knew all about the conflict between the families, but he had never bothered to bring the subject up with Mariolino because Peppone's principle was 'as long as a comrade serves the Party, then for all I care he can serve the Queen of Peru as well. A comrade just has to be a communist from the neck up.'

Which is why he confined himself to saying, 'Are you here to get her head straightened out?'

'There's no need, Signor Podestà,' answered the girl.

This business of calling him 'Podestà' instead of 'Mayor' was another piece of Gina mischief, and Peppone had never been able to put up with it. It made him feel like a petty Fascist boss.

He came aggressively up to her and put an enormous black-stained finger under her nose.

'You watch how you talk to me,' he shouted, 'or I'll wring your neck like a hen.'

'Yes, like one of those hens that you and your thugs stole from us for your May Day celebrations,' retorted the girl, unperturbed. 'There's no need to get so angry. We knew perfectly well that you did it for democracy and they were Fascist hens.'

The idea of purging the Filotti's hen house had been a personal initiative of Smilzo's dating back to 1945. The liberation of the Filotti hens was part of the amnesty along with all the rest.

But every so often, when things were especially delicate politically, the local reactionaries brought up the wretched story of the Filotti family's hens, and the one who lost on the deal every time was poor Smilzo, who got a sack load of kicks from Peppone.

Peppone came even closer, Mariolino pulled the girl tightly to him to defend her, and then Peppone noticed the stitches in Mariolino's forehead and the beaten face of the girl.

'What the hell happened?' he asked.

Mariolino made his report and Peppone went over to the tractor to scratch his head.

'A bloody mess!' he observed finally. 'I can't see why you'd want to get yourselves beaten up like this. There are so many women and so many men . . .'

'And so many political parties too,' the girl interrupted him in a hard voice. 'Why are you so stubbornly attached to the one that makes ninety percent of the people around here hate you?'

'Ninety percent? Not likely, young lady! We've got sixty percent behind us,' claimed Peppone.

'We'll see at the next election!' retorted the girl.

Peppone cut the debate short.

'Never mind that. This is your business. It's got nothing to do with me, and I don't want it to. I'm Secretary of the Party, not secretary of some dating service.'

'You are the Mayor!' said the girl.

'Indeed I am, and proud of it! So what?'

'Then you should marry us, right now,' exclaimed the girl.

'You're crazy. You should be locked up! I'm a mechanic,' sneered Peppone after a moment's perplexity, sticking his head back under the bonnet of the tractor and returning to the job of dismantling it.

The girl turned mockingly to Mariolino.

'So,' she exclaimed in a loud voice, 'this is the famous Peppone who's not afraid of anybody!'

Peppone pulled his head out from under the bonnet.

'This has got nothing to do with being afraid! This is about the law, and I can't marry you in a garage. And besides, there are rules that I don't keep in my head. Come to the Town Hall tomorrow. We'll sort everything out. I don't see why you need to get married at ten thirty at night. I've never seen such an urgent pair of lovers.'

'It's got nothing to do with love,' explained Mariolino, 'it's a matter of necessity. We've run away from home and we're not going back. But we can't leave the village if we aren't married. When we're sorted out with the law and with our consciences, then we'll catch a train and be off. We'll get to wherever we get to, and it'll all be good because we're starting from nothing.'

Peppone scratched his head.

'I get it,' he muttered. 'It all makes sense. But you'll have to wait till tomorrow. We'll see how to manage it all then. For tonight you sleep here in the garage, on the truck, and the girl can sleep at my mother's house.'

'I'm not sleeping away from home if I'm not married!' exclaimed the girl.

'Nobody says you have to sleep,' replied Peppone. 'You can stay awake saying your rosary and praying for America. Yes, because whether you like it or not, we've got the atom bomb now too.'

He took a newspaper out of his pocket and brandished it at her.

Mariolino took the girl's arm.

'Thanks, Boss, we'll come back tomorrow,' he said. They went out and Peppone stood there with the paper in his hand.

'To hell with the atom bomb and all!' he shouted, crumpling up the paper and chucking it away.

A hundred years ago, when the river was in full spate, it burst the main dyke and the water came up as far as The Poplars, regaining in one minute a piece of land which men had spent three centuries stealing from it. In a hollow between the dyke and The Poplars was the old oratory, a little church with a low, squat tower, and the water had overwhelmed it, with the aged sexton inside, and left it entirely submerged. After a few months someone had the idea of retrieving the bell which was still in the drowned bell-tower, and so he dived into the water pulling behind him a long rope with a hook at the end of it. Then, because he was taking so long to come back to the surface, the others who were on the river bank had started pulling the rope, and they pulled and pulled without reaching the end of the rope, as if he'd dived into mid-ocean. Finally the hook came up with nothing attached to it. And just at that moment the faint ringing of a bell come up from the depths of the river.

The sunken bell was heard again a few years later, on the night when a man called Tolli drowned himself in the river. Then it was heard when the daughter of the landlord of the Bridge Inn threw herself into the river. Probably no one had heard anything at all because it is impossible to hear a bell ringing when it's buried at the bottom of a river, but the legend continued.

In the Lower Plain, legends are borne by the water: every so often, the current draws into itself a ghost and casts it adrift upon the fields.

A hundred and fifty years earlier, during another flood, one of those floating mills which you can still see anchored in the middle of the river (painted in black and white checks with 'God preserve me' written on the front of the cabin which straddles two barges) sank, and the lame miller went down with it, an evil-minded old man whom God rightly sent to the Devil. But his ghost remained wandering upon the water. And sometimes late on a grey winter afternoon, the mill would appear and drop anchor beside some village or other, and the limping miller would come ashore and walk through the fields picking up newly sown grains of wheat one by one, filling sack after sack. Then he'd grind the grain and throw the flour to the wind, making a mist you could cut with a knife, and that year the land would produce no grain.

Nobody believed this nonsense, but everybody thought of it on winter nights when they heard the wind moaning or the distant howling of a dog.

The night of the betrothal of our Romeo and Juliet was one of those to make people think of the drowned lame miller and the sunken bell.

Towards eleven o'clock someone knocked at the door and Don Camillo jumped out of bed. It was one of the Filottis.

'Gina's disappeared!' he said in agitation. 'The old man wants you right now!'

The gig flew along the dark roads, and Don Camillo found the whole family in the big kitchen, even the children in their nightshirts and with eyes like saucers.

'We heard the window banging in Gina's room,' explained old Filotti. 'Antonia went to look and found the room empty. She'd got out through the window. There was this note on her chest of drawers.'

Don Camillo read the note, which was very brief:

'*We're going away. We shall either get married in church like Christians or we shall get married in the old oratory and then you'll hear the bell ringing.*'

'It can't have been more than an hour ago,' said the old man. 'At nine forty, when Giacomo's wife brought her a candle, she was still in her room.'

'A lot can happen in an hour,' muttered Don Camillo.

'And you know nothing about this, Don Camillo?'

'What could I know about it?'

'So much the better. I was afraid those wretches had come to you and made you feel sorry for them. They can go to hell, damn them!' the old man yelled. 'Let's go back to bed!'

Don Camillo slammed a half ton fist on the table.

'To hell with bed!' he shouted. 'And to hell with you, you senile old fool. We've got to find them!'

Don Camillo went to the door and everybody, even the army of women, even the children, followed him, leaving the old man in the immense deserted kitchen.

The wind was blowing hard on the main dyke, but below it, on the strip of land between the dyke and the water, the air was as still as if it had been caught in the bare branches of the acacias. The boy and girl walked in silence and only stopped when they reached the edge of the water.

'The old oratory is down there,' said Mariolino pointing.

'They'll hear the bell ringing,' murmured the girl.

'Damn the lot of them!' muttered the boy.

'Don't damn anyone,' sighed the girl. 'When you're about to die you mustn't curse people. We're damned if we take our own lives. It's a terrible crime.'

'My life is my own and I'll do what I want with it,' retorted the boy bitterly.

'Maybe the old sexton and the lame miller will be our witnesses,' sighed the girl.

A little wave came onto the sand and wetted their feet.

'It's cold like death,' sighed the girl with a shiver.

'It only lasts a moment,' answered the boy. 'We'll swim to where it gets deep, then we'll hug each other tightly and let ourselves slip down.'

'They'll hear the bell ringing,' whispered the girl, 'and it will ring louder than it ever did before, because this time there are two at once going to see the old bell-ringer. We'll hug each other tightly and no one can say anything about it.'

'Death will bring us closer together than the priest or the mayor could,' said the boy.

The girl didn't answer. The river by night has the pull of the abyss, and a thousand girls in every century have found themselves by the bank of a river, and have started to walk slowly towards the water and slowly gone on walking until the water has covered them.

'We'll hold hands as we walk,' whispered the girl. 'When the ground suddenly slips from under our feet, that will be where the oratory lies, and we will embrace.'

They held hands and began their horrifying, inexorable march.

Don Camillo had left the farm, followed by the entire Filotti clan, and had reached the road to the river.

'We'll split up there by the electricity transformer, half on this side of the dyke and half on the other side. That way half of us will work our way upstream and half downstream. If they haven't already got to the river they won't be able to reach it now.'

Electric torches, candles, lanterns, oil lamps, even acetylene bicycle lamps: everyone had a light of some kind and went on in silence.

And so it was that after a hundred yards they came to a point where the road was joined by a little side road, and so they bumped into another search party, the whole Wasteland family, apart from the old man, and Peppone was leading it. Nothing miraculous about this for the simple reason that, before Don Camillo left the presbytery on the Filotti's gig, he'd told his old servant to run to the Mayor's house and let him know what was happening so he could notify his Bolsheviks at the Wasteland.

The two leaders stopped in front of each other and looked at each other fiercely. Peppone took off his hat and greeted Don Camillo.

Don Camillo responded by taking off his own hat and the two search parties went on side by side. It was like a scene from a novel with all those lights in the night.

When they had reached the dyke, Supreme Commander Don Camillo said, 'We'll go up and then divide.'

'Yes, Duce,' replied Peppone. And Don Camillo glared at him.

One step . . . two . . . three; the water was now up to the young people's knees, but they no longer felt how cold it was. And the horrible march was continuing implacably when voices came suddenly from the dyke, and the two of them turned sharply to see the dyke filled with lights.

'They're looking for us!' said the girl.

'They'll kill us if they catch us!' exclaimed the boy.

Ten more steps, and they'd be at the edge of the trench where the sunken church lay. But now death and the river had lost their fascination. Lights and people were reconnecting them violently with life.

With one leap they were on the bank and then on the dyke. Beyond it were the empty fields and woods. But they were spotted immediately and so the chase began. The lovers ran along the top of the dyke and the two search parties were set loose to advance below them on either side of the dyke.

They were overtaken, and then at a yell from Peppone, who was puffing like a regiment of bulls at the head of the riverside column, the two bands of searchers climbed back up the dyke and came together. With the arrival of Don Camillo, who was advancing at full steam with his cassock up by his stomach, the pincer movement was complete.

'You good-for-nothing!' yelled one of the Filotti women, coming towards Gina Filotti.

'You wretch!' shouted one of the Wasteland women coming threateningly towards Mariolino of the Wasteland.

The Filottis seized their girl, the others their young man, and there was a furious uproar of female voices. But up came Peppone and Don Camillo, each of whom had an alarming rod of oak wood in his hand.

'In the name of God!' said Don Camillo.

'In the name of the law!' yelled Peppone.

Everyone fell silent, formed a long procession, and set off home with Juliet and Romeo, the *promessi sposi*, the newly betrothed, leading them. Behind them came Don Camillo and

Peppone carrying oak staves. And behind them, side by side, the silent lines of the two families.

As soon as it had come down from the dyke, the procession had to stop because the way was barred by old Filotti who raised his fists to the sky at the sight of his granddaughter. And at the same moment, naturally, the old man from the Wasteland arrived and made as if to fly at his grandson. There they were, miraculously side by side, glaring ferociously at each other, with a combined age of a hundred and fifty-six, but as full of fury as a couple of teenagers.

The two search parties spread themselves in silence along the two sides of the road and everyone raised their lanterns. The two old men squared up, clenched their fists, and began to pound each other's heads: but their animosity outweighed their strength, and after the first assault they went back to looking askance at each other and clenching their fists. Filotti even had the nerve to blow on his knuckles as he'd done as a boy to give his fist more power.

So Don Camillo turned to Peppone and said, 'Go on.'

'I can't, I'm the Mayor. It would make the thing political.'

So Don Camillo stepped forward, gently put his right hand on Filotti's neck and his left on the other's neck, and with a sharp, precise blow struck the head of one against the head of the other.

There were no sparks to be seen because the bones were too old, but the sound could be heard some way off.

'Amen,' said Peppone, resuming his march.

And so this story came to an end as all stories do. Years have gone by and the wire fence that divides the Toretta from the Wasteland still has that famous hole, and a little child can have fun going back and forth through it. And old Filotti and the old man from the Wasteland are finally side by side without quarrelling, and indeed the gravedigger says he's never seen two dead people get on so well together.

The Painter

GISELLA WAS A WOMAN in her forties, one of those women who, if they come across a group of people gathered in a piazza, go straight into top gear and charge through the crowd with their heads down, yelling 'Get him! Get him! Put him up against the wall! Hang him! Rip his guts out!' without for one moment caring whether the group has gathered because a criminal has been caught, or simply because they want to hear a travelling salesman telling them a load of drivel about shoe polish.

She was one of those women who always march at the head of the pack in a procession, draped in red and singing ferociously, and who, when some bigwig gives a speech at a rally, jump up and down screaming at the speaker: 'You're beautiful! You're a God!' (Although speaking only to one man, there's enough amorous frenzy in the voice of such women to embrace the entire Party Executive, and the propaganda department too!)

For us, Gisella was the very personification of proletarian revolution, and as soon as she heard that trouble, big or small, had broken out at some farm, she ran straight there to 'galvanise the masses'. If the farm was a long way off she'd jump on her husband's racing bike, and if anyone on the road yelled something after her, she'd reply that only upper-class pigs have dirty linen to hide, while real people can show even their bare backsides with heads held high.

When the farm workers went on strike, Gisella agitated widely on foot, by bike and in the surveillance squad's truck. So, early one evening, two weeks after the agitation had ended, someone put her head in a sack, dragged her behind a hedge, lifted the curtain and painted her bottom red.

Then he dumped her there with her head still in the sack and went sniggering on his way.

This was a serious matter because, apart from the fact that Gisella had to spend an age washing away the shame by sitting in a basin filled with petrol, Peppone saw the whole incident as a mortal offence to the proletarian masses. He flew into a rage, called a rally, yelled words of fire against the unknown reactionary delinquents, and proclaimed a general strike in protest.

'Everything is to be stopped,' he shouted finally. 'Everything closed, everything blockaded until the designated authorities have arrested the perpetrators!'

The marshal got four *carabinieri* from his station onto the case, but tracking down people who stick women's heads in sacks of an evening in open country and paint their bottoms red is like looking for a needle in a haystack.

'Signor Mayor,' said the marshal to Peppone after the first day of the search. 'Be patient. There's no need for you to go on with this strike. Justice can do its work without strikes.'

Peppone shook his head.

'Until you've caught this delinquent, everything stops!' he replied. 'Everything!'

The investigation was resumed at dawn the following morning, but since Gisella hadn't been able to see who had painted her because of the sack covering her head, the only participants with anything to say about the crime were therefore the painted part of her anatomy and the sack. The marshal took hold of the sack, studied it inch by inch with a magnifying glass, weighed it, measured it, sniffed it, and kicked it around with the utmost brutality. But, in general, the eloquence of sacks is very limited and this was the most anonymous and taciturn sack in the entire universe. So the marshal sent for the district medical officer.

'Take a look yourself,' he said. 'Pay that woman a visit.'

'And what am I going to find? For a start, the injured part has been treated with petrol. But beside that, we aren't dealing with the usual kind of painter, the kind who signs their pictures when they've finished them.'

'Let's not put too much thought into this, Doctor,' answered the marshal, 'because if we start thinking about it, it'll make us laugh, and then we won't be able to think about it at all. But there are people around here with no sense of the ridiculous who are stirring the whole thing up into a tragedy, paralysing life for an entire community.'

The doctor went to visit Gisella, and returned an hour later.

'She has a bit of hyperacidity in her stomach, and her tonsils are slightly enflamed,' explained the doctor with a shrug. 'I've taken her blood pressure, if you're interested. And that's all I can tell you.'

The four *carabinieri* returned towards evening. Not one footprint, not a single clue. Nothing.

'Very well then!' jeered Peppone fiercely when he heard the outcome. 'From tomorrow, the bakeries will be closed too. We'll distribute flour, and people can make their own bread at home.'

Don Camillo was enjoying the fresh air sitting on his bench in front of the presbytery when he suddenly found Peppone standing in front of him.

'Reverend,' said Peppone darkly and in his most dictatorial manner, 'call the bell-ringer and tell him to go up to the tower and stop the clock. Everything must stop here, even the clock. I'm going to show those cowards how to organise a general strike! Everything stops!'

Don Camillo shook his head.

'Everything stops, starting with the Mayor's brain.'

'The Mayor's brain is working perfectly!' yelled Peppone.

Don Camillo lit a half cigar.

'Peppone,' he said gently, 'you think your brain is working but your extreme partisanship has put a road block on it which stops you realising that you're making yourself completely ridiculous. And I think that's a pity. If I saw you being walloped on the backside with a stick, God forgive me, I wouldn't mind a bit. But seeing you look ridiculous makes me feel sorry for you.'

'The judgement of the clergy is of no importance to me!' shouted Peppone. 'The clock will be stopped, or do I have to stop it myself with a burst from my machine gun?'

Peppone's voice and gestures revealed a desperate fury, and Don Camillo was touched.

Standing up, he said, 'The bell-ringer's not here. Why don't you and I go up?'

They climbed the ladders of the tower, went into the clock chamber and stopped in front of the mechanism, one of those old ones with great big cogwheels.

'Look,' said Don Camillo, pointing to a wheel, 'all you have to do is put this peg there and the whole thing stops.'

'Yes, yes . . . it's got to stop,' exclaimed Peppone who was now in a sweat.

Don Camillo leaned against the wall near a window that looked out onto the fields.

'Peppone,' he said, 'a simple man had a sick child, and every evening the little boy became feverish, but they had no way to bring his temperature down. The thermometer always read nearly forty, and so the simple man, who wanted to do something for his child at any cost, took the thermometer and crushed it under his foot.'

Peppone went on watching the mechanism of the clock.

'And now, Peppone,' said Don Camillo, 'you want to stop the clock, but I'm not laughing at you. Imbeciles will laugh, but I feel sorry for you in the same way I feel sorry for that father who stamped on the thermometer. Peppone, tell me honestly: why do you want to stop the clock?'

Peppone did not answer.

Don Camillo spoke very seriously: 'You want to stop the clock because it's on the tower and you see it a thousand times a day. Wherever you go, the clock on the tower watches you, like the sentry in a turret in a prison camp. And it's no good you turning your head and looking in another direction because you can still feel that gaze weighing on your neck. And if you shut yourself away at home and hide your head under your pillow, that look passes through the walls and, what's more, the chiming of the clock reaches you, bringing you the voice of time, bringing you the voice of your conscience. If you are afraid of God because you have sinned, there's no point in taking the Crucifix from above your bed and hiding it. God is still there and He will speak to you all your life in the voice of your remorse. Peppone, there's no point in stopping the clock on the tower. You won't stop time. Time goes on. The hours pass, the days pass, but now every moment is to be stolen by you.'

Peppone lifted his head and swelled his chest.

'Deflate yourself, you puffed up ball of smoke!' shouted Don Camillo. 'Go on then, stop the clock. You won't stop time, and the harvests will languish in the fields, the cows will perish in the stables, and there'll be less and less bread on men's tables. War is the most hideous of wrongs, but if wicked people want to invade your country and plunder your property and take away your freedom, you must defend yourself. Going on strike means defending your most sacred rights, defending your bread, your freedom and your children's future. And yet you are the wicked warmonger here, attacking those who are no different from you, just so you can protect your foolish partisan pride. It's a war of prestige, the cruellest and most hateful kind of war.'

'Justice . . .'

'There are laws, accepted by you, which protect the citizen from top to toe, inside and out. There's no need for a party to intervene and protect the backside of a third rate La Pasionaria. Stop your strike instead of stopping the clock.'

They went down, and when they reached the ground floor Peppone confronted Don Camillo.

'Don Camillo,' said Peppone, 'we two can speak freely. Tell me the truth. Was it you?'

Don Camillo sighed.

'No, Peppone. I am a priest and as such I cannot stoop so low. The most I could have done is paint her face red, but that would have been devoid of meaning.'

Peppone looked him in the eye.

'I confined myself,' said Don Camillo, 'to sticking the sack over her head, tying her up and carrying her behind the hedge. Then I went off to mind my own business.'

'And who was behind the hedge?'

Don Camillo started to laugh, but Peppone spoke seriously. 'When we were both risking our lives, I trusted you and you trusted me. Let's do what we did back then. The matter will stay between us two.'

Don Camillo shrugged.

'Peppone, it was a poor oppressed and tormented creature, an unhappy creature who for years had suffered the pains of hell in silence, and who came to his parish priest for help. How could I not listen to his heart-rending plea? Behind the hedge was Gisella's husband.'

Peppone pictured Gisella's husband, that thin, haggard little man who had to mend his own trousers and cook for himself while his wife went around 'galvanising the masses', and he shrugged. Then he recalled that Gisella's husband was one of those 'Christian workers', and he frowned.

'Don Camillo,' he said in a grim voice, 'did he do it as a Christian Democrat?'

'No, Peppone. As a husband. Only as a husband.'

Peppone set off to call everybody back to work.

'As for you, though ...!' he exclaimed, pointing a threatening finger at Don Camillo as they went through the door of the tower.

'I did it for the encouragement of art,' explained Don Camillo spreading his arms.

The Festival

IT WAS LATE when Peppone sent the text over, and then old Barchini the newsagent-cum-printer took five hours setting the type, which meant that by the end of it he was worn out and so sleepy he was barely able to stand. Nevertheless he found the strength to bring a proof copy to the presbytery.

'What's this?' asked Don Camillo, suspiciously eyeing the sheet of paper which Barchini had spread out on the table.

'A thing of beauty,' grinned Barchini.

The first point which caught Don Camillo's eye was 'democrasy' spelt with an 's', and he pointed out that a 'c' was what was needed.

'That's good,' replied old Barchini appreciatively. 'As soon as I take it off I'll move the 's' down to 'faccionalism' in the second-to-last line. I had to give it two c's because I'd run out of s's.'

'I wouldn't bother,' muttered Don Camillo. 'Leave it as it is. It's always better to make more of democracy than factionalism.'

He began to read the proclamation carefully: it turned out to be the programme of events for the Party's Press Festival, with some additional matters of a socio-political character.

'What does it mean here, at item 6: "*Artistic and Patriotic Cycling Contest for mixed couples with the cities of Italy represented bisexually allegorically*"?'

'Well,' said Barchini, 'this is a bike race where every male competitor carries a girl on his crossbar. And every girl is dressed as an Italian city. One represents Milan, another Venice, another is dressed as Bologna, another as Rome, et cetera. And each cyclist is dressed in the typical style of the city. So the one with Milan on his crossbar is wearing a workman's overall because of industry. The one with Bologna is dressed like a farm worker because of agriculture in Emilia-Romagna. The one with Genoa is dressed like a sailor, and so on.'

Don Camillo asked for some other clarifications.

'And this? "*A politico-satirical people's shooting gallery.*"'

'I don't know, Don Camillo. It's something they'll put up in the piazza at the very last moment. They say that after the race of the cities it'll be the most important part of the day.'

Don Camillo had preserved his *sang-froid* up till now, but when he came to the last lines of the poster, he let out a cry.

'No! It cannot be!'

'I'm afraid it's true, Don Camillo. It really is. On Sunday

morning, Peppone and the other Branch leaders will go around the main streets of the village hawking the Party newspaper.'

'It's a joke!' exclaimed Don Camillo.

'Oh no it isn't. They've done this in all the major cities of Italy! And the newspaper sellers have been regional Party leaders, editors, and even members of Parliament. Haven't you read about it?'

When Barchini had gone, Don Camillo walked up and down his room for a while, and then went to kneel before Jesus at the high altar.

'Jesus,' he said, 'make Sunday morning come quickly.'

'Why so Don Camillo? Do you not think time is travelling fast enough in its natural course?'

'Yes, but there are occasions when minutes seem like hours.' He thought about this for a moment, and then added, 'But in other circumstances, hours seem like minutes, and so that's a compensation. Leave things as they are for now. I'll wait for Sunday in the normal way.'

Jesus sighed.

'What wicked thought is running through your brain?'

'Wicked thought? Me? If innocence could possess a human face, I would only have to look in the mirror and say, "Behold, Innocence".'

'Maybe it would be better to say, "Behold, a fib"!'

Don Camillo crossed himself and stood up.

'I won't look in the mirror,' he said, rushing off.

Sunday morning finally arrived, and after early Mass Don Camillo went to put on his best cassock, polished his shoes, carefully brushed his hat, and forcing himself not to run, made his way softly softly to the main street of the village.

It was crammed with people, and everyone was strolling about aimlessly, though it was clear that they were waiting for something.

Before long the booming voice of Peppone could be heard from afar.

'It's the Mayor selling newspapers!' everyone shouted, seized with sudden anxiety, and they all squeezed onto the pavement as if a procession were about to pass.

Don Camillo placed himself in the front row and swelled his chest in order to seem even taller than he was.

Peppone appeared with a great bundle of newspapers under his arm, and every so often one of his men – who were deployed along the route – detached himself from the crowd and went to buy one from him. Everybody else was speechless because Peppone was yelling like a newspaper seller, which made them want to laugh, but he was looking to left and right with such a villainous expression on his face that the desire to do so vanished instantly. The situation, with his cry echoing in the silence, and all the people packed motionless along the walls, and that hulk of a man walking alone in the middle of the deserted street, was not so much laughable as tragic.

Peppone passed in front of Don Camillo, and Don Camillo let him go by. Then unexpectedly his enormous voice was heard like a shot from a cannon:

'News vendor!'

Peppone stopped dead. Then he turned his head slowly and gave Don Camillo his fiercest Comintern glare. But Don Camillo was unperturbed. He calmly stepped towards Peppone, feeling in his pocket for his wallet.

'*Roman Observer*, please,' he said casually, but loudly enough to be heard half way to the next province.

Peppone turned fully round to face Don Camillo. He said nothing, but an entire speech by Lenin could be read in his eyes. Then Don Camillo seemed to snap out of a trance and flung out his arms with a smile.

'Oh, I beg your pardon, Signor Mayor,' he exclaimed. 'I was miles away, and mistook you for a newspaper vendor. Ah, I see now, you're selling *your* newspaper. Please do give me a copy.'

Peppone ground his teeth and slowly handed a copy of the newspaper to Don Camillo, who put the paper under his arm and started leafing through his wallet. He took out a 5,000 lire note and offered it to Peppone.

Peppone looked at the banknote, then looked Don Camillo in the eye and puffed up his chest.

'Of course, of course,' said Don Camillo taking back the note. 'Stupid of me to think you could give me change for this.' He pointed to the bundle of papers which Peppone was carrying under his arm. 'You poor thing. You can't have had much change coming in, when you've still got all those papers to sell.'

Peppone refrained from violence. He stuck the bundle between his knees, shoved a hand in his pocket, pulled out a fat handful of banknotes, and began counting out the change from Don Camillo's 5,000 lire.

'I'll have you know this is the fourth pack of papers I've sold,' Peppone hissed as he carried on leafing banknotes from his wallet.

Don Camillo smiled smugly.

'I'm delighted to hear it. But 4,500 will be enough. Please keep the rest: the honour of buying a newspaper from the Mayor is worth a lot more than 500 lire. And besides, you'll be giving me the pleasure of helping a newspaper which, in spite of your noble efforts, hasn't been able to achieve a large enough circulation to keep it afloat.'

Peppone was sweating.

'Four thousand nine hundred and eighty five!' he shouted. 'Not a penny less, Reverend! We don't need your money.'

'Oh I know, I know,' said Don Camillo ambiguously as he pocketed the money.

'And what do you mean by that?' yelled Peppone clenching his fists.

'For Heaven's sake, I don't mean anything,' said Don Camillo, opening the paper while Peppone got himself back together again.

'U – ni – tà,' Don Camillo spelled out. 'Oh! How strange! It's written in Italian.'

Peppone gave a brief roar and then went on his way, yelling in fury as if he were declaring war on the western powers.

'I'm sorry,' stammered Don Camillo. 'Don't be angry. I honestly thought it would be written in Russian.'

That afternoon, when they came to tell him that the speech was over and the festivities had started, Don Camillo went out to entertain himself by parading his enormous shoulders up and down the piazza.

The allegorical bike race turned out to be a splendid event. First past the finishing post was Trieste, who was sitting on the crossbar of Smilzo's bike, and everyone had been talking about Trieste all morning because during the Branch meeting some people had said it would be better not to include Trieste, given the political background, at which Peppone started barking that his brother had died in the war to liberate Trieste, and that not including Trieste in the race was like saying his brother had been a traitor to the people. So they'd put Trieste in, represented by Smilzo's girlfriend Carola wearing the tricolor, with a halberd on her admirable chest. And Smilzo was dressed as a First World War infantryman, with a helmet on his head, and an 1891 rifle strapped over his shoulder. He was half-dead from the heat, but Peppone had ordered him to finish first. 'You have to do it, for me and for my brother,' Peppone had said, and so Smilzo came first, but they had to give him artificial respiration because he was drowning in his own sweat.

Don Camillo, seeing Trieste arrive on the crossbar of the infantry bike, seemed to go crazy with enthusiasm. And he enjoyed the sack race and the pot breaking (piñatas), and when they said the 'Politico-satirical shooting gallery' was open, he rushed through the crowd to get there.

An appalling crush of people had formed around the stall, but this didn't trouble Don Camillo who was like a Panzer tank when he got going. It must have been a hilarious show because everyone was laughing and yelling.

In fact it was all very simple: the idea was to throw balls at some great big wooden dummies – figures five feet tall – painted caricatures. But painted by someone who really knew what he was doing, an artist from the city, and the key thing was that they satirically portrayed the principal representatives of the political parties of the centre and the right.

And the biggest dummy portrayed Don Camillo.

He recognised himself immediately, and the portrait was genuinely funny, so he could see what all the laughter was about.

He said nothing, clamped his jaws shut and stood watching with folded arms.

A young lout stepped forward with a red kerchief around his neck, bought six balls and started to throw them. There were six targets and the one furthest to the right was Don Camillo. The young man threw with great accuracy, and he knocked over a figure each time. Down went the first, then the second, then the third, then the fourth. But as the number of dummies went down, so did the volume of noise from the crowd, and when the fifth fell, there was total silence.

It was the turn of Don Camillo's dummy.

The young lout glanced out of the corner of his eye at the flesh-and-blood Don Camillo standing beside him, one step away, then put the ball back on the stand rail, and walked away.

People started murmuring, but nobody else stepped up. And all of a sudden Peppone appeared.

'Give me some,' he said.

The stall-keeper had set up all the figures again and he placed six balls on the rail in front of Peppone. Peppone started to throw, and the crowd drew back. The first figure fell. Then the second, then the third. Peppone was throwing with ferocity, with rage.

The fourth figure fell. The fifth fell. The dummy of Don Camillo alone remained on its feet.

Don Camillo slowly turned his head and his eyes met Peppone's. An entire conversation took place in a few seconds between those eyes, and Don Camillo's side of it must have been quite extraordinarily eloquent because all the colour drained from Peppone's face. But this didn't mean a thing: Peppone merely rolled up his sleeves, settled himself firmly on his feet, eyed the figure of Don Camillo, slowly brought back his arm, and fired.

A shot like that would have flattened not just a target made out of wood, but an ox, so great was the fury with which Peppone had hurled the heavy ball. And the force of the throw was such that after hitting the dummy, the ball bounced back again.

But the dummy didn't fall over.

'The hinge has got stuck,' explained the young man in charge of the shooting range, after looking behind the dummy.

'Typical underhand Vatican tricks,' sneered Peppone,

putting his jacket back on and walking off, while the crowd, as if waking in relief from a nightmare, started to laugh again.

Don Camillo walked away too. And late that evening, Peppone turned up at the presbytery.

'Listen, I had a rethink,' he explained grimly, 'and after you'd gone, I got them to remove your figure because I didn't want it to be taken as an insult to religion. I'm only against you when it comes to politics. The rest doesn't interest me.'

'Good,' replied Don Camillo.

Peppone went to the door.

'As for throwing the ball at you, well I'm sorry about that now, in a way. Still, it turned out all right.'

'Yes,' answered Don Camillo. 'It turned out all right. Because if my image had been knocked down, you'd have gone down too. I had a punch ready that could have felled an elephant.'

'I knew that,' muttered Peppone. 'Nevertheless, the prestige of the Party was at stake, and I had to take a shot. Besides, you made a fool of me this morning in front of everybody.'

Don Camillo sighed.

'That's true.'

'Well then, we're even,' decided Peppone.

'Not yet, Peppone,' muttered Don Camillo, handing out something to Peppone. 'Give me back the 5,000 lire note from this morning and take this one instead. This morning's one was forged.'

Peppone put his hands on his hips.

'Are you or are you not a total scoundrel? Never mind chucking balls at your effigy. You need a few bombs dropped on your head! What am I supposed to do now, when I've handed over all the money to the official from the Federation who was here today with the speaker?'

Don Camillo put his money back in his wallet.

'I'm so sorry to hear that,' he sighed. 'I shall never have a moment's peace for as long as I live, thinking of the harm I've done to your party!'

Peppone left so as to avoid compromising himself.

The Old Schoolmistress

SHE WAS THE VILLAGE'S national monument, the old schoolmistress, a tiny, skinny woman who everyone had known forever because she had taught the ABC to fathers, sons and sons' sons, and now she lived alone in a little house just outside the village, and only managed to keep going on her pension because whenever she sent someone to the shops to buy two ounces of butter or meat or some other food, they charged her for two ounces but always gave her seven or eight.

It was more of a problem with eggs because even a schoolmistress 3,000 years old who has lost her ability to judge weights is going to notice when she asks for two eggs and is given six instead. But then the doctor cured the difficulty because, meeting her one day, he told her that she seemed very poorly, and after asking a few questions ordered her to give up eggs completely.

Signora Cristina kept everybody in awe. Even Don Camillo gave the old schoolmistress a wide berth. Ever since his dog had unfortunately jumped into her garden and smashed a pot of geraniums, whenever they met the old woman threatened him with her stick and shouted that there was a God even for Bolshevik priests!

She couldn't stomach Peppone, who when he was a little boy used to come to school with his pockets full of frogs, fledglings and other unwelcome things, and one morning had arrived astride a cow, together with that bonehead, Brusco, playing the part of his groom. She left the house very rarely and never talked to anyone because she hated gossip, but when they told her that Peppone had become mayor and was making proclamations, that got her out. And when she came to the piazza she stopped in front of a poster pinned to the wall, put on her glasses and read the whole thing from top to bottom, scowling ferociously. Then she opened her bag, took out her red and blue pencils, marked the mistakes, and wrote at the bottom of the poster, '4/10 – Ass!' And all the village's most powerful Reds were standing behind her, watching with grim faces, folded arms, and tightly set jaws. But nobody dared say a word.

Signora Cristina's woodshed was in the garden behind her house, and it was always well supplied because someone would often climb over her hedge at night and throw a couple of logs or a bundle of kindling onto the pile. But it was a cold winter and the schoolmistress had too many years weighing on her small bent shoulders to be able to go outside without breaking a rib. So nobody saw her about, and she didn't even notice when she ordered two eggs and they sent her eight. And one evening, as Peppone was holding a council meeting, someone came to tell him that Signora Cristina had sent for him, and could he please hurry up because she didn't have time to die at his convenience.

Don Camillo had already been summoned, and had run straight there because he knew she only had a few hours left. He found a big white bed with a tiny old woman inside it, so small and so thin that she looked like a baby. But the old schoolmistress hadn't lost any of her marbles, and she chuckled when she saw the huge black bulk of Don Camillo.

'You'd like it, wouldn't you, if I now confessed to having committed all kinds of nastiness. I'm afraid not, my dear Signor Priest. No, I called for you because I want to die with a pure soul, and without grudges. Therefore, I forgive you for breaking my pot of geraniums.'

'And I forgive you for calling me a Bolshevik priest,' whispered Don Camillo.

'Thank you, but there's no need,' retorted the little old woman. 'Because it's the spirit of the thing that counts, and

I called you a Bolshevik priest in the same way that I called Mayor Peppone an ass, with no intention of causing offence.'

Don Camillo gently began a long speech to help Signora Cristina understand that this was the moment to put aside all human self-importance, even the smallest vestige, because in order to have any hope of going to Paradise . . .'

'Hope?' interrupted Signora Cristina. 'But I am certain of going there!'

'And that is a sin of presumption,' said Don Camillo gently. 'No mortal can be certain of having lived according to the laws of God.'

Signora Cristina smiled. 'No mortal except Signora Cristina,' she answered. 'Because tonight Jesus Christ came to Signora Cristina to say that she would go to Paradise! And that's why Signora Cristina is certain. Don't tell me you know more than Jesus Christ!'

Before a faith as formidable as this, as precise and unequivocal, Don Camillo could barely catch his breath, and went into a corner to say his prayers.

Then Peppone arrived.

'I forgive you for the frogs and the other nasty things,' said the old schoolmistress. 'I know you, and I know that you aren't wicked deep down. I shall pray to God to forgive your gross crimes.'

Peppone flung out his arms. 'Signora,' he stammered, 'I've never committed any crimes.'

'Don't tell fibs!' retorted Signora Cristina severely. 'You and the other Bolsheviks have banished the King, abandoning him on a far away little island to starve to death together with his children.'

The schoolmistress began to weep and, seeing such a tiny old woman weep, Peppone felt like howling.

'It's not true,' he exclaimed.

'Yes it is,' replied the schoolmistress, 'Signor Biletti told me, and he listens to the radio and reads the newspapers.'

'Tomorrow I'm going to smash his face in, the filthy reactionary!' whined Peppone. 'Don Camillo, tell her it's not true.'

Don Camillo came over and gently explained, 'You've been

misinformed. It's all been made up. Desert islands and dying of hunger. All made up, I assure you.'

'So much the better,' sighed the little old woman more calmly.

'And in any case,' exclaimed Peppone, 'it wasn't just us who banished him. There was a vote, and the result was that there were more people who didn't want him than people who did want him, and so he went away, and no one did anything to him. That's how democracy works.'

'What a democracy!' replied Signora Cristina sternly. 'One does not banish kings.'

'I'm sorry,' answered Peppone in confusion.

What else could he have said?

Signora Cristina rested for a little while and then spoke again. 'You are the mayor,' she said, 'and this is my last will and testament. The house is not mine, and you can give my few rags to whoever needs them. Keep my books yourself because you need them. You must do a lot of composition exercises and studying of verbs.'

'Yes, Signora,' replied Peppone.

'I want a funeral without music because music is trivial. And I want a funeral with no carriage, like in the old days. With the coffin carried on pall bearers' shoulders, and I want the flag on the coffin.'

'Yes, Signora,' replied Peppone.

'My flag,' said Signora Cristina, 'the one over there by the wardrobe. My flag, with the royal coat of arms.'

And that was all, because then Signora Cristina whispered, 'God bless you, my boy, even though you are a Bolshevik.' And then she closed her eyes and never opened them again.

Next morning Peppone called all the representatives of the parties to the Town Hall. And when he had them all in front of him he said that Signora Cristina was dead and that the Council would express the gratitude of the people by honouring her with a solemn funeral.

'I am telling you this as Mayor, and I have called you here as Mayor and interpreter of the will of all the citizens, so that they won't criticise me tomorrow for acting off my own bat. The fact is that Signora Cristina expressed as her last wish that

she should have her coffin carried by pall bearers, and have
the flag with the royal coat of arms draped on it. Here and
now, everyone can say what they think. The representatives of
the reactionary parties can do us the favour of keeping quiet
because everybody knows perfectly well that they'd love it if
there was a band playing the so-called "royal march".'

The first speaker was from the Party of Action, and he spoke
well because he had a degree.

'For the sake of one deceased person, we must not cause
offence to the hundred thousand dead whom the people have
sacrificed in order to create the republic!' And so on, with
great warmth, in an unbroken stream, concluding that Signora
Cristina had worked with the monarchy, but for the fatherland,
and therefore nothing could be more just than to cover her
coffin with the unadorned version of the flag which represents
the fatherland today.

'Hear hear!' agreed Begollini, the socialist who was more
Marxist than Marx. 'The age of sentimentality and nostalgia is
over: if she wanted the flag with the coat of arms, she should
have died sooner!'

'Oh, this is mere stupidity,' exclaimed the pharmacist, leader
of the Historic Republicans. 'You should be saying that the
public display of that emblem in a funeral today could provoke
feelings of resentment which would rob the ceremony of its
true nature, transforming it into a political demonstration and
diminishing, if not destroying, its noble significance.'

Then it was the turn of the Christian Democrats'
representative.

'The wishes of the dead are sacred,' he said in a solemn voice.
'And the wish of the deceased lady in question is especially
sacred for us because we all love and revere her, and regard
her prodigious activity as an apostolic mission. And precisely
because of this reverence and our respect for her memory, we
are of the opinion that one should seek to avoid the smallest act
of disrespect which, even if it had quite the opposite intention,
would rebound to the discredit of the deceased. Therefore we
too associate ourselves with the others in advising against the
use of the old flag.'

Peppone gravely assented with a nod of his head. Then he
turned to Don Camillo, who had also been summoned.

'What does our parish priest think?'

Don Camillo was pale.

'The parish priest thinks that before he speaks he would rather wait to hear the opinion of the Signor Mayor.'

Peppone cleared his throat and began to speak.

'In my capacity as Mayor,' he said, 'I thank you for your collaboration, and as Mayor I endorse your view that we should avoid using the flag requested by the deceased. However, since it is not the Mayor who commands in this village but the Communists, as the leader of the Communists I'm telling you I don't give a damn for your views, and Signora Cristina will go to the cemetery tomorrow with the flag she wants because I respect her dead more than I respect all of you living, and if anyone of you has an objection I'll chuck him out of the window! Does Signor Priest have anything to say?'

'I yield to violence,' replied Don Camillo with a shrug, having come once again into the grace of God.

And so the next day, Signora Cristina went to the cemetery in a coffin carried on the shoulders of Peppone, Brusco, Bigio and Fulmine. And all four of them were wearing kerchiefs red as fire around their necks, but on the coffin was the old schoolmistress's flag.

This is the sort of thing that happens there, in that strange village where the sun pounds people's heads like a hammer and where people are known more for their brawn than their brains, but at least they respect the dead.

Five Plus Five

POLITICS HAD MADE things go badly wrong, and even though nothing in particular had happened, when Peppone came upon Don Camillo he made a grimace of disgust and turned his head away.

Then during a speech in the piazza, Peppone made some offensive allusions to Don Camillo and even called him 'the Bishop's carrion crow'.

Finally, after Don Camillo responded with some rhymes in the parish newsletter, someone deposited such a large cartload of manure outside the presbytery door that he had to leave the house by a ladder from his window. On the pile there was a note saying, 'Don Camillo, fertilise your head.'

So began a war of words, both on paper and on walls, a war so heated and violent that a nasty stink of menace filled the air. Then, after Don Camillo's final word in the newsletter, people said, 'If Peppone's lot don't respond to that, it will surely be the end of it.'

Peppone's lot didn't answer. Instead they shut themselves away in a troubling silence which seemed like the calm before a storm.

One evening Don Camillo was in the church absorbed in his prayers, when he heard the little door of the bell-tower creak, and he didn't even have time to get to his feet before he found Peppone standing in front of him.

Peppone had a gloomy expression on his face and was keeping one hand behind his back. He looked drunk, and his hair was flopping over his forehead.

From the corner of his eye, Don Camillo glanced at a candelabra to one side of him, and having carefully calculated the distance, he leaped to his feet, and there he was with his hand tightly around the heavy bronze implement.

Peppone clenched his teeth and looked Don Camillo in the eye, while Don Camillo tensed every nerve in the certainty that the moment Peppone revealed what was hidden behind his back, the candelabra would go flying like an arrow.

Peppone slowly drew his hand from behind his back and offered Don Camillo a long, narrow package.

Full of suspicion, Don Camillo made no move to take the package, and so Peppone put it onto the altar rail, tore off the blue paper, and revealed five long wax candles, each as thick as a vine stem.

'He's dying,' explained Peppone in a grim voice.

Now Don Camillo remembered being told that Peppone's four or five year old son was ill, but he hadn't made much of it because apparently it was something minor. And now he understood Peppone's silence, and the lack of retaliation.

'He's dying,' said Peppone. 'Light them right now.'

Don Camillo went into the sacristy to fetch some candelabras, slipped the five big wax candles into them, lit them and arranged them in front of the altar, before the figure of Christ crucified.

'No,' said Peppone bitterly, 'that bloke up there is part of your inner circle. Light them in front of her over there.'

On hearing the Madonna being called 'her over there', Don Camillo gritted his teeth and could barely overcome the urge to crack Peppone's skull, but he said nothing and went to arrange the candles in front of the statue of the Virgin Mary in the little chapel on the left.

Then he turned to Peppone.

'Tell her!' rasped Peppone.

So Don Camillo knelt down, and in a low voice he told the Madonna that Peppone was offering her those five big candles so that she would help his sick child.

When he stood up again, Peppone had disappeared.

Passing the high altar, Don Camillo quickly crossed himself and tried to scuttle off, but the voice of Jesus stopped him.

'Don Camillo, what is the matter?'

Don Camillo flung out his arms in the greatest humility.

'I'm sorry the poor wretch swore like that,' he said. 'And that I couldn't find the strength to say anything to him. How do you reason with a man who's lost his head because his son is dying?'

'You did very well,' answered Jesus.

'Politics is a terrible thing,' explained Don Camillo. 'You mustn't take against him. You mustn't be hard on him.'

'And why would I judge him harshly?' whispered Jesus. 'By honouring my Mother, he fills my heart with sweetness. I am not entirely happy that he called her "her over there".'

Don Camillo shook his head.

'You misheard,' he protested. 'He said, "Light them all in front of the Blessed and Most Holy Virgin who is in that chapel there." Think about it! If he'd dared to say a thing like that, children or no children, I'd have kicked him right out of the church!'

'I am very glad of that,' replied Jesus with a smile. 'Very glad indeed. But in speaking of me, he said "that bloke up there".'

'I can't deny that,' admitted Don Camillo. 'But even so, I'm convinced that he meant it as an affront to me, not to you. I'd swear to it, that's how certain I am.'

Don Camillo went out, and three quarters of an hour later came back filled with excitement.

'Didn't I tell you?' he cried, laying a package on the altar rail. 'He brought me five candles to light for you too. What do you think?'

'This is wonderful,' answered Jesus, smiling.

'They're smaller than the others,' Don Camillo pointed out, 'but it's the thought that counts. And you've got to remember that Peppone isn't rich, and what with all the expense on medicine and doctors, he's up to his ears in debt.'

'It is all wonderful,' repeated Jesus.

The five candles were lit straight away and they shone so brightly that there seemed to be fifty of them.

'And you could even say they give more light than the others,' observed Don Camillo.

And they really did give more light than the others because it was Don Camillo who had bought them, running into the village and getting the chemist out of bed, and putting them on tick because Don Camillo was as poor as a church mouse. And Jesus knew all this very well and didn't say a word, but a tear slipped from his eyes and drew a line of silver in the black wood of the cross. Which meant that Peppone's child was safe.

And so he was.

The Dog

THE BUSINESS with the dog really upset the village.

One night a bleak, protracted lament was heard coming from far away, from the dyke by the river, and the people shivered and said, 'It's him!'

Heading upriver from Don Camillo's neighbourhood, there were three small villages spread along the dyke – La Rocca, Casabruciata, and Le Stoppie – and when, months and months earlier, word came that every night in Le Stoppie a dog was howling like a wolf but nobody had ever seen it, everyone thought it was a drunkard's tale. Then the thing moved downstream, and it was said that the dog was now howling every night on the dyke at Casabruciata, and the noise was starting to be a nuisance. Then people learned that that the dog was terrorising La Rocca, and now everyone believed it, so whenever the howling of the dog was heard coming from the dyke, people jumped up in their beds, and quite a few of them came out in a cold sweat.

The next night the same thing happened again, and a lot of people crossed themselves, because that wasn't the cry of an animal, but the lament of a human being.

People went to bed with their hearts pounding and didn't get any sleep because they were waiting for the howl and, since it kept on happening, it was decided that there should be a sweep of the area. And one morning twenty men took shotguns and raked the dyke and its vicinity, and fired shots into every bush that moved, but they didn't find a thing. And that night they heard the same old tune.

The second sweep was equally fruitless, and they never made a third because, what with all this mystery, people were starting to be afraid even by day.

The women came running to Don Camillo and begged him to bless the dyke, but Don Camillo said no. When you have dog-trouble, you go to the dog-catcher, not the priest.

'They're scared stiff in the Vatican too,' said a good-looking girl called Carola who was Smilzo's girlfriend.

So Don Camillo pulled up a stick from his garden and set off, followed some way behind by the women, who stopped at a certain point and waited while he went on to the dyke. He searched to the right and to the left, battered all the bushes with his stick, and finally reappeared.

'There's nothing there.'

'Well, it wouldn't have cost you much to hit it with a blessing as well while you were there,' exclaimed Carola.

'If you don't watch how you speak, I'll hit you and the whole Women's Union with my blessing,' Don Camillo warned her. 'If the dog's annoying you, put cotton wool in your ears, and that way you'll sleep as well as I do. The trouble is, if you want to sleep well at night you need a clear conscience, and many of you don't. It would do you good to show your faces in church more often.'

Carola started singing 'The Red Flag', which had a rather abrupt finale because Don Camillo sent her on her way with the help of his stick.

The dog howled again that night and even Don Camillo, whose conscience was in excellent order, was unable to sleep.

The next day he met Peppone.

'They told me you went looking for the dog yesterday,' said Peppone. 'I went too, just now, and I didn't see anything.'

'If the dog howls at night down by the dyke, it means the dog is there at night,' muttered Don Camillo.

'And so?'

'And so anyone who wants to find it should go onto the dyke at night, when the dog is there, and not by day when the dog isn't there.'

Peppone shrugged.

'And who's going down there at night?' asked Peppone. 'Everybody around here's as scared as if it was the devil himself.'

'You too?' enquired Don Camillo.

Peppone hesitated for a moment.

'And you?' he asked.

They walked side by side in silence. Then Don Camillo stopped.

'If I could find someone prepared to come with me, I'd go,' he said.

'So would I,' retorted Peppone. 'I'd go too if I could find someone to go with me. Hard to find anyone though.'

'That's true,' admitted Don Camillo, shamelessly refusing to notice that if they were both looking for someone to go with them, the matter was automatically settled.

There were a few moments of embarrassment, and then Peppone flung out his arms in resignation.

'All right, let's meet this evening after nine o'clock.'

They met after nine o'clock and walked cautiously through the vine rows, and if there'd been an amplifier handy, the beating of their hearts would have sounded like a machine gun at full blast. When they reached a bush at the foot of the dyke, they lay in wait silently with their shotguns in their hands.

Hours went by: it was as silent as the grave, and the moon stuck its nose out from behind the clouds and lit up that sadness.

And then came the long spine-chilling howl that stopped the hearts of Don Camillo and Peppone. It was coming from the river, and the two of them cautiously left the undergrowth and looked over the dyke as if from a trench.

The lament came again, and without a doubt its source was a cluster of reeds poking out of the water about twenty yards away. Don Camillo and Peppone fixed their eyes on the reeds which were against the light because the moon was blazing on the water, and all at once they clearly saw a black shadow move, and took aim. The moment the howling began they each fired a shot and the howl changed into a whimper of pain.

Now their fear vanished and the two of them jumped out of their hiding place. Don Camillo pulled up his cassock and went into the water, followed by Peppone.

Reaching the middle of the reeds they found a wounded black dog, onto which Peppone shone his torch.

It wasn't an ill-natured creature and it licked their hands, and Peppone instantly lost the desire to break its neck.

'You got it in the leg,' said Peppone to Don Camillo.

'We got it, one way or another,' specified Don Camillo.

Peppone took the dog by its collar and lifted it up: underneath it was a floating sack, entangled in the reeds. Don Camillo lifted the sack, a huge army sack made of waterproof canvas which the water had rendered hard as iron.

Peppone bent down and used a little billhook to cut the wire from the mouth of the sack, but immediately stood up again, turned pale, and looked at Don Camillo.

'Same old story,' said Don Camillo. 'Someone killed a man, who knows when, put him in a sack and threw the sack into the river. The man had a dog, and the dog jumped into the water and followed the sack as the current carried it downstream. The sack first gets caught up in reeds opposite Le Stoppie, then opposite Casabruciata. By day the dog hides, or goes to look for food, and by night comes back to be with its master. People have only heard it when the sack has stopped near a village, so who knows how long it's been howling night after night?'

Peppone shook his head.

'But why was it howling?' he asked. 'And why did it only howl at night?'

'Maybe because when the conscience wants to make itself heard it can make use of even a dog's voice, and because the voice of conscience is most clearly heard at night.'

The dog had lifted its head.

'Conscience!' said Don Camillo aloud.

The dog answered with a whimper.

No one was ever able to identify the unfortunate in the sack because time and water had destroyed all his features. After so much voyaging he came ashore in consecrated ground.

The dog died too, and Don Camillo and Peppone buried it in a hole as deep as hell, so it would rest in peace.

But in the villages and remote farmhouses scattered along the river there are still people who wake in the night with their hearts pounding, jump up, and sit on their beds with their foreheads like ice because they've heard the dog howling and will hear it howl for the rest of their lives.

Autumn

O N THE AFTERNOON of the third day of the month, Barchini the newsagent-cum-printer appeared at the presbytery.

'Still no sign of anyone,' he said. 'It's obvious they don't intend to do anything.'

'There's still time,' objected Don Camillo. 'It's not even four o'clock yet.'

Barchini shook his head.

'Even if it's a short text, it'll take me three hours to set. Then there's the correcting, and then the printing. And it's murder printing by hand, one sheet at a time. But you can rely on me, Don Camillo. Whatever happens, I'll let you know.'

Just to be sure, Don Camillo waited another hour. Then, since he'd heard nothing more from Barchini, he slipped on his overcoat and went to the Town Hall. The Mayor, naturally, wasn't there, so Don Camillo headed determinedly for Peppone's garage, and there he found him absorbed in reattaching a nut to a bolt.

'Good evening, Signor Mayor.'

'There's no Mayor here,' replied the other grumpily, without even lifting his eyes from his work. 'The Mayor's in the Town Hall. Here there's no one but Citizen Giuseppe Botazzi, who's breaking his backbone trying to earn his daily bread while everybody else goes off to have fun.'

Don Camillo stayed calm.

'True,' he retorted. 'But may one request a favour of Citizen Giuseppe Botazzi, or has an order arrived from the Comintern to say that Comrade Peppone must act like an oaf and make himself unavailable to the public?'

Peppone broke off from his work.

'Let's hear it,' he muttered suspiciously.

'Well then, it would be much appreciated if Citizen Giuseppe Botazzi would be so kind as to say to Comrade Peppone that when he next meets the Signor Mayor, he might ask him to send his parish priest Don Camillo a copy of the poster which the Council has had printed on the occasion of November the Fourth, so that Don Camillo can pin it up on the notice board of his community centre.'

Peppone resumed his work.

'Tell the Signor Parish Priest that what he should stick on the notice board at his leisure club is a photograph of the Pope.'

'That's already there,' explained Don Camillo. 'But a copy of the poster would be useful, so that tomorrow I could read it to the children and explain the significance of the Fourth of November.'

'Now just a minute!' sneered Peppone. 'The Reverend, who knows Latin and has studied history books weighing 100 pounds each, needs Peppone the mechanic, who only got as far as the third year of primary school, to give him ideas for explaining November the Fourth? I'm sorry, but it won't work this time. If you think you and your gang of priests in civvies can amuse yourselves by analysing the mistakes in my grammar, you've got it wrong.'

'It's you that's wrong,' Don Camillo protested calmly. 'I have no intention of amusing myself by looking for grammatical mistakes in the writing of Peppone the mechanic. I simply want to explain to my children what the village's highest authority thinks about the Fourth of November. I, the parish priest, when I speak about the Fourth of November, wish to be in agreement with you, the Mayor. Because there are some things which everybody ought to agree upon. So it's not a question of politics.'

Peppone knew Don Camillo inside out, and confronted him with his hands on his hips.

'Don Camillo, let's go easy on the poetry and cut to the chase. Drop the story about the poster for your notice board and tell me what you're really after.'

'I'm not after anything. I just want to know whether you have or haven't made a poster for the Fourth of November. If you haven't, then I could help you put it together right now.'

'Thanks for the kind thought, but I haven't made a poster and I'm not going to!'

'Orders from the Department of Propaganda?'

'Orders from nobody!' shouted Peppone. 'Orders from my conscience, and that's that! The spirit of the people is already full of wars and victories. The people know only too well what wars are like, without any need to celebrate them with speeches and proclamations.'

Don Camillo shook his head.

'You're on the wrong track, Peppone. This has nothing to do with celebrating war. It's about paying homage to those who suffered in this last war and sacrificed their lives for us.'

'*Balle*! You give yourself the excuse that you're remembering the dead and the suffering, so you can make filthy militarist, warmongering, monarchist propaganda! The heroism . . . the sacrifice . . . the dying man throwing his crutches at the enemy . . . "The Bells of San Giusto and Trento and Trieste", "The Song of Mount Grappa", "The Festival at Santa Gorizia," the "murmuring Piave", the victorious headlines, "our ineluctable destinies": it all stinks of monarchism and militarism, and all it's good for is to make young people get above themselves, and to create nationalist propaganda and stir up hatred of the proletariat. So Istria and Dalmatia and Venezia Giulia will go up in flames, along with Tito and Stalin and the Comintern, and America, the Vatican, Jesus Christ, the enemies of religion et cetera et cetera until the point comes where the proletariat are the only enemies the fatherland has left, so they'll have to bring back the empire!'

Peppone had grown more and more heated as he spoke, and was gesticulating as if he was addressing a rally. And when he had finished, Don Camillo calmly said, 'Bravo, Peppone. There's an entire article for *Unità* in that. But putting all this aside, are you going to answer my question: will you or won't you be doing something to commemorate the victory?'

'I've already given years of military service for the victory, and that's enough! They took me from my mother when I was still a boy, they stuck me in a trench, starved me and covered me in lice and slime. Then they made me march night after night, under water with a ton of stuff on my back, they made me go into battle when bullets were pouring down like hailstones, and when I was wounded they told me to sort it out for myself. I've been a porter, a gravedigger, a gunner, a nurse, a mule, a dog, a wolf and a hyena. Then they gave me a hankie with a picture of Italy on it, a cheap cotton suit, and a piece of paper saying I'd done my duty, and home I went to beg work from the people who'd made millions on my back and the backs of all the other poor wretches!'

Peppone broke off and raised his index finger solemnly.

'This is my proclamation,' he concluded, 'and if you want to finish it off with a quotation from actual life, put this in red: that Comrade Peppone is ashamed of having fought to make those filthy pigs rich, and the only thing that would make him proud today would be if he was able to say, "I was a deserter!"'

Don Camillo shook his head. 'Pardon me for asking, but why did you go up into the mountains in '43?'

'What's that got to do with it?' shouted Peppone. 'That's another matter altogether. It wasn't His Majesty who commanded me to go! I went of my own free will. And there are wars and wars!'

'I understand,' murmured Don Camillo. 'An Italian always prefers to fight against his political opponents.'

'Don't talk nonsense, Don Camillo,' yelled Peppone. 'When I went up there I wasn't doing politics. I was defending my fatherland.'

'What?' exclaimed Don Camillo. 'Did I really just hear you say the word "fatherland"?'

'There are fatherlands and fatherlands,' explained Peppone. 'The '15–18 fatherland was one thing, the '43–45 one was another.'

The church was packed for the Mass dedicated to the souls of the Fallen. There was no sermon. Don Camillo simply said, 'At the end of Mass the children of the community centre will go and lay a wreath at the monument.' And at the end of Mass everyone formed a column behind the children, and the silent procession wound its way through the village to the piazza. The piazza was deserted, but someone had laid two large wreaths at the foot of the little monument to the Fallen; one with a ribbon in the colours of the Tricolour and the words, 'The Council', while the other consisted entirely of carnations, and on the ribbon were the words 'The People'.

'The gang brought them while you were saying Mass,' explained the proprietor of the café in the piazza. 'They were all there except Peppone.'

The children's wreath was laid, and the gathering broke up without any speeches.

On his way home, Don Camillo met Peppone, and barely recognised him because it was pouring with rain and Peppone was muffled in his greatcoat.

'Did you see the wreaths?' asked Don Camillo.

'What wreaths?' asked Peppone indifferently.

'The ones by the monument. Beautiful.'

Peppone shrugged.

'Oh, it must have been the lads' idea. Are you unhappy about it?'

'What do you think?'

By the presbytery Peppone was about to go on his way, but Don Camillo caught his sleeve.

'Come in for a drink. I promise it won't be poisoned.'

'Another time,' muttered Peppone. 'I want to go home. I'm not feeling well. I haven't even been able to work today. I'm cold, and shivering all over.'

'Shivering? It's the seasonal flu. The only medicine is a glass of wine. And I've got some really strong aspirin too. Come on in.'

And Peppone went in.

'Take a seat while I go and get the bottle,' said Don Camillo.

When he came back a moment later with the wine and glasses, he found Peppone sitting down, but still wearing his greatcoat.

'I've got a raging fever,' explained Peppone. 'I'd rather stay covered up.'

'Do whatever's most comfortable.'

He handed Peppone a brimming glass and two white tablets. 'Get them down you.'

Peppone swallowed the aspirin and washed them down with wine. Don Camillo went out for a moment and came back in with an armful of logs which he chucked onto the fire.

'A warm blaze will do me good too,' said Don Camillo, getting the fire going.

'I've been thinking about what you told me yesterday,' said Don Camillo as the flames leapt up. 'From where you stand, you're right. I had a completely different experience of the war. I was a young priest fresh out of the seminary when I found myself in the middle of it. Lice, hunger, military service, bullets, misery, exactly like you. I didn't take part in combat, you understand. I went out collecting the wounded. But it was different for me. It was my job, and it was a job I'd chosen. It wasn't like that for you, you hadn't chosen to be a soldier. Which is just as well, because people who choose to be soldiers are a bad lot.'

'Well, that's not always true,' muttered Peppone. 'There are good people even among the officers. And then you have to remember, when the time comes to risk your neck, even some of the stinkers who go around wearing a monocle will risk it without any fuss.'

'That may well be,' continued Don Camillo, 'but whereas it was my job as a priest to treat wounded men and give Extreme Unction to the dying, while bullets flew overhead, for you it was no better than a swindle. A priest's job is to prepare souls to go to Paradise, by way of the Vatican. So when a priest finds himself in the middle of a cholera epidemic or an earthquake or a war, it's all grist to the mill. It's the land of plenty for someone who earns his living saving souls. But for someone like you, what is there to save in a war? Only your skin!'

Peppone tried to move away from the fireplace which had become an inferno, and with two aspirin in his body and a greatcoat on it, he was on the brink of exploding with the heat.

'No, Peppone,' said Don Camillo. 'If you move, the game's up. The whole point of aspirin is to make you sweat. The more you sweat, the sooner you get better. Drink another glass of wine on top of it. It's cool and it will ease your thirst.'

Peppone drank two glasses of wine and mopped his brow.

'That's right,' continued Don Camillo. 'I understand perfectly that a man who is forced to risk his neck for no reason wants nothing more than to clear off out of it. In those circumstances, a man who deserts isn't a coward; he's simply a human creature obeying his instinct for self-preservation. Drink up, Peppone.'

Peppone drank. He was dripping, and seemed to be on the brink of bursting.

'You can take off your coat now,' Don Camillo advised him, 'so that when you go out, you can put it back on and not feel the change from hot to cold.'

'No, I'm not feeling hot.'

'I'm someone who likes to reflect on things,' Don Camillo went on. 'You were absolutely right not to put up a poster. It would have been against your principles. Yesterday I was just thinking selfishly of my own situation. For me, the war was interesting. It offered me an occupation. Take this, for example: in my compulsion to save souls and show myself in a good light to the Eternal Father, when I heard myself being called by a man who'd caught a bullet between our trench and the Austrians', I jumped out of the trench and went to tell him the usual things that you say to the dying, and he died in my arms. A couple of bullets grazed my head, it was nothing. But that goes without saying.'

'I know about that,' said Peppone grimly. 'I read about it in the army paper they brought to the trench instead of food, the pigs! They gave you a medal too, if I'm not mistaken.'

Don Camillo turned and looked at a little display case hanging on the wall.

'I put it there,' he said. 'There are too many medals going around.'

'You've got every right to wear it,' protested Peppone, after swallowing another glass. 'Anyone who hasn't stolen his medal has the right to wear it.'

'Let's not talk about these things. You rightly have a completely different idea of war. But take off your greatcoat, Peppone!'

Peppone was so hot that he looked like a Noah's flood of

sweat, but he was as stubborn as a mule, and he didn't remove his coat.

'In the end,' concluded Don Camillo, 'your scorn for everything to do with jingoistic rhetoric, and your maxim that the whole world is your fatherland, makes you more right than the others. For you a day like Victory Day is a tragic date because the winners of a war are more likely to start another than the losers. Is it true that in Russia they give medals to deserters and punish those who perform acts of courage in war?'

'Ha!' cried Peppone. 'I knew you'd find a way to make this political! I knew it!'

Then he suddenly calmed down. 'This heat's killing me,' he sighed.

'Then take your coat off!'

Peppone finally removed his coat, revealing the silver medal he'd been awarded in the '15–18 war pinned onto the lapel of his jacket.

'Well,' said Don Camillo taking his silver medal out of its case and pinning it onto his cassock. 'That's an idea.'

The old servant appeared and said, 'It's time.'

'We can go and have a bite to eat,' said Don Camillo.

So they ate, and they also drank a considerable quantity of bottles of wine, ending up with toasts to goodness knows how many long-dead generals from the first war.

Then towards evening, Peppone put his coat back on and headed for the door.

'I hope you won't be so shameless as to exploit this moment of weakness.'

'No,' answered Don Camillo. 'Even on the day I have to hang you, nobody will stop me hanging you with respect.'

'We'll see about that when the second wave comes!' muttered Peppone darkly as he vanished into the gloom of the evening.

The shades of the dead whirled about in the uncertain light of a grey sky straight out of "The Festival of Santa Gorizia". It looked like an allegorical painting by Plinio Nomellini.

Fear

PEPPONE FINISHED reading the newspaper which came with the afternoon post, while Smilzo was sitting on a barrel in a corner of the garage waiting for orders.

'Get the truck,' said Peppone, 'and bring the team here in an hour.'

'Something serious?' enquired Smilzo.

'Get a move on!' shouted Peppone.

Smilzo started the Dodge and set off. After three quarters of an hour he was back with the twenty-five men of the team. Peppone got in too and they soon arrived at the People's Palace.

'You stay here to keep an eye on the truck,' Peppone ordered Smilzo. 'Shout if you see anything suspicious.'

When they were in the meeting room, Peppone told them the news.

'Here,' he said, slamming his great hand on the enormous headline, 'we've reached the point of no return. This is it. The forces of reaction have been unleashed. They're shooting our comrades and throwing bombs at all the Party HQs.'

He read out some extracts from the paper, which was *Milano-sera*, a Milanese afternoon news sheet.

'And remember, it's not one of our Party newspapers saying these things. It's an independent paper and this isn't made up. It's right here on the front page!'

Brusco growled, 'If they're having to report this in the damned independent papers, which are always far to the right and oppose us whenever they can, just imagine what must really be going on. Think about it: it's got to be even worse than they're saying! I can't wait to read tomorrow's *Unità*.'

Bigio shrugged.

'There might be less in it,' he said. 'The comrades at *Unità* are on the ball, but they're highly educated, cultured people who do a lot of philosophising, and they tend to play down this sort of thing so the people don't get stirred up.'

'Educated people who take care to stay within the rules and not break the law,' added Gigotto, the Redskin.

'Poets, more than anything else!' concluded Peppone. 'But they're people who deal punches with their pens that would pin the Eternal Father himself to the wall.'

They went back to discussing the situation and re-read the most important pieces of news and opinion from the Milanese newspaper.

'The Fascist revolution is under way,' said Peppone. '"Action Squads" are springing up every minute and burning the co-operatives and ordinary people's houses. They're stabbing people and expelling them. The newspaper says there are "Fascist HQs" and "*squadristi*": no beating about the bush. If it was just a matter of the usual voters' indifference, or capitalism, or monarchy, or stuff like that, they'd be talking about "reactionaries" and "nostalgia" et cetera. Here they're talking openly about Fascism and action squads. And don't forget, this is an independent newspaper. We must be ready to confront every eventuality.'

Lungo said that in his opinion they should move before the others did: they knew every one of the reactionaries and the members of the previous Council. 'We go house to house and whack them. That'll shut them up.'

'Bah,' Brusco objected, 'seems to me we'd be on the wrong side of the law straight off. It says here in the paper that we should respond to the provocations, not provoke them. Because if we provoke them, that gives them the right to respond to the provocations.'

Peppone agreed. 'If we have to whack anybody, we should whack him fairly and democratically.'

Night had fallen. In the autumn down by the river, evening begins at ten in the morning, and the air is the same colour as the water. They continued the discussion calmly for another half hour, when all at once they heard a bang which made the windows rattle.

They went out and found Smilzo sprawled on the ground behind the truck like a corpse, with blood all over his face. They entrusted the lifeless body to the caretaker's wife and jumped into the truck.

'Let's go!' yelled Peppone as Lungo took the wheel.

They shot off, and after a mile or so Lungo turned to Peppone. 'Where are we going?'

'Hmm?' murmured Peppone.

'Where are we going?'

They braked and gathered their thoughts. Then they reversed, went back to the village and stopped outside the Christian Democrat HQ. They found a table, two chairs and a portrait of the Pope, and threw the whole lot out of a window.

Then they jumped back into the truck and headed for l'Ortaglia.

'It must have been that coward Pizzi who threw the bomb that killed Smilzo,' said Redskin. 'He's been eaten up with fury against us since we argued about the farm workers' strike. He said, "You haven't heard the last of this."'

They surrounded the house, which stood all by itself. Peppone went in.

Pizzi was in the kitchen stirring polenta. His wife was laying the table and his son was kneeling by the fire, putting logs on it. Pizzi looked up, saw Peppone, and realised that something was up. He looked at the little boy who was playing at his feet.

'What do you want?' he asked.

'Someone's thrown a bomb outside our HQ and killed Smilzo!' yelled Peppone.

'Nothing to do with me,' replied Pizzi.

His wife came forward.

'Take the boy away,' said Pizzi.

The woman grabbed the boy and left the room.

'You said you'd make us pay when we were arguing over the farm workers' strike. You're a filthy reactionary.'

Peppone stepped forward threateningly, but Pizzi took a step back, seized a revolver from the mantelshelf and pointed it at Peppone.

'Stop there, Peppone, or I'll shoot you!'

At that moment, someone who'd been lurking outside opened the window and fired a shot. Pizzi fell to the floor, and in his fall fired a shot from his revolver into the ashes of the hearth . . .

The woman closed her dead husband's eyes and put her hand over her mouth. The boy flung himself on his father and started to howl.

Peppone's men rushed outside to the truck and drove away in silence. Before reaching the village they got out and went off in dribs and drabs.

People had gathered outside the People's Palace, and Peppone bumped into Don Camillo just as he was coming out.

'Is he dead?' asked Peppone.

'It would take more than that to finish off a hard case like him!' answered Don Camillo with a sneer. 'You've made proper fools of yourselves destroying the Christian Democrats' table. You'll be a laughing stock!'

Peppone gave him a grim look.

'There isn't much to laugh at, my dear Reverend. We're talking about bombs!'

Don Camillo looked at him with interest.

'Peppone,' he said, 'there are two possibilities: either you're a scoundrel or you're a moron.'

In fact Peppone was neither. He simply didn't know that the bang hadn't been a bomb, but the Dodge's spare tyre, the reconditioned one which was at the back under the flatbed of the truck. What had struck poor Smilzo on the head was a great lump of rubber.

Peppone went to look under the truck and saw the disembowelled tyre. Then he thought of Pizzi stretched out on his kitchen floor and the woman with her hand over her mouth so she wouldn't scream, and the boy who did.

For the moment, people were laughing. Then, an hour later they weren't, because word was going round the village that Pizzi had been wounded.

He died the following morning, and when the *carabinieri* went to question his wife, the woman stared at them, her eyes wide with terror.

'Did you see anyone?'

'I was in the other room. I heard a shot and found my husband on the ground. I didn't see anything else.'

'Where was the boy?'

'He was already in bed.'

'Where is he now?'

'I've sent him to his grandmother.'

Nothing more could be made of it. The revolver turned out to be missing a cartridge. The projectile which had killed Pizzi had entered one temple, and the calibre of the bullet was identical to the one from the revolver which had been in Pizzi's hand. The conclusion was suicide.

Don Camillo read the report and the statements of the relatives which confirmed that Pizzi had been anxious for some time about a big sale of seeds which had gone badly, and that he had often expressed the wish to do away with himself. Then Don Camillo went to consult Jesus.

'Jesus,' he said sadly, 'this is the first death in the village for which I cannot hold a funeral service, and justly so because anyone who kills himself is killing one of God's creatures and damns himself, and – if we are going to be strict about this – would have no right to rest in a churchyard.'

'Certainly, Don Camillo.'

'But if we do tolerate his burial in a churchyard, he must go there unattended, like a dog, because anyone who renounces his humanity lowers himself to the level of the animals.'

'This is deeply sad, but it must be so.'

The next morning, which was Sunday, Don Camillo preached a terrifying sermon on suicide. It was pitiless, tremendous, implacable.

'I wouldn't go anywhere near the corpse of a suicide,' he concluded, 'not even if I knew that my doing so would restore him to life!'

Pizzi's funeral took place the next afternoon. The coffin was loaded onto a plain, third class carriage that wobbled. And behind it, on two carts, were Pizzi's wife, son and two brothers. When the vehicles entered the village, people closed their shutters and peeped through the cracks.

Suddenly something happened that took the breath away:

Don Camillo emerged unexpectedly with two altar boys and the cross, took up his position in front of the carriage, and set off singing psalms.

On reaching the courtyard of the church, Don Camillo gestured to Pizzi's brothers that they should take the coffin off the carriage and carry it into the church. Here Don Camillo celebrated the offices of the dead and blessed the corpse. Then he went back to his position in front of the funeral carriage and walked all the way through the village, singing psalms. There was not a soul to be seen.

At the churchyard, after the coffin had been lowered into the grave, Don Camillo swelled his chest and cried out in a voice of thunder, 'May God reward you for your honest life, noble Antonio Pizzi.'

Then he threw a handful of earth into the grave, blessed the coffin, slowly left the churchyard, and went back through the fear-haunted village.

'Jesus,' said Don Camillo when he was back in the church. 'Do you have anything to rebuke me for?'

'Yes, Don Camillo: when you accompany a dead person, it is not appropriate to carry a pistol in your pocket.'

'I understand, Jesus,' replied Don Camillo. 'If I wasn't going to carry it in my hand, I should have slipped it into a sleeve.'

'No, Don Camillo, you leave this kind of equipment at home, even if you are accompanying the corpse of someone who has . . . committed suicide.'

'Jesus,' said Don Camillo, 'do you want to bet that a committee of my congregation's most bigoted Pharisees will write indignantly to the Bishop, telling him that I've committed a sacrilege, accompanying a suicide to the cemetery?'

'No,' replied Jesus, 'I don't want to bet because they've already started writing the letter.'

'By this action I've drawn everybody's hatred upon myself: the people who murdered Pizzi; the people who know perfectly well, as everyone does, that Pizzi was murdered but who would find it convenient if nobody cast doubt on the suicide; and Pizzi's own relatives who would prefer it to be thought that they hadn't the least idea it wasn't suicide. One of his brothers asked me, "But isn't it forbidden to bring a suicide into church?" And then there's Pizzi's own wife who is afraid, not for herself, but for her son, and is keeping quiet to save his life.'

The side door creaked, Don Camillo turned round and Pizzi's son appeared. The boy came and stood in front of Don Camillo.

'I thank you in the name of my father,' he said in the grave, hard voice of a grown man. Then he left as silently as a shadow.

'There,' said Jesus. 'That is someone who doesn't hate you, Don Camillo.'

'But his heart is filled with hatred for whoever killed his father, and it's a hellish chain which no one can break, not even you who allowed yourself to be placed on the cross for the sake of damned mad dogs like these.'

'The world hasn't ended yet,' replied Jesus serenely. 'The world has barely begun, and Up Above we measure time in billions of years. There's no need to lose your faith, Don Camillo. There is time, there is time.'

The Fear Persists

AFTER HIS NEWSLETTER came out, Don Camillo found himself all alone. 'I feel as if I'm in the middle of a desert,' he confided to Jesus. 'And it's no different when I have a hundred people around me because, although they're right there, only half a yard from me, there's a sheet of plate glass half a yard thick between them and me. I can hear their voices, but they seem to be coming from another world.'

'It is fear,' answered Jesus. 'They are afraid of you.'

'Of me?'

'Of you, Don Camillo. And they hate you. They were living warmly and peacefully in the cocoon of their cowardice. They knew the truth, but nobody forced them to acknowledge it because nobody had made it public. You have acted and spoken in such a way that they *must* recognise the truth. And that is why they hate and fear you. You see the brethren obeying the orders of the tyrant like sheep, and you shout, "Rouse yourselves out of your lethargy! Look at people who are free! Compare your lives with free people's lives!" And they will not thank you. They will hate you, and if they can they will kill you because you compel them to notice what they knew already, but through their desire for a quiet life were pretending not to know. They have eyes but do not want to see. They have ears but do not want to hear. They are cowards but they do not want anyone to say so. You have made an injustice public and put people in a serious dilemma: if they say nothing, they accept the oppression; if they do not accept it, they must speak out. It was so much more comfortable being able to ignore the oppression . . . Does all this astonish you?'

Don Camillo shrugged. 'No,' he said. 'It would astonish me if I didn't know that you had been put on the cross for telling people the truth. It just makes me sad.'

Then a messenger came from the Bishop.

'Don Camillo,' he said, 'Monsignor has read your newsletter and knows about the reaction it has provoked in the village. He was pleased by the first issue, but he hopes very much that the second will not contain your obituary. Here is his letter.'

'This is outside my jurisdiction,' said Don Camillo. 'He should petition not me but God.'

'And he is doing just that,' said the messenger. 'And he very much wants you to know it.'

The marshal of the *carabinieri* was a man who knew how the world works. He met Don Camillo by chance and said, 'I read your newsletter. The bit about the tyre tracks on Pizzi's threshing floor is very interesting.'

'Hadn't you noticed them?'

'No,' replied the marshal. 'I didn't "notice" them because as soon as I saw them, I had a bit of chalk thrown here and there; and so, by comparing the patterns with the wheels of the various vehicles, I happened to discover that the tyre-prints were left by the Mayor's Dodge. What's more, I happened to observe that Pizzi shot himself in the left temple while he had the revolver in his right hand and, rummaging in the ashes of the hearth, I found the bullet which had come from Pizzi's revolver, whereas Pizzi was killed by a bullet coming through the window.'

Don Camillo frowned at him. 'Why didn't you tell anyone?'

'I told it to the right person, Reverend. And they replied that if I had gone ahead and arrested the Mayor, the matter would immediately have taken on a political character. These things run aground when they turn political. We need to wait for the right moment: and you have given it to me, Don Camillo. I don't want to load the responsibility onto other people. I simply want to avoid the danger of the thing running aground because some people make it political.'

Don Camillo replied that the marshal had acted very well indeed.

'I can't give you a pair of *carabinieri* to watch your back, Don Camillo.'

'That would be a sick joke!'

'I know. But if I could, I'd give you a whole battalion,' muttered the marshal.

'There's no need, marshal. The Eternal Father will watch my back.'

'Let's hope he looks after you better than he looked after Pizzi,' commented the marshal.

The investigation resumed the next day, and various landowners and tenants were ferociously interrogated. And when one of them, Verola, protested indignantly, the marshal answered him with the utmost calm.

'*Signore mio*, new evidence suggests not a suicide but a homicide, and given that we can rule out attempted robbery, and we can rule out a politically motivated crime, as Pizzi was apolitical, so we must direct the investigation towards those who had relations, whether commercial or social, with Pizzi and who might be nursing hatred towards him.'

The business went on like this for some days and the people under interrogation were outraged.

Brusco was furious, but kept quiet.

Finally he said, 'Peppone, that villain is playing with us as if we were children. You'll see: when he's questioned everyone, even the midwife, two weeks later he'll come to you and ask you, all smiles, if you wouldn't mind him questioning one of us. And you won't be able to say no. And he'll question the man and everything will go sky high.'

'You must be joking!' cried Peppone. 'Not even if they pull out my fingernails!'

'They won't question you or me or anyone else we might think of. They'll question the very one who'll spill the beans. They'll question whoever it was who fired the shot.'

'Don't talk rubbish,' sneered Peppone. 'We don't even know ourselves who fired the shot.'

And that was true. No one had seen which of the twenty-five men in his team had fired. When Pizzi fell they had all jumped into the truck and had left without saying a word, and not a word had been spoken about the crime ever since.

Peppone looked Brusco in the eye, and said, 'Who fired that gun?'

'Who knows? Maybe it was you.'

'Me?' shouted Peppone. 'And how could it be me when I wasn't even carrying a gun?'

'You went into Pizzi's house by yourself. Nobody saw what you did in there.'

'But the shot was fired from the window. Someone must know who was stationed by the window.'

'At night all cats are grey. Even if somebody did see, he saw nothing. Only one person saw the face of whoever fired, and that's the boy. Otherwise the family wouldn't have said he was in bed. And if the boy knows, then Don Camillo knows too. If he didn't know for sure, he wouldn't have done and said what he's said and done.'

'Damn whoever brought him here!' yelled Peppone.

Meanwhile the circle was being closed, and every evening the marshal methodically went to tell the Mayor the latest developments in the investigation.

'I cannot put it more clearly than this, Signor Mayor,' he said one evening, 'but that's where we are. There seems to be a woman mixed up in this.'

'There can't be!' countered Peppone. But he would gladly have throttled the marshal.

It was late evening and Don Camillo was keeping himself busy in the empty church. He'd put up a stepladder on the highest altar step. A crack had opened in the wood of one arm of the cross, along the grain, and Don Camillo, after filling the crack, was now staining the white plaster of the filler with a little varnish.

All at once he sighed, and Jesus quietly asked him, 'What is the matter, Don Camillo? You've seemed weary these last few days. Do you feel unwell? A touch of 'flu perhaps?'

'No, Jesus,' Don Camillo confessed without lifting his head. 'It's fear.'

'Fear? What on earth are you afraid of?'

'I don't know. If I knew what I was afraid of, I wouldn't be afraid,' replied Don Camillo. 'Something's not right, something hanging in the air, something I can't defend myself against. Twenty men attacking me with rifles in their hands don't scare me. They just annoy me because there are twenty of them, and I don't have a rifle. If I found myself out at sea and unable to swim, I'd think "in a minute I'll drown like a rat," and I wouldn't like that at all but it wouldn't frighten me. When you can think about a danger you don't feel fear. Fear is what you feel about dangers that you can sense but not know. It's like walking blindfold along an unknown road. A nasty business.'

'Have you lost faith in your God, Don Camillo?'

'*Da mihi animam, cetera tolle*. The soul belongs to God, bodies belong to the earth. Faith is great, but this is a physical fear. My faith might be huge, but if I go for ten days without a drink, I feel thirst. Faith consists in bearing that thirst, accepting it with a serene heart as a test imposed by God. Jesus, I am ready to bear a thousand fears like this for your love. But I still feel afraid.' Jesus smiled. 'Does that make you despise me?'

'No, Don Camillo, if you did not feel fear, what would be the point of your courage?'

Silence alarms people in the villages on the banks of the river because it feels like a threat. Don Camillo was carefully applying his paintbrush to the wood of the cross, and as he looked at the hand of Christ pierced by the nail, it seemed to him all of a sudden that the hand was coming to life. At that moment a shot echoed around the church.

Someone had fired from the little side chapel.

A dog barked, and then another. There was a distant burst of machine gun fire. Then the silence returned.

Don Camillo looked with alarm at the face of Jesus.

'Jesus,' he said, 'I felt your hand on my forehead.'

'You are delirious, Don Camillo.'

Don Camillo looked down again and stared at the hand pierced by the nail. Then he felt something like a shudder as the can and paintbrush dropped from his fingers.

Jesus's wrist had been pierced by the bullet.

'Jesus,' said Don Camillo breathlessly, 'you pushed back my head and your arm took the bullet that was intended for me!'

'Don Camillo!'

'The bullet didn't stay in the wood of the cross!' shouted Don Camillo. 'Look where it has ended up!'

High up on the right, opposite the little window, there was a display case with a silver heart inside. The bullet had broken the glass and fixed itself in the centre of the heart.

Don Camillo ran to the sacristy to find a tall ladder and stretched a piece of string from the hole which the bullet had made in the glass of the window and the hole in the heart in the display case. And the string passed less than a foot from the nail in the hand of Jesus.

'My head was right there,' said Don Camillo. 'Your arm was hit because you pushed back my head! This is the proof.'

'Calm down, Don Camillo.'

But Don Camillo couldn't possibly calm down, and if he hadn't been hit by a raging fever God only knows what would have happened next. And God – who did indeed know – sent Don Camillo a raging fever which left him stuck to his bed like a wet rag.

Thriller and Romance

THE WINDOW through which the shot had been fired opened onto the little meadow belonging to the church, and the marshal and Don Camillo were outside the chapel examining the scene.

'Here's the evidence,' said the marshal pointing to four holes which stood out against the whitewash, a foot or so under the sill of the now notorious window. He took a little knife out of his pocket and probed one of the holes until something came out.

'It looks straightforward to me,' said the marshal. 'The gunman was positioned some way off and fired a round from his machine gun at the lighted window. Four bullets ended up here in the wall, but one made a hole in the window and came in.'

Don Camillo shook his head.

'I told you it was a pistol shot, and fired from here. I'm not so senile that I can't tell the difference between a pistol shot and a round from a machine gun! First there was a shot from a pistol, and from here. Then there was a burst of machine gun fire from further away.'

'So the spent cartridge should be somewhere nearby!' returned the marshal. 'And there isn't one.'

Don Camillo shrugged.

'You'd need the music critic from La Scala to tell by the pitch if a shot came from an automatic pistol or a revolver. If whoever shot at me used a revolver, he'll have taken the cartridge away with him.'

The marshal started to hunt all around and in the end found something on the trunk of the cherry tree which stood five or six yards from the side of the church.

'One of the bullets scarred the bark,' he said. And that was clearly the case.

He scratched his head in puzzlement.

'Bah,' he said finally, 'let's do a bit of forensic science.'

He took a pole and stuck it in the earth, right against the wall, in front of one of the holes in the plaster; then he started to walk across the meadow, every so often looking back at the trunk of the cherry tree which had been struck by the bullet, and moving to left or right according to whether or not the tree was obscuring the pole against the wall. And so there came a point where he found himself right by the hedge, and on the other side of the hedge there were a ditch and a cart track.

Don Camillo came and joined him, and the two of them started to search the ground, one each side of the hedge. They didn't search for long. After five minutes, Don Camillo said, 'Look here,' and there was a machine gun cartridge. Then they found the other three.

'That proves what I've been saying,' exclaimed the marshal. 'The fellow fired through the window from here.'

Don Camillo shook his head. 'I don't know anything about machine guns,' he said, 'but I know that other guns don't fire their bullets in curves. Take a look for yourself.'

A *carabiniere* came up and informed the marshal that all was calm in the village.

'Thanks very much!' commented Don Camillo. 'Nobody was shooting at them! They were shooting at me!'

The marshal took the *carabiniere*'s musket and, lying on the ground, aimed it at the first pane of the chapel window, close to where he remembered the bullet-hole being.

'If you shoot, where will you hit?' asked Don Camillo.

It was child's play. Starting from there and passing through the chapel window, a bullet would have to have smacked into the first confessional on the right, three yards from the church door.

'Unless it was a very well trained bullet, it couldn't have passed through the altar, not even if you threatened to cut its throat,' concluded the marshal. 'Which means, Don Camillo, that when you get mixed up in something, it causes enough grief to make us all tear our hair out! Wasn't one gunman enough for you? No, *Signore*, you need two. One to shoot you from under the window, and another to shoot you from behind a hedge 150 yards away.'

'Well, that's the way I am,' said Don Camillo. 'No expense spared.'

The same evening, Peppone gathered all his top brass and most trusted lieutenants from all the Council districts. He looked grim.

'Comrades,' he said, 'a new fact has turned up to complicate the local situation. An unknown gunman shot at "our" self-styled parish priest, and the forces of reaction are exploiting this incident to raise their heads once again and throw more mud at the Party. The forces of reaction, cowardly as always, don't have the courage to talk openly, but we know they're murmuring in corners and saying we are responsible for the shooting!'

Lungo raised his hand and Peppone gave him the nod.

'First of all,' said Lungo, 'we could tell the forces of Signora Reaction to demonstrate that there really was an attempt on the priest's life. Because so far we've only got his word for it. And since there weren't any witnesses, it could well have been the Signor Reverend himself who fired the revolver so he could write slanders against us in his hateful newsletter. Let's see the evidence.'

'Hear hear!' agreed the assembly. 'Lungo's right.'

Peppone addressed them again.

'One moment! What Lungo says is true, but we mustn't rule out the possibility that the incident is a real one. Knowing the personality of Don Camillo, I cannot honestly say he's someone who uses underhand methods . . .'

He was interrupted by Spocchia, the section boss from Molinetto. 'Comrade Peppone, remember that a priest is always a priest. You're letting yourself be conned by sentimentality. If

you'd listened to me, his odious newsletter would never have
come out, and the Party wouldn't now be damaged by these
scurrilous insinuations about Pizzi's suicide. Show no mercy to
the enemies of the people! Showing mercy to the enemies of
the people is a betrayal of the people!'

Peppone slammed a fist onto the table.

'I don't need lessons in morality from you!' he yelled.

Spocchia was unimpressed. 'And if,' he shouted, 'instead
of standing in our way, you'd let us take action while we still
could, we wouldn't now have a heap of crooked reactionaries
under our feet! I . . .'

Spocchia was a thin young man of twenty-five, with a bush
of hair rising in waves and slicked back at the sides, ending in
a kind of crest at the back the way it's worn by oafs from the
north and roughnecks on the west bank of the Tiber. He had
small eyes and thin lips.

Peppone confronted him angrily. 'You are a moron!' he said,
looking Spocchia in the eye.

The other man turned pale, but said nothing.

Going back to the table, Peppone said, 'Making use of
an incident based purely on the assertion of a priest, the
reactionaries are plotting new ways to harm the people.
Comrades, we must be determined as never before. To the
ignoble insinuations . . .'

At this moment a strange thing happened which had never
happened before. Peppone started listening to himself. It
seemed that he, Peppone, was down in the audience listening
to what Peppone was saying.

('. . . the selling of flesh, the enemies of the people recruiting for
reaction, the starving farm-workers . . .')

Peppone listened and gradually it felt as if he was listening
to someone else.

('. . . the monarchists . . . the treacherous clergy . . . the
reactionary government . . . America . . . Plutocracy . . .')

'What does "plutocracy" mean?' thought Peppone. 'Why's
he talking about plutocracy when he doesn't even know the
meaning of the word?'

He looked around and saw faces he barely recognised.
Shifty eyes, and the shiftiest were those of young Spocchia. He
thought of Brusco, his most loyal follower, and tried to catch

his eye, but Brusco was at the back with his arms folded and his head down.

(*'. . . let our enemies know that in us the spirit of the Resistance has not been weakened . . . The weapons we once seized to defend our liberty . . .'*)

Now Peppone felt as if he was yelling like a madman. Then the applause brought him round.

'That's what we wanted,' Spocchia whispered to him as the meeting broke up. 'You know, Peppone, all you need to do is whistle and it'll start. My boys are ready. At an hour's notice.'

'Bravo, bravo!' replied Peppone, slapping him on the back, though he'd rather have cracked his skull. Who knows why?

Only he and Brusco were left, and for a while they said nothing.

'Well?' cried Peppone at last. 'Lost your tongue? Aren't you even going to tell me whether I spoke well or not?'

'You spoke very well,' answered Brusco. 'Very well indeed. Better than ever before.'

Then the curtain of silence fell between them again.

Peppone was doing the accounts in his ledger, when all of a sudden he grabbed a glass paperweight, hurled it onto the floor with great force and yelled a long, complicated and exasperated oath.

Brusco looked at him.

'I made an ink blot,' Peppone explained as he closed the book.

'It's the pens we get from that thief, Barchini,' observed Bruso, carefully not pointing out to Peppone that since he'd been writing in pencil the story of the ink blot didn't add up.

When they were outside in the darkness, Peppone stopped at the crossroads as if there was something he wanted to tell Brusco. Then he abruptly said, 'Well, see you tomorrow.'

'Tomorrow, Boss. Good night.'

'Bye, Brusco.'

It was nearly Christmas and high time to get out the Nativity set from its box, clean it up, touch up the paint and mend any chips. Even though it was late, Don Camillo was still at work in the presbytery. He heard a tap on the window and after a bit went to open the door because he saw it was Peppone.

Peppone sat down while Don Camillo went back to work, and the two of them said nothing for quite a while.

All at once Peppone exclaimed angrily, 'God dammit!'

'Have you nowhere but the presbytery to go and blaspheme?' enquired Don Camillo calmly. 'Couldn't you have got your swearing done at the office?'

'You can't even swear in the office,' muttered Peppone. 'Because if you swear, you have to explain why.'

Don Camillo was busy touching up St Joseph's beard with white lead.

'There's no place for a decent citizen to live in this world any more!' exclaimed Peppone after a while.

'And how does that concern you?' asked Don Camillo. 'Have you turned into a decent citizen?'

'I've always been one.'

'Oh wonderful! I'd never have guessed.'

Don Camillo went on painting St Joseph's beard. Then he moved on to his robe.

'Will you be doing that for much longer?' enquired Peppone furiously.

'If you give me a hand we'll get it finished in no time.'

Peppone was a mechanic with hands like shovels and enormous fingers that he had trouble bending. But when you had a clock that needed mending, Peppone was the man to go to. Because that's how it is: great big men are ideal for the most delicate jobs. He could paint the trim on the bodywork of a car and the spokes of a wheel as one born to it.

'Can you believe this? I'm painting Nativity figures now!' he muttered. 'You must have mistaken me for the sacristan.'

Don Camillo fished around in the box and pulled out a little pink thing the size of a sparrow, which was the Infant Jesus himself.

Without quite knowing how, Peppone found the little statue in his hand, so he picked up a paintbrush and set delicately to work. He was on one side of the table and Don Camillo on the other, but they couldn't see each other's faces because of the glare of the lamp between them.

'This world is only fit for pigs,' said Peppone. 'You can't trust anyone, if there's something you want to tell them. I don't even trust myself.'

Don Camillo was deeply absorbed in his work: the Madonna's face needed to be completely repainted. Delicate stuff.

'And do you trust me?' he asked casually.

'I don't know.'

'Try telling me something, and you'll see.'

Peppone finished the Infant Jesus's eyes, which was the hardest part. Then he touched up the pink of the little lips. 'I want to jack it all in,' he said. 'But I can't.'

'Who's stopping you?'

'No one's stopping me! I could beat off a regiment with a crowbar.'

'Are you scared?'

'I've never been scared in my life!'

'I have, Peppone. Sometimes I get scared.'

Peppone dipped his brush.

'Well, sometimes I do too,' said Peppone. And that's exactly what he had just been feeling.

Don Camillo sighed.

'The bullet passed four inches from my forehead,' he told Peppone. 'If I hadn't moved my head back at exactly the right moment I'd have been done for. It was a miracle.'

Peppone had now finished the Infant Jesus's face and was refreshing the pink of his body.

'I'm sorry I missed him,' Peppone muttered. 'But he was too far away, and the cherry trees were in the way.'

Don Camillo's brush stopped moving.

'Three nights ago,' Peppone explained, 'Brusco was keeping an eye on Pizzi's house to make sure the gunman didn't get hold of the boy. The boy must have seen who shot his father from the window, and the gunman knows it. Meanwhile I was keeping an eye on your house because I was sure that the man knows you know who shot Pizzi.'

'Who is he?'

'I don't know,' replied Peppone. 'I saw him from a long way off, going towards the window of the chapel. But I couldn't fire until he did something. As soon as he fired, I did too. But I missed.'

'Thank the Lord,' said Don Camillo. 'I know how you shoot, and now I can say there were two miracles.'

'Who is it? You and the boy are the only ones who know.'

Don Camillo slowly said, 'Yes, Peppone, I know, but nothing in the world can make me violate the secret of the confessional.'

Peppone sighed and went back to his painting.

'Something's not right,' he said suddenly. 'It feels as if everyone's looking at me differently, now. Everyone, even Brusco.'

'It'll be the same for Brusco, and for all the others,' replied Don Camillo. 'Everyone's afraid of everyone else, and whenever anyone speaks it's as if they're having to defend themselves.'

'Why's it like this?'

'Let's not get political, Peppone.'

Peppone sighed again.

'I feel like I'm in prison,' he said gloomily.

'There's a way out of every prison on this earth,' answered Don Camillo. 'Prisons are only for the body. And the body doesn't count for much.'

The Infant Jesus was finished now, and with his fresh colour, so pink and bright, he almost shone in the enormous dark hand of Peppone.

Peppone looked at it and seemed to feel warmth from that little body on his palm. And he forgot the prison.

He put the pink Infant Jesus on the table with great care, and Don Camillo put the Madonna near him.

'My little boy is learning the Christmas poem,' announced Peppone proudly. 'Every evening I hear him going through it with his mother at bedtime. He's a phenomenon.'

'I know,' Don Camillo admitted. 'And he learned the poem for the Bishop wonderfully too.'

Peppone froze. 'That was one of your worst skulduggeries!' he exclaimed. 'You still haven't paid for it.'

'Paying and dying always come in their due time,' observed Don Camillo.

Then he put the little figure of the ass next to the Madonna leaning over the Infant Jesus.

'Here's Peppone's son, here's Peppone's wife, and here's Peppone,' said Don Camillo touching the ass last of all.

'And here's Don Camillo!' exclaimed Peppone, taking the figure of the ox and putting it next to the group.

'Huh! Beasts always understand one another,' concluded Don Camillo.

Leaving the presbytery, Peppone found himself in the dark night of the Po valley, but he was completely at ease now because he could still feel the warmth of the pink Infant Jesus in his hand.

Then he heard the words of the poem again, and by now he knew it by heart.

'When he recites it to me on Christmas Eve, it'll be magnificent!' he rejoiced. 'And when the democracy of the proletariat is in charge, we mustn't touch poetry. In fact, we should make it compulsory!'

The river flowed slowly and placidly, just two steps away, at the foot of the dyke, and that was a poem too, a poem which began when the world began and is still going on. And it took a thousand years to shape and smooth the smallest of the billions of stones on the riverbed.

And so only after twenty more generations will the water have smoothed a new pebble.

And a thousand years from now people will rush at 3,000 miles an hour in machines with super-atomic rockets . . . to do what? To arrive at the end of the year, open-mouthed in the presence of that same plaster Infant Jesus touched up one evening long ago by comrade Peppone with his paintbrush.

Biographical Afterword

KNOWN AS Giovanni to English readers, but christened Giovannino, Don Camillo's creator was born at Fontanelle in the Valley of the Po in 1908, the son of a schoolteacher mother and entrepreneur father, who had a shop which sold among other things, bicycles, the principal mode of transport in the valley. Giovannino means 'Little John'. Being given such a name was the first joke of his life, for he grew to be a big man.

The laughter stopped for a brief moment in 1925/6, when his father, having moved the family to Parma twelve years earlier, succumbed to the economic depression under the Fascist rule of Benito Mussolini, who in 1922 had been summoned to be Prime Minister by Victor Emmanuel III, Italy's King.

At high school, Giovanni's creative talents were recognised and nurtured by an instructor called Cesare Zavattini. Giovanni was illustrating posters and proof reading for a local daily newspaper, *Corriere emiliano*, even before he left to take up a place at the University of Parma. It was indeed soon clear that his interest in journalism, his work on the newspaper and his contributions to a number of other publications (articles as well as cartoons), would soon overtake any academic pretensions. He became Editor of *Corriere emiliano* in 1929.

In the 1930s, with Italy caught up in the worldwide depression, he met and fell in love with Ennia Pallini. In 1936, after undertaking his national service, he moved to Milan to take up a position on the satirical magazine *Il Bertoldo* as a staff writer, after Zavattini had approached the publisher Angelo Rizzoli on his behalf. In 1940, he and Ennia were married and their first child, Alberto, was born.

'We got married and it cost me an "aquilotto" (five silver lira),' Giovanni recalled. 'A modest amount, but the ceremony was not even worth that. It took place in the Santa Francesca Romana Church in Milan, immediately after a rich wedding. The church was still full of flowers, the altar covered with candles, and lush red carpet stretched out from the altar to the door. As we entered, we heard a shout and groups of little altar-boys went into a frenzy. And, while one group took away the flowers, the second group stripped the altar of all the silver plated statues, and the third group rolled away the red carpet just as we walked down the aisle, in such a way that we didn't even step on it! It was a very quick ceremony, with brutal commands: "Stand up!", "Kneel!", "Sit down!", "Kneel!", "Yes!", "Ring!" . . .'

There was no shortage of material to inspire the satirist in Italy at this time, and although *Bertoldo* could not afford to be too provocative – (these were the days of heavy censorship by the Fascist government) – the magazine had a certain 'remark', as Giovanni put it, and the editor was frequently in hot water with the authorities.

Benito Mussolini, Prime Minister since 1922, had by 1930 transformed the country into a dictatorship, sweeping the opposition aside and making a powerful friend of Adolf Hitler, who was impressed by his rise, and in particular his imperialist policy in Africa.

With the terrible loss of life suffered by Italy in the First War, many Italians dreaded the impact of the *Pact of Steel*, as Mussolini's alliance with Hitler, signed in May 1939, was called. Revealing his own uncertainty that Italy was going to win the fight with Britain and France, Mussolini delayed a Declaration of War until 1940, and within months it was clear that Italy was but a dispensable pawn in Germany's grand plan.

Giovanni, meanwhile, not content with taking pot-shots at the Fascist regime in *Bertoldo*, had finally got himself arrested by the political police for howling in the streets at night. 'I got drunk because my brother was missing in Russia and no one had any news of him,' he said. 'That night I shouted a lot and said things which I saw written on two sheets of paper the next morning when I was arrested by the Political Office.' He was drafted into the army to prevent any more trouble.

In 1943, after America joined the war, the Western powers invaded Italy and Mussolini's Nazi-aligned, Fascist regime was overthrown. The Armistice was signed that September, whereupon Giovanni was left stranded at the mercy of his former German partners in the field of battle at Alessandria. German forces moved swiftly to relieve Italian soldiers of their weapons before they could be relieved of them by the Allies.

Given the choice to collaborate or be shipped off to a prison camp in German-occupied Poland, Giovanni adopted the slogan: 'I will not die even if they kill me,' and chose the latter, using his own instruments as journalist, writer, sketcher and cartoonist to become one of the 'animators' of the Italian Resistance. Together with intellectuals and artists, he read the news to his fellow prisoners, held conferences and made theatre. 'In the various lagers [prison camps] he went through,' wrote Paride Piasenti, President of the National Association of Former Prisoners, 'Guareschi was an example of dignity, of unshakable constancy, morality and of faith in freedom.' Many years later, at Giovanni's funeral, a few moments before the coffin was lowered, the priest, Onorio Canepa, came forward and spoke in a low voice: 'He was my prison mate in the Nazi lagers. In those unlucky days he was able to help 10–20,000 or more inmates.'

Giovanni recorded his experiences as a prisoner-of-war in *Diario Clandestino* (*My Secret Diary*). Written 'to relieve the sadness of his unlucky fellow prisoners', it is regarded by his family as his most important work.

The Resistance – made up of freedom fighters with a variety of political and national allegiances – attracted communists, socialists, liberals, Christian Democrats, Catholics, monarchists, republicans, anarchists, Yugoslavs, Russians, Ukrainians, Dutch, Spaniards, Greeks, Poles, Germans disillusioned with National Socialism, Britons and Americans (ex-prisoners or advisors deployed by the SAS, SOE and OSS) and former officers of the Royal Italian Army – a tinder box of internecine political rivalry.

A legend at this time was a certain Don Camillo Valota, a priest whose first ministry was undertaken in the mountains where Resistance fighters holed up in between operations. At the Alpine village of Sondalo, Don Camillo became a catalyst for unity within one such disparately ideological group. Wherever he went, Resistance fighters flocked to hear him speak, and he persuaded them to look to the inner man, to their own conscience rather than to any political or religious ideology – in practical terms, to bury their differences in the common cause to rid the country of Fascism.

Readers of the fictional Don Camillo stories may recognise the ideals of this charismatic priest in them, and it has been reported that Don Camillo Valota's path did indeed cross that of Giovanni in a prison in Milan, when he was *en route* to Poland and Don Camillo Valota was *en route* to the Nazi concentration camp at Dachau, having been arrested for helping Jews escape from Switzerland. However, Giovanni's son, Alberto, can find no evidence of their meeting: 'In the thousands of letters that my father wrote and received, from 1936 to 1946, the date of the first story of the series *Mondo piccolo*, the name of Don Camillo Valota never appears and my father never spoke of him…'

Alberto writes that the character of Peppone was in fact inspired by a well-known Marxist trade union leader John Faraboli, who, like Giovanni, was born in Fontanelle di Roccabianca, and began his political career there by founding the League of Farmers and becoming its president. As for the fictional Don Camillo, his inspiration was Don Lamberto Torricelli, archpriest of a small town a few kilometres from Parma called Marore. Torricelli was 'a big man, two metres tall with hands big as shovels', just like the literary Don Camillo. He had been a great comfort to Giovanni as a young man, helping him with his studies when economic meltdown had overwhelmed the family.

These two influences on the youthful Giovanni – John Faraboli and Lamberto Torricelli – presented in microcosm what would become the post-war world where communism was openly in conflict with Christianity.

Come the end of the war, Giovanni returned to Italy to find revolutionary fervour arising from a different quarter. Democrazia Cristiana (the Christian Democrats), led by sometime Resistance fighter Alcide De Gasperi, was the party in control. The principal opposition was the Communist Party, controlled by Josef Stalin from Party Headquarters in Russia. With the Italian monarchy democratically deposed by the Italian people in 1946, Stalin, who had shown his measure in the brutal purges of his party between 1937 and '38, began working to absorb Italy into the Soviet orbit, along with other countries in central and eastern Europe.

Giovanni chose the moment to start up a weekly satirical magazine, *Candido*. Famously, 'in a happy moment of satiric inspiration', he drew a cartoon of a Communist as a man

with an extra nostril to exhale the copious amounts of hot
air created by a ceaseless diet of propaganda. It so caught the
public imagination that it is remembered in Italy to this day.

Candido went on to play a pivotal role in the defeat of the
Communists in the 1948 elections, the *Times* reporting that the
election was won 'by De Gasperi and Guareschi together'. But
Giovanni held no candle to any particular political ideology, so
that after he had dispensed with the communists he began to
criticise the Social Democrats and De Gasperi instead. He also
targeted the culture of consumerism which began to take hold
of the nation after America gave billions of dollars to Italy and
other countries (including Britain) to win support in its fight
against Moscow-controlled communist parties in Europe and
China.

It was not in Giovanni's nature to do anything but provoke
whoever was in power. Right from the start, long before he
met Valota, when he was at school and his father decided he
should become an engineer, Giovanni, for the very enjoyment
of going the opposite way, had determined to become a lawyer.

To be creative *is* to go the other way, to think outside the
box, to break out of prejudiced humdrum ways of thinking and
doing things. Giovanni wanted people to look at all politicians
– even at politics itself – with a new pair of eyes. And there is no
better way to do that than by using humour. He began to write
the Don Camillo stories the year after the war ended.

'I remember the day, the day before Christmas Eve 1946,' he
said. 'Due to the holidays, the work had to be finished earlier
than usual. But apart from contributing to *Candido*, I used
to write little stories for *Oggi*, another of the firm's weekly
newspapers. So, on that day before Christmas Eve, as usual, I
found myself in trouble up to my eyes: it was already evening
and I hadn't written the piece that was missing to complete
the last page of my newspaper yet. In the afternoon, I had
just managed to write a piece for the other weekly newspaper,
and the piece had already been put in order and paged! "The
Candido has to be completed immediately!" the distributor
told me. So I pulled out the piece I wrote for *Oggi*, reordered
it in bigger type, and flung it into *Candido*. As soon as my
article was published, more and more letters arrived from my
twenty-four readers, so I decided to write a second chapter on

the story of the fat priest and the fat communist mayor from Bassa.'

Twice Giovanni's political work led him into serious trouble. In 1950, *Candido* published a cartoon by Carlo Manzoni in which the President of Italy, Luigi Einaudi, was pictured surrounded by a presidential guard (the *corazzieri*) of giant bottles of Nebbiolo wine. Einaudi personally managed the manufacture of Nebbiolo wine at the farm he owned near Dogliani, boasting that he used the most advanced agricultural developments. So offended was he at the cartoon that he had Giovanni arrested. In court he received a suspended sentence.

By this time, books of the Don Camillo stories were becoming bestsellers in Italy and 'the cinematographic adventure' of *The Little World* was about to begin – a series of seven black-and-white films were made between 1952 and 1965, French-Italian co-productions released simultaneously in both languages. To this day, these films are screened in Europe and accessed on YouTube throughout the world.

Giovanni, perhaps still a little shocked at the treatment he had received over the Einaudi affair, and increasingly independent financially, decided to move from Milan back home to the Lower Plain, the setting which had inspired the characters of the Don Camillo stories. He chose Roncole Verdi, a small town fifty miles or so west of Fontanelle, where he'd been born forty-four years earlier. He bought some land and built the house he had been dreaming of for years.

Over the following two years he 'designed and had the furniture built, was engaged with the garden, and bustled about with nails and tools: these are the most beautiful memories,' says his son Alberto, even if it meant that he had to commute to Milan three days a week. 'Those years were really the only ones serene for our parents, for in 1954, our father was again tried and this time imprisoned.'

This time Giovanni was charged with libel after he published photocopies of two wartime letters from former Prime Minister Alcide De Gasperi asking the Allies to bomb the outskirts of Rome in order to demoralise German collaborators. After a two-month trial a court found in favour of De Gasperi. Giovanni declined to appeal and was committed to prison in

Parma's San Francesco jail. He received twelve months for the libel, another month for the penalty of the previous sentence over the Einaudi business, and then six months' probation at home.

Giovanni took it on the chin: 'In 1953 I run into a bigwig and I will spend, in San Francesco prison in Parma, thirteen months,' he said. 'And, to tell the truth, I will be treated like the most esteemed professional robbers, thieves, rapists, murderers . . .'

This was serious and lunacy at the same time. A prison officer was assigned to censor and stamp his mail. So great a threat did the judiciary believe Giovanni presented to the State that when he received a magnolia leaf by post (sent to him in June as a sign of the oncoming summer), it too was stamped by the censor. Conditions in prison were atrocious; he suffered worse, he said, than he did in the lagers. He lost weight, his cell was one of the coldest, in winter the temperature reached minus twenty degrees. He was allowed neither a newspaper nor, at first, materials with which to write. After months he was allowed a typewriter; paper provided was stamped and had to be handed in before eight o'clock each evening.

After 400 days, Giovanni said: 'I don't hate anyone, but I didn't imagine that Italians could be so aggressive against a simple journalist. The SS who were carrying out surveillance on me during my time in the lagers were angels in comparison.'

When he received news of De Gasperi's death he wrote: 'I am here, silent and alone, sitting near the river bank. But I am not waiting for my enemy's corpse to pass. I do not consider anybody to be my enemy. Nobody succeeded in stirring up my hate! I only wait for the corpse of one year's lost life to pass. And if, meanwhile, any other corpse passes, I do not rejoice nor worry. It does not concern me: only God regulates these matters, and God never makes mistakes. My heart is clear and light.'

By 1956, on account of this experience, Giovanni's health had deteriorated and he began to spend time in Switzerland, in 1959 making a second home at Cademario, a village in the district of Lugano in the Swiss canton of Ticino. By now he had retired from the post of Editor of *Candido*, although he remained a contributor until the magazine closed in 1961.

Controversy continued to attend him, however. In 1962–3 he was invited to make a documentary called *La Rabbia* (*Rage*), with the film director Pier Paolo Pasolini, a passionate Marxist and self-declared atheist. They were to take half the film each to address society's ills in this era of great intellectual ferment and transition, and to pit their views against one another. Giovanni took the opportunity to criticise the soulless materialism that was degrading art for commercial ends, and the pointless sensationalism of aiming for the moon when there were so many problems here on earth – this planet, 'where the Son of God chose to be born, to suffer and to die as a man'. When the film was released in 1963, it was unaccountably withdrawn after a very short time and Giovanni's half, which some say eclipses that of Pasolini, mysteriously disappeared.

It was not until 2008, at the Venice Film Festival, that the film again came before the public eye, but only Pasolini's half. The ensuing controversy, which enveloped Giuseppe Bertolucci, the director of the *La Rabbia* restoration project and head of the committee for the centennial celebrations of Giovanni's birth, only abated when *La Rabbia* was shown to great public acclaim at the Fiuggi Family Festival in 2009, with both parts intact. More recently, the film has been made available as a DVD.

Giovanni died on the 22nd of July, 1968, in Cervia on the east coast of Italy, where he had taken to spending the summer months. He suffered a fatal heart attack.

The feeling in Italy was that he had, throughout his life, been treated shabbily by the authorities. The word was that Don Camillo had done for Italy what Cervantes' *Don Quixote* did for Spain, and might be described similarly as 'the genius of the Italian nation'.

In Britain, in 1982, the novelist Graham Greene lent his weight to the view when he published his novel, *Monsignor Quixote*, which features friendly bickering between a Catholic priest and a Communist mayor, who like Don Camillo and Peppone, share a genuine affection for each other, even if they are ideological enemies.

The town chosen as location for the Don Camillo films,

Brescello in the Lower Plain, today has a museum dedicated to Don Camillo and Peppone, and includes a Russian T34 Tank. Pilgrims to the Lower Plain should also know that the Club of Ventitrè keeps the Guareschi archive, declared 'of great historical interest' by the Ministry for Arts, Culture and Environment, at Roncole Verdi, where Giovanni lies buried in the churchyard, a town which owes its name to being the birthplace of the composer Giuseppe Verdi.

Between 1946 and 1966 Giovanni wrote 346 stories featuring Don Camillo. The first book, *The Little World of Don Camillo*, was published in America in 1950 by the Catholic publishers Pellegrini & Cudahy. It was an immediate bestseller, so much so that the company itself was taken over by a bigger publisher, Farrar, Strauss & Giroux, which then sold the series in the UK, to Gollancz who published it in hardcover and to Penguin in paperback.

Again they became immediate bestsellers. The final volume, an omnibus edition appearing in 1980, coincided with a series on television. Then someone informed Giovanni's son, Alberto, of an academic thesis by one Crespi Simone of the University of Bergamo, which claimed that nineteen of the stories in the original *Little World of Don Camillo* had been omitted from the English translation. This came as a complete surprise. No-one on the Italian side had ever checked the English translation. Further research indicated that only 132 of the Don Camillo stories – just over a third of the total number that Giovanni had written – had ever appeared in English.

It is intended that this authorised edition of the first of Giovanni's books will be followed by similarly faithful translations of his work, which will eventually lay before his English-language readers the first complete Don Camillo edition.

Any translator of the prankster Giovannino Guareschi must grapple with the verbal tricks he plays. Adam Elgar shows himself equal to these in this volume, but has left one dimension untouched – the author's tendency to choose names for Peppone's gang that have a certain allegorical, or at least descriptive, meaning in the original Italian.

Says Elgar, 'The reason for Guareschi's choices is not always clear, but I suspect there are a few private jokes, or possibly he was making fun of some real communists whom he knew. *Peppone* means "Big Joe", clearly an allusion to Stalin; *Brusco* means "rough"; *Smilzo*: "skinny, lanky"; *Spiccio*: "brisk, swift"; *Bigio*: "grey"; *Fulmine*: "lightning"; *Stràziami*: "torture me", "tear me";[1] *Spocchia*: "overweening arrogance". Two characters briefly mentioned as part of the march at the start of the story, 'Trespassing', have no allegorical meaning to their names, but I suspect they could be identified by Guareschi's circle: *Roldo dei Prati* – Roldo from the meadows, who has a raging fever, and *Bilò* with the wooden leg. As far as I can tell, the young man who becomes known as Redskin (Pellerossa) has no special significance to his real name – *Gigotto*, though "giga" means "jig".'

We hope to gather more and more information about the foibles of this intriguing artist and very human man as the series unfolds.

piersdudgeon@gmail.com, September 2013

---

[1] Mario Tschinke adds that *Stràziami, ma di baci sàziami* are the words of a popular Tango of 1926.